Democracy Studio

Practical guide to artificial intelligence on citizen engagement.
Case studies in Taiwan, Israel, and Estonia.

By Julien Carbonnell

PLAN :

FOREWORD

I destinate my work in priority to urban professionals or insiders who experience a growing complexity at all levels of city development. I aim to enlighten the sorely needed practice of balanced network initiatives as leadership in smart-city planning. While urban demography increases to unprecedented levels, promoting social acceptability and understanding of the urbanization processes is a priority to prevent oppositions, lousy faith, vandalism, or widely any hostile attitudes from inhabitants.

My field research consisted of comparing the citizen engagement in decision-making in Taiwan, Israel, and Estonia. In the first part of this thesis, I define the research question and the methodology used. I present my case studies and share the first insights out of them. In the second part, I use different algorithms and computational models to analyze the data collected on the case studies and simulate the citizens' interaction in smart cities. Modeling complex adaptive systems gives me a broader understanding of the formation of public opinion outside of my datasets. In total, I collected 807 answers to survey studies, about 65 interviews, and 148,163 tweets. My approach to urban research consists of spending some months in cities that feature interesting cases on my topics: smart-city, digital democracy, and civic technology. By comparing very different cultural backgrounds but replicating the same research protocol in a close time, I allow myself to perceive and reveal more about this worldwide phenomenon of the digital transformation of cities and democratic societies. Systemic digital devices such as smartphones and the internet are globally surrounding our contemporary peoples. It gives them new powers and opportunities to live more efficiently by using high-speed calculation daily. It also offers the latest generation a brand new definition of self-being worldwide.

In 1992, M. Crozier and E. Friedberg defined the pathway of a researcher in three steps. The first step consists of addressing the context with distance, the second of making a detour by stakeholders' interiority, and the third of recovering its externality. In the tradition of phenomenology studies, this process of personal commitment asks the researcher an unconditional openness attitude and a temporary suspension of any preconceived opinions on the topic of investigation. It also asks for a practical jump in the object of study. No need to say that my in-person jump took an unexpected turn between March 2020 and June 2021, while the sanitarian measures deployed worldwide were trying to address an answer to the global pandemic. Luckily, the travel restrictions didn't compromise my research so much: I played with the calendar to pass borders when they were open and experienced lockdowns in 4 different countries. By chance, internet-based studies are a significant part of my research. The whole business world and public servants that traditionally do not hang so much on computer meetings all moved online during that time. So I have virtually attended conferences, joined focus groups on my topics, and led my one-to-one interviews by videocall.

Studying humans implies accepting to walk by a range of mysteries and accepting sensitive personal feelings as a source of knowledge. Giving transparency to the digital transformation of the cities is a way to observe democracy in its essence, to monitor and document governance in action and reconnect decision-making in the digital era to the first ideals of direct democracy from Antic Greece. My primary concern is to help find a way to engage multi-stakeholders in decision-making on their urban environment. To attract populations with an added value in the global competition between cities, local governments often question their national frame policies. Observing the causal relationships which generate urban situations, I wish to establish universal laws on the digital transformation of cities which could serve developing cities.

SUMMARY

I wrote my doctorate thesis from field research. The day I received the agreement from the university to join the urban research laboratory, I left my flat and started to plan a three years trip as a digital nomad. While most Ph.D. students complain about the stress and frustration of their final graduation, I honestly think I had the best time of my adult life.

While pervasive computers and information technologies profoundly change our way of life, no previous generation of humans ever experienced such an integrated, peaceful and global world. To catch the sense of this worldwide phenomenon of the digital transformation of cities and democracies, I chose a phenomenological approach of science. The researcher dives into a living context and uses its sensitivity to observe what appears to its consciousness. Engage first in the complex wholeness of what happens, strengthening the subjective link between the researcher and its environment. The tools and concepts of thinking available to our minds structure our ability to perceive the world. By giving us perceptions of an unknown world, the digital interfaces have deeply shaken the ontophanic culture we were used to living in. To catch the complexity of the digital phenomenon, enlighten the sense of what we perceive (and what we are) in front of the interfaces, we need to embrace uncertainty and experiment outside the laboratories. The phenomenology suggests a suspension of preconceived understandings to avoid cultural bias. It makes the phenomenologist researcher a disinterested but not disengaged spectator.

Crossing the experiences in very different societies is a way to test hypotheses about human behavior and culture. The comparative studies consist of identifying similarities and differences between populations to isolate local specificities from global theories. It implies a few protocol regulations and many local collaborations. I added computational models to reinforce the findings with data evidence and deploy my research protocol in more cities in the years to come. Each case studies takes the shape of a report including a monograph on the geopolitical context, a list of key local stakeholders, a survey to random inhabitants, a social network analysis, and a series of one-to-one interviews with local experts. Working on cross-cultural studies implies having a sensitive knowledge of the local phenomena, applying statistical analysis to the data collected, and finally linking both by an effort of sedimentation of thoughts. This method is more sensitive to the complexity and the historical specificities of each case than a rigid description. It helps to understand the emergence of a phenomenon while cross-sourcing information sources in each case increase the level of validity of the findings. The originality of my research method, the newness of the topic, and the innovative tools used added to the boldness of doing it as an independent, brung me lots of support on my field investigations.

In part 1 of this thesis, I present the research question, define the concepts and the methodology. The smart-city promoters claim to develop a citizen-centric urban development model, supposedly inclusive, sustainable, and socially ethical. In practice, each city addresses the need for citizen engagement in local democracy, depending on the existing public infrastructures and the resources they dispose of at the moment. My goal is to develop a practical method for the digital engagement of citizens, transferable to most cities. I am willing to answer how the digital transformation of cities improves the power of influence of the citizens on their local governments while making decisions on the future of their towns. My primary hypothesis is that public investment in IT supports the digital transformation of citizenship and democracy. Civil society initiatives favoring open-data and open-source software increase the educational level needed in the population to make it a success. Collecting data ethically on citizens and social networks allows the scientists to understand the social dynamics of a city better and build effective predicting models on the population. Such repositories of data and research are crucial resources to feed a startup ecosystem and develop an economy of knowledge and innovation. Stakeholders of different categories may have opposite interests.

Still, it is necessary to engage them in consensual decision-making because none could reach enough power in a democracy to act alone. Computational simulations help to understand the collective dynamics of decision-making under the influence of multi-stakeholders with diverging interests.

Chapter 1 investigates democracy as the most adapted frame to allow all stakeholders to participate in the future of their cities. It first presents a synthetical history of citizenship and democracy concepts. From antic Greece to contemporary times, the role of the citizen has evolved along the European middle-age and the 18th century republican revolutions. Nowadays, the state of democracy questions the concepts of consensus and the general interest. The second step presents the contemporary criticism on post-democratic regimes, sometimes called the citizen crisis, and questions the later mutation of citizenship in a distant relationship with the institutions. A generation of upcoming citizens adapted to the global apathy of political lives. It developed new strategies of influence over their electives, empowered by social media and the internet. These new powers don't come without risk. There is notably a growing ability to manipulate public opinion by faking independent citizen identity while belonging to professional or class interests. Finally, a third step presents the innovations in voting and decision-making experimented by online communities. Entrepreneurs and hackers conceptualized decentralized autonomous organizations without representatives but collectively regulated. This perspective proposes to overpass the classical left/right, communitarian/liberal debate by opening new economic markets in the sense of shared ownership in entrepreneurial communities.

Chapter 2 introduces the last trend of urban developments, leaned on the overall development of communication and information technologies. The first part defines the smart city as a way to use data to improve urban living. Data is knowledge, and a new knowledge economy is booming in the cities. But collecting data means recording peoples' daily lives, and it questions the ethic of our societies. Are data-driven democracies trustworthy? It is needed to take a look at the forces at work in our contemporary society. The technology push/market pull paradigm presented is relevant to understanding how the innovation spreads in our cities through a direct market/civil society deal. In the second part, I develop the principle of collaborative management of urban projects from an overview of its stakeholders: public sector, private business, research & innovation, civil society, and media industry. I will also present a widespread collaboration agreement in the development of smart-city projects by public-private partnerships. A survey study has written the third part of this chapter of the RIL—the Finnish Association of Civil Engineers. It questions the success conditions of urban innovations, borrowing the concept of Key Success Factors to the science of management applied here to urban projects. It concludes that the participation of the most significant number of stakeholders is the best condition to ease urban transformations.

Chapters 3 and 4 share more information about the theoretical background and the research methodology used in my research. I want to develop social science research updated to the new possibilities offered by the technical progress. The field is relatively new and keeps evolving with the growth of social media and automation tools, so I tend to strengthen the demonstrability of my research with solid data analysis and a triangulation of the data sources. Humans are not considered autonomous entities anymore but rather interconnected informational organisms which share a global ecosystem with biological agents and technical artifacts. In this context, the city can be taken as an integrated socio-technical system. The actor-network theory helps me create relevant categories of stakeholders, which will be used in further machine learning and agent-based models. The actor-network theory is a theoretical and methodological approach to social science. Everything in the social and the natural worlds exists in constantly shifting networks of relationships. Since stakeholders of decision-making in urban transformations can be taken as interacting agents playing a challenging role of leadership among society, the actor-network theory is of good background support to my research. Consequently, places, events, organizations, processes are seen as much essential as humans in creating social situations. They all interact with each other and dynamically influence the ongoing direction taken by the system as a whole. In the second part of this thesis, from chapters 7 to 11, I will demonstrate how to use artificial intelligence such as machine learning to build predictive models on a city and agent-based modeling to simulate the output of the complex adaptive system of intelligent agents interacting. Profiling analysis of the data collected by survey and social network scraping will deduct the parameters of the multi-stakeholder dynamics. My approach uses concepts and tools crossed from both social and computer science. The representation of ego-networks, featuring node centralities, community detection, or link prediction, is a direct application of network science in urban research. The linguistic analysis will complete the comparative cultural study—the whole research validity benefits from using surveys, data analysis, and one-to-one interviews to cross-fertilize.

Chapter 5 is a foreseen of digital tools and methods used to gather stakeholders' participation in my research. I am validating my protocol of research by testing it on side studies. The first findings also help me define my population with more precision and serve as a warm-up lap in reaching the targets by emails and on social networks. The first survey study has been conducted on my French LinkedIn network. It is a sound out on their interest and practices of decision-making in urban planning. I collected 158 participants, balanced men/women, mainly in their '50s, working as executives in the private sector. 2 of 3 passed a Master's Degree. They use the internet many times a day, are not members of any political party. 81% of them say to be ready to block an urban project that does not match their values, and 87% would like to engage in decision-making on local urbanism but run out of time. 85% imagine that they could do it more easily online, with a convenient web app. The second study is a mixed survey and calls on 100 civic technology developers worldwide, with most French and American ones. It presents the digital developments of a range of young leaders at a median age of 32 years old, already engaged or concerned by offline politics. Their enterprise, startup, or non-profit organization is in most cases less than five years old and hires full-time salaried workforces financed by sales, grants, or investors. Most of them keep committed to governance by a state on which 80% of them imagine having a positive impact. They are not keen on automation and bots or artificial intelligence making decisions in place of citizens. The third study is a comparative survey between civic hackers from the USA, Taiwan, and Russia. I am collecting more information about the motivation to volunteer in the digital transformation of politics. A comparison of three web communities: Code for America, g0v, and Teplitsa tell a worldwide seek for self-fulfillment in life, meeting new people, and the continuous advance of personal skills.

But the cultural and political heritage in democracy and citizenship influence the management choices and the way to express political engagement. The local job market is also structuring the background of the willingness to working without a paycheck.

In chapter 6 I first explain how I chose my case studies in Taipei (Taiwan), Tel-Aviv (Israel), and Tallinn (Estonia). The logic underlying these choices was to catch a comparative study of three cities with similarities despite very different cultural, historical, and geopolitical backgrounds in Asia, the Middle-East, and North-Eastern Europe. After the first months of online research, I also already collected my first feedback. Some cities appeared to be more welcoming than others by the intermediary of potential local collaborators. Startup ecosystems have been decisive in my choices as an independent researcher bypassing the gatekeepers of academic formalities. Once I chose Taipei, Tel Aviv, and Tallinn as my three case study cities, I listed each category's main representative stakeholders and official networking organizations, places, and events for each city. And I follow with an in-depth comparison of the three case studies. Finally, it looks like Taiwan, Israel, and Estonia have a lot in common in their digital transformation. After having been occupied by foreign rulers for centuries, all three finally took advantage of this interbreeding. They all benefited from the nationalist emancipations to settled an authentic cultural identity, even if the pathway followed by the three are all different. I can see a significant comparison point in terms of geopolitical contexts. All three are small democratic regimes pushed into digital innovation to separate themselves from a considerable power somewhat authoritarian at the border. Nowadays, they keep struggling for independence or at least against the ambitions of domination of their neighbors. What happened in Hong Kong in 2020 increases Taiwan's concern about the assumed expansion of China in the area. The violent riots in Jerusalem in May 2021 recall that Israel is not at peace, and even if four countries of the Arabic league suspended their boycott of Israel last year, 12 out of 19 countries of the Arabic league maintain it. The Estonian government faces struggles to integrate its Russian population. And at the same time, Russia keeps considering East-Baltic as an area of privileged interest. Taiwan, Israel, and Estonia are all considered the few economic miracles, which succeeded in incredible growth quickly. All three invested in a strategic human resource in the context of a lack of any natural one. Supported by the advent of IT, they all became vibrant hubs for technological innovation and startups. In the three cases, the newly created state has been the first to ask entrepreneurs to develop innovative solutions, helped in promoting them worldwide to reach foreign markets, and keep supporting entrepreneurs through a series of facilities. The citizen engagement culture is not the same. Still, it resulted in the three cities in tailored services and e-citizenship devices to move the digital transition of democracy forward. Finally, the three towns developed a proper model of smart-city where the citizens can find room for expressing their opinion and influencing decision-making at a local level.

In part two of the thesis, I deliver in-depth data analysis and build different computational models from the data collected in the case studies. I present five artificial intelligence models: three machine learning ones and two agent-based models. First, I have had to clean and transform the data to interpret and conduct different calculations on the potential relationship between variables. I have been able to identify many correlations, which allows me to point regular patterns in citizen engagement and answer to some hypotheses with certainty. Then I am using different algorithms to predict various aspects of citizen engagement. I finally use probabilistic techniques to test how much I can infer my findings outside of my datasets.

Chapter 7 is a ranking model for citizen engagement in smart cities. The variables have been collected from the citizen's point of view, on a survey basis, in which they could tell how much they feel engaged, how much they trust the public sector, private companies, academics, or other civil society actors, and who influences them the most in their decision-making. They were asked if they want to engage more, how much, and by which channel of engagement. From these variables, I have created a class of highly engaged citizens, aggregate them by the city to finally rank cities on their citizen engagement score. Once trained on a subset of my data, the artificial neural network algorithm called Multi-Layer Perceptron achieves a satisfying performance in automatically detecting the highly engaged citizens in the dataset with more than 95% accuracy. At the same time, some strong correlations are noticed, leading to validating some hypotheses and denying some clichés. For example, the age and the willingness to use a voting app as a channel of engagement show no relationship. Gender does not affect the engagement feeling, but generation does. The youngest citizens feel more engaged than the oldest. And this tendency is confirmed by the length of stay: the one citizens having stayed less in the city usually feel more involved than the ones living there for a longer time. More surprising to me: the engagement feeling has no relationship with meeting peers in the neighborhood. In terms of the validated hypothesis, I can tell that the citizens who felt the most engaged wish to engage more. As well as those who feel the most engaged share their opinion in public more openly, which gets them in contact with other opinions, so they tend to change their opinion more easily. To build my predictive model, I combined different variables relevant to the definition of a highly engaged citizen in a Smart-City. A recursive feature elimination technique allowed me to select the best combination of data to avoid redundancy and increase the algorithm's performance. It appears that the three most important variables to detect highly engaged citizens are the level of engagement feeling, the number of sources of information used to shape an opinion, and the total messaging apps used to communicate with peers. These pieces of data have been the input for four classification algorithms of Machine Learning: Logistic Regression, K-Nearest Neighbours, Multi-Layer Perceptron, and Support Vector Machines. These four models have been used to predict the results of 2/3 random samples out of my data after training on 1/3. Three predictive models on four reach a satisfactory accuracy score. Still, the best of them is the Multi-Layer Perceptron; an Artificial Neural Network used to classify data points. However, the inferential statistics do not conclude on the allowance to generalize my classification model outside of my datasets because of the imbalance in the spread of highly engaged citizens between my three case study cities.

Chapter 8 is a predictive model for public opinion based on Twitter lexical content mining. While 78% of my participants express an interest in engaging more in the decision-making for the future of their cities, most of them say a lack of time. They would be open to the use of adapted channels for engagement. Indeed, if you've spent some time in citizen's meetings and neighborhood reunions, you've undoubtedly noticed that they often lack diversity: most active people can't join. They are either at work, at the gym, or taking care of the children or diner. The youngest citizens are not joining either. Most of them "are not interested in politics." As a result, actual citizen engagement is often biased by the unbalance of representativeness between citizens. It usually attracts higher proportions of activists, political professionals, retired people, freelancers looking for an opportunity, and unemployed people. A straightforward explanation of this situation is that in-person meetings at a particular hour in a specific place can't match other personal commitments for the broadest part of the population. Given this fact, I have been tempted to reach people's opinions directly where it is spontaneously expressed: on social networks. For this study, I have been collecting tweets in my three case studies, riding up to 2013 and 2012, which means almost all of what has been published on my cities of interest since the beginning of the social platform. I have then used opinion mining algorithms to detect the sentiment attached to each tweet and many other lexical features. After looking at the correlation between variables, I can assume some exciting relationships. If the limited length of tweets tends to frame the messages published, users behave on their own. They do not follow the same systematic rule. However, the grammatical rules of the language, and the length of words, are more determinant. Some features such as the average number of stop-words are highly dependent on subjectivity, while others such as the average number of punctuation are not. The average number of stopwords is positively correlated with all sentiment scores and bags-of-words. Sentiment scores are all strongly correlated to each other, positivity globally more strongly than negativity. Sentiment scores and the weight of BoWs are correlated to each other. Some hypotheses have been tested: the smart city index of the IMD business school has no relationship with citizen engagement on Twitter. The use of specific lexicons to urban topics is not correlated either to citizen engagement, even if it shows a significant correlation with some lexical variables such as the average number of stop-words or some sentiment scores—however, the hypothesis saying that sentiment scores are solid independent variables to predict citizen engagement on Twitter is validated. Consequently, the more citizens express a subjective opinion about their city on Twitter, the more the city can be considered highly engaged. So, after defining a highly engaged tweet from both sentiment polarity and subjectivity scores, I have created a categorical variable called "highly engaged" to classify the 20% cities having the citizens the most engaged. As a precision on my case studies, Taipei has 1589 highly engaged tweets out of a total of 17,341, representing 9.76%. Tel Aviv has 1485 engaged tweets out of 17,628, meaning 8.42 % of the total, and Tallinn has 705 active tweets out of 6,299, or 11.19% of the total. I used this variable as the target of my four machine learning models. I found that the K-Nearest Neighbours classifier is the one model achieving the best performance in predicting the classification of highly engaged cities from the citizen engagement on Twitter. So far, I haven't been able to prove the statistical validation of this predictive model since there is a too big difference in standard deviations between my three samples.

Chapter 9 is also based on Twitter analysis, but this one focuses on the topology of networks. Who is connected with who, and which probability for new connections to form? This study aims to detect the most influential users across each city's network and predict the evolution of the dynamics of citizen engagement influenced by the multiple stakeholders of a smart city. My research question here is to know if the popularity of the social platform depends on the level of engagement. I am also trying to see if I can predict the influence of a user on the whole city's network from graph-based machine learning algorithms. Some basic human observation will provide the first insights: the number of followers and the followers/followings ratio, average likes, comments & RT per tweet, comments & RT per account, network associations between categories of stakeholders (public sector, private business, academics, civil society, media). Using algorithms on the datasets can lead to much deeper analysis: node-level measures such as centrality and position in the network, edge-level statistics and probabilities of non-edges to form an edge, and network-level structures: communities of nodes and effectiveness label propagation. By investigating the topologies of my networks, I have been able to detect significant insights relevant to the further steps of the thesis. A look at the structures of connections between categories of stakeholders revealed that the public sector and the media industry do not have a complete network of networks between cities. In contrast, the private sector (corporate and startups) has the strongest one.

Academics and civil society have an existing but weak connection across cities. The categories having a strong categorical relationship assure a better resilience to edge/node deletion and a better information flow between them. Surprisingly the public sector and the media, two professional communicators, are the less connected across cities. I can argue that they focus instead on local engagement than an international one, while corporate companies and startups are thinking globally to grow their market shares. Otherwise, the number of tweets is correlated with the number of followers and the maximum number of likes received. The number of nodes and the number of edges are related to the number of tweets, which means that the size of an ego network is proportional to the user's activity. Still, the number of followers is not correlated to the number of nodes, neither to the number of edges nor to the size of the network. So, the size of a network is not helping in terms of popularity. Since the average shortest path length shows a clear correlation with the number of followers, I assume that the most popular users also can spread information more widely, thus being influential on the network as a whole. On another note, the number of tweets (engagement metric) has a better multi-correlation with other variables than the number of followers or the maximum likes received (popularity metrics). This confirms my assumption that the popularity on the network is hardly predictable. Finally, the rage on the social network measured with the number of followers or the maximum likes received does not react as expected: it is not systematically related to the engagement level in the network. Other factors may enter into a collision with the performance as an influencer on Twitter. This finding echoes previous assumptions from my research, saying that civil society, for example, is granted more trust than the media industry and corporate companies. However, professional stakeholders often have much more significant networks and a better tactic of class engagement which confers them more power of influence. Suppose the number of connected components and the maximum degree centrality is well correlated to the other variables. In that case, both achieve a terrible performance taken as a unique independent target to predict from other variables with a linear regression algorithm. Finally, I am using graph-based machine learning to make inferences of two kinds: node classification into communities and link prediction.

Chapter 10 is an agent-based model simulating the formation of the opinion of neutral citizens under the influence of highly engaged ones. An agent-based model (ABM) is a class of computational models for simulating the actions and interactions of autonomous agents to assess their effects on the system as a whole. Such computational simulation allows me to learn more about the dynamics of a crowd of citizens interacting in a complex system of mutual influences. In the first part of this study, I experimented with the original voting model from NetLogo library, the usual integrated development environment for ABM. In this model, each agent has eight neighbors and is randomly assigned an opinion at the setup, blue or green. All agents update their opinion at the same time, according to the majority opinion around them. In case of equality in the neighbors: four blue and four green, the agent will stick to its previous state. When you run the model, you can see that gradually and more and more clearly, clusters of opinions arise. Blue cells and Green cells, which were perfectly mixed randomly from the initial state, tend to progressively aggregate by color until a stable distribution emerges where clear boundaries are visible. Some parameters can be changed to which lead to different outputs: when each agent is asked to change its opinion in case of equality in the neighborhood, the society keeps vibrating in a constant instability of borders, and when the agents are invited to take the opinion of the minority in their area systematically, the distribution of opinions tends to aggregate themselves in big masses until one takes the advantage on the other and finally turns the whole population to its color. After that, I am entering the code of the original model to test different variations of the parameters, notably unbalancing the initial distribution of opinions. The experiment shows very clearly that it can never reverse an initial slight imbalance. The minority class remains from a 60/40 initial distribution; but it almost disappears from the simulations starting at a 70/30 distribution. In the second part of the study, I am developing my citizen engagement model from scratch, using the empirical data collected in my survey study. Each agent is attributed some initial parameters: a graduate opinion between -1 and 1, representing any topic of public interest. An engagement score is inspired by the combination of variables from chapter 11. The manual setup allows determining the quantity of highly engaged citizens in the population. And a social status starts at 1 for all agents. Still, it increases each time an agent interacts with another, progressively giving more power of influence to the agents engaging the most. Two facilities ensure the effect of these parameters: an engagement score above 75% confers an increased vision giving the agent the ability to reach an agent twice farther than the others, and a speed of moving which increase proportionally to the social status giving the agent more chance to get in touch with more peers to influence them. Different patterns emerge along with the runs: after some time, a sentiment (positive or negative) takes advantage of the other. It ends up turning the whole population to its side. The final result is susceptible to slightly unbalanced opinion distribution at the setup. But the engagement score and social status facilities have the potential to reverse an initial unbalance. Engagement score and social status took individually both increase the opinion formation. Still, they don't constantly get a better result when combined. The initial percentage of highly engaged citizens affects the formation of public opinion. It has the potential to reverse an initial unbalance. However, it is not regular: some values can reach an optimal speed in forming opinions while others get the worst results. For example, 20% of highly engaged citizens result in the fastest formation of public opinion. In comparison, a proportion of 30% takes fourth more time. The social status tends to counterbalance the power of influence of the highly engaged citizens and allows a better prediction of the public opinion. Finally, the model proves that the formation of thought in a population is susceptible to highly engaged citizens benefiting from an experience in political engagement and a social reward such as social status.

Chapter 11 integrates all data analysis in an agent-based model simulating the spread of individual opinions and influences on a social network. I am using data integration in profiling each stakeholder category: public sector, corporate companies, startups, academic research, civil society, and media. Five parameters have been built from nineteen variables out of three sources of data collection. In the Stakeholder Engagement model, one representative of each stakeholder category will try to influence a population of undecided users. It has been coded in Python programming language and aims to observe how the users of a social network can take advantage of others and how it potentially affects public opinion. To simulate the ability of stakeholders to influence the decision-making at a society scale, I have created four attributes from different combinations of variables: engagement represents the networking activity, trustability represents the level of trust one is granted by the others, influenceability says how much one is sensitive to others' opinion, and recovery is the capacity of someone to recover from an influence. Influenceability is a constant value, while engagement and trustability vary along with the simulation, depending on the agent activity. Recovery is stable in itself but under the influence of the experience gained each time an agent recovers from an influence. The more an agent is experienced, the more easily it can recover from an influence. Giving the first look at these parameters, it seems that the corporate companies are the most engaged in networking. At the same time, the startups get an impressive recovery capacity. The public sector has the highest trustability, but the academics the lowest one, aside from civil society, which also has the highest influenceability score. I can already invalidate the hypothesis that civil society has more power of influence at a network level: professional users globally have more opportunity to build a prominent and dense network and adopt the best communication strategy, balancing their trustability with the public opinion. In this model, the agents of a network with a strong argument will try to influence the neutral ones to get engagement points that confer an increased influence. I am validating different hypotheses with this ABM. In the formation of opinion, clusters appear, which stabilize sub-group opinion between nodes. The whole population never turns to a single thought: a few neutral or opposite ideas always remain. Before a threshold value of average node degree between 3 and 4, no opinion takes a dominant advantage over the other ones. With the moderate node degree at 2, it takes a long time and many tries for a stakeholder to fully convert a neutral user to a strong opinion. But an increase in average node degree will increase the speed of the formation of thought to a stable state. The average node degree increases the rate of opinion formation. It decreases the proportion of neutral or opposite remaining and allows domination of one opinion on the others. Before a threshold value between 2 and 3 average node degrees, positive and negative tends to stabilize at an equivalent rate. Thus the hypothesis saying that network topology has an impact on opinion formation is validated. Some stakeholders have more chances than others to turn the whole population into their opinion. So even if we start with three positive and three negative stakeholders, the entire population will not turn out depending on who has what statement. Thus the hypothesis saying that some stakeholders have more power of influence on the public opinion is validated. When a single stakeholder has a contrary opinion than the other ones, its chance to influence the whole network depends on its attributes, of course, giving him more or less power of influence on the others, but also its position in the network. Indeed, the more central it is, the more chances it has to take advantage of the network or maintain a significant minority nested in the whole network. Thus, the hypothesis that there are strategic positions in the network that significantly increases one stakeholder's chances of spreading its opinion to the entire network is validated. A regular conspiracy theory says that professional interests manipulate people. I have attributed all population nodes an opinion, and the contrary view to the six categories of stakeholders in my model. Despite their advantageous parameters, which give them an increased power of influence, the professional stakeholders haven't been able to reverse the opinion of the mass population and have rapidly aligned their idea to the majority. Thus the hypothesis of the conspiracy scenario saying that a coalition of stakeholders can reverse the thought of a population when it is formed is wrong.

As a final discussion on this cross-cultural study, I have strengthened the findings out of my computational models by linking the outputs of each city with the keen understanding developed along with my stays and recorded in monographs. All in one, it appears that Tel Aviv is the most excited on a word-to-mouth way of information to make a decision, and the one using public space the most to get in touch with others; Tallinn is the city with the most expressive and engaged tweets overall, while Taipei releases easily on its city council and public consultant to build a bottom-up approach of governance. All in one, like a city, like a social network: Tel Aviv is vibrant, welcoming, and noisy, while Tallinn is dense and faithful to its users, while Taipei is the most neutral but shows the most effective results at the end.

In an epilogue, I take a distance from my thesis built on developed countries from the advent of CIT in the '90s. I am questioning myself on the replicability of these economic development models in less developed countries.I chose the African continent to take another perspective on civic technologies and smart cities. Africans are currently finding their way to live the digital experience and are profoundly reinventing the African continent. Cities, democracies can benefit widely from the opportunities knocking at their doors. The spatial technologies allow an assessment of the existing situation and a better analysis of the local realities of the territories. It helps understand the situation widely, with simple elements. The recording technology will manage the resources better, plan a resilient development, and establish standard norms by partnerships from a shared vision based on solidarity. While Africa's financial services industry logs impressive growth as more banks target the continent's emerging middle class, and a growing interest to invest in African emerging economies comes from the African diaspora worldwide, there is still a lot to do in terms of building a shared vision for the future of the continent. Urbanization and digitalization are opportunities to develop economies. Still, they can't go without finding consensus between the peoples, the governments, and the private investors.

INTRODUCTION: Researcher nomad, a field man.

"Contemporary philosophy looks like a chess game where players ignore that some moves are possible and always play the same moves obsessionally. I suggest that it would be more interesting to get conscious of the possibility of playing other moves, already played in the past, which we have lost the souvenirs." Claude Romano *(2012)*

Several philosophers commonly consider a few revolutions in humankind: the Copernican revolution told the human he is not at the center of the universe. The Darwinian revolution told the human he is part of the animal species. The Freudian revolution told the human that he does not control his consciousness. In the last two or three decades, computation and ICT profoundly changed our vision of the world. Humans are no more autonomous entities but rather interconnected informational organisms that share a global ecosystem with biological agents and technical artifacts. We are probably living the fourth revolution of thought.

A phenomenological approach of city science

To catch the sense of this global phenomenon of the digital transformation of cities, I applied some philosopher's practice bringing back nearly-forgotten concepts in science, called phenomenology. Suppose the empirical approach of research consists of using rational images of what is observed. In that case, the phenomenological approach goes more in-depth in the living of the experiment by asking the researcher to put his judgments in brackets for the time of the observation.

In the following, I first argue how to use phenomenology as the science of what appears to one's conscience. Then I explain how sensitive ecosystems work and how the technology became a perceptive device to feel the world one lives in. In the last point, I'm developing what attitude it asks of the researcher.

a. A phenomena is the shape of a meaning

If phenomenology can be considered the science and the theory of the living experience, where a researcher dives into a context and uses its sensitivity to observe what appears to its consciousness, the underlying goal of this method is to trace the source of living phenomena. The observation interprets a specific vision of things. It is done on more or less precise theoretical notions in the background. An event erupting in time catches the attention of the observer. On the contrary, a fact will be regular and repeated, captured by an observer, and converted into reportable data. Differently, the phenomena designate what shows up to someone in this world and consider how it shows up.

Hans-Dieter Gondek and László Tengelyi give a commonly approved definition of phenomena: a phenomenon is the shape of meaning, conceived as a sensitive appearance emerging from a human living, and phenomenology is defined as the science of observing phenomena and their origins. Edmund Husserl (1959–1938) is considered the father of modern phenomenology. He wanted to elaborate a science that goes straight to the things themselves. Husserl suggested engaging first in the complex wholeness of what happens, then keeping a personal link with our living. Suppose an empirical scientist uses rational experiments to test hypotheses to create new knowledge. In that case, the phenomenologist considers a broader experience from what he feels sensitively in an observation context. As knowledge is built in the interaction with the object of study, perception is made in the interaction with the phenomenon.

But phenomenology remains a science, and its findings are valid to other scientists. The goal is not only to refurbish all that relates to sensitivity, affectivity, the spontaneity that used to be downgraded to an infra-rational level in science but also to promote these diverse dimensions of existence and understanding constitutive elements, fully integrate into human reason. Edmund Husserl refused traditional empiricism, which pretends to build knowledge from a bottom-up analysis of sensations and observations, and the transcendental concepts come from a top-down reason. He promoted the third way, arguing that the experience of living precedes conceptual thinking and its requirements. And this primary perception opens on the truth, in essence, overpassing the underlying assumptions of the later-acquired consciousness. The phenomenology offers the possibility to enlighten an original layer of signification shaded under the intellectual concepts.

b. The technique as a perception tool

The Romanian philosopher and theologist Mircea Eliade (1907–1986) invented the term ontophany to designate how our being-in-the-world appears to us by the intermediary of cultural myths and history. Our perception of the world grows in a "bubble" in which our ability to perceive is structured by the tools and concepts of thinking we dispose of. Each technical generation can be seen as an underlying framework for the perception, which introduces a qualitative renewal of the way humans feel to be in the world. It means that the technical ecosystem in which we live at a given date influences the world's phenomena we perceive.

Before they become tools and devices we can use, the techniques are structures of perception that shape our existence. An invisible matrix, produced by history and culture, in which flows our possible experiment-of-the-world and the possibility to transcend it. Like the animals live their existence in a proper perceptive ecosystem which results directly from their specific (related to species) sensorial devices, the humans live in the sensitive ecosystem issued from the systemic tools of their period of history. By giving us perceptions of an unknown world, the digital interfaces have deeply shaken the ontophanic culture we were used to living in. Stephane Vial introduced digital ontophany to update this concept to a digital era where actual beings appear to us by digital intermediates. Being native of a generation is not much a question of birthdate but perceptive devices at our disposal. Experiencing digital living means being paired to the world by digital devices.

Our pre-linguistic experiences have set necessary structures and intelligibility lineaments, autonomous from the linguistic schemes of conceptual thinking. Some fundamental learnings such as colors and sounds, for example, are a necessity rooted in prior experiences, which owns its proper reason, not derived from social conventions. Phenomenology starts by assuming a logic-of-the-world in itself since our consciousness perceives the world as a phenomenon. To catch the complexity of the digital phenomena, to enlighten the sense of what we perceive (and what we are) in front of the interfaces, we need to overpass the concept of virtual. The question is no longer to know if our online experiences are real. The only reality we can live in nowadays is a hybrid of digital and non-digital ones.

c. An unconditional openness attitude

Studying phenomena consists in a suspension of the judgment regarding our natural attitude on space and time, on our beings, and our opinions of this world. At the same time, we keep anchored to the natural world as a source of information to receive an internal and external experience. Indeed, adopting a rigorist perspective on the human object of study is under-ranking it at a passive state, which means losing the essence of human tasks.

The phenomenological approach of geography studies opposes itself to a passive conception of the human. While personal motivations characterize the socio-spatial activity of the human, the humanist geographer prefers to describe a situation without reducing it to a study of forms and numbers, and phenomenology allows the geographer to interact with its ecosystem.

The considerable difficulty in adopting a phenomenological approach comes from the wideness of the phenomenological field, forcing the researcher to an unconditional openness to the world displayed in front of his eyes and inviting him to engage his subjectivity in its aim.

No remarkable reduction is obtained by empirical exercises but by an effort of thought. In a first step, one exercises imaginary variations to recognize the relations and the dependencies between objects of study. In a second step, one observes the constitution of the essences inside the phenomena and the sense given by one's consciousness. And the third step consists of a process of meaning sedimentation, where the new meaning is impossible until a deeper invariable is reached: the founding essence of what has been observed expresses its sense.

Suppose our perception of the world depends on conceptual schemes. In that case, it depends on linguistic particularities and differs from one culture to another. Two different conceptual frameworks describing the same phenomena from two different cultural backgrounds may not refer to the same perception of the same world. Local particularities emerge in the worldwide digital transformation, depending on the needs, contextual elements, and cultural background.

A phenomenological approach consists of a temporary suspension of the preconceived understanding of a phenomenon, avoids the bias induced by cultural attributes, and encourages the phenomenologist researcher to become a disinterested but not disengaged spectator.

Comparative method to Cross-Cultural Urban Studies

Comparative Studies or Cross-Cultural Studies specializes in anthropology and sister sciences (sociology, psychology, economics, political science) that uses field data from many societies to test hypotheses about human behavior and culture. It consists of identifying trends shared between cases to build a comparison between them and allows scientists to isolate and bring to light local specificities to grow generalization and global theories. The temptation to international understanding intensifies in a context of worldwide innovation such as the internet and increases cross-national collaborations or scientific exchanges.

To overpass local specificities in a global phenomena understanding, comparative research methodology implies a few protocol regulations and a certain level of personal immersion for the researcher to catch the complexity of factors, configurations, relationships of a study context.

a. A common protocol of research:

Building inference on urban development at the wide-scale of global cities implies a considerable data record. At the time of "Big Data," it is not hard to find such repositories openly shared on the web. Still, most of them are usually sparse and already overly exploited. They are suitable for training studies but not enough to feed the ambition to find something new to say about. As I wanted to look at the digital transformation of citizenship and democracy in very different cultural contexts, I chose to collect my datasets and build my analysis models. It asked me to find many local collaborations to anchor my context understanding to the field and strengthen the validity of my crafted work by using computational tools whose scientificity makes no doubt. In the end, I expect to have built strong data analysis models which can be deployed in many smart-city contexts.

My protocol of research is a constant reporting template applied to each case study:

- a monograph of the cultural, historical, geographical and political context,
- an identification of the local dynamics, featuring key stakeholder identification,
- a survey to the inhabitants pointing to the availability and their willingness to take part in decision-making on local urban planning and the future of the city.
- both lexical and topological social network analysis,
- a series of one-to-one interviews of experts.

The work on cross-cultural datasets is an exercise of pattern discovery at the scale of the data. It suggests getting a sensitive knowledge of the topic and the case studies written in individual monographs, then focusing on the data analysis, which means applying statistical reduction, correlation, and prediction to observe what sense comes out of it, and finally describe the links between the tendencies discovered in the datasets and their context of emergence described in the monograph. It is a process of reinforcement learning where each step brings new sensitivity levels, allowing the researcher to build an upper level of analysis among its case studies.

b. Monographs comparison in urban science:

Comparing things is essential to basic scientific and philosophic inquiry. Still, the primary issue in comparative research remains: the datasets in different countries may define things differently or may not use the same categories. Since I collect my data, I do not depend on any third-party work or collaboration. After analyzing my datasets and bringing to light some local specificities, I focus on establishing the societal coherence of each case study city, then lean from one to the other to build generalities on my topic.

The method of comparison by monographs is more sensitive to the complexity and the historical specificity of each case than a rigid description frame. Monographs are in-depth case studies written by crossing different sources of information to help understand a context of the emergence of a phenomenon before identifying by comparison, what the different situations converge or diverge, and eventually, what factors make them divide. Cross-national comparison isolates the national policy impact on society, and cross-sourcing information increases the level of validity of the findings.

As for the statistical analysis of the data collected in each case study, the overall idea is to extract the information packed in complexity by discovering patterns in the datasets and transform it into a comprehensive blending for further use. Interesting groups of data records can be brought together (Clustering), unusual records (Anomaly Detection), and dependencies (Association Rule Learning) can then be seen as a kind of summary of the input data, which I may use in Machine Learning and Predictive Analytics.

c. Personal immersion in field studies:

Furthermore, while observing the complexity of factors, configurations, relationships constituent of an urban context, it is asked to the researcher to reach a sensitive experience of the locals' living. While the researcher reads about a context and meets locals with no preconceived opinion and confronts it to the daily reality he experiences during its stay, he progressively gets an overall understanding of the local perspective to a topic and becomes able to extract what makes the most sense in the data records from what does not echo much.

When we compare social dynamics in such cities, it is usually to attest to phenomena happening in each of them, to identify the differences that can influence the effect of these macro-trends. In a global context where national spaces are questioned in their ability to contend interpersonal relationships and international competition between the cities to implement the latest urban innovations to attract value-added populations, it appears relevant to scale the governance research at the scale of the town.

I do not list a precise range of information or an anticipated set of stakeholders I would like to meet or involve in my studies. Even In the first time of my research, I don't lead a term to term comparison trying to isolate this or that variable. I will focus on establishing societal coherences specific to each city. Then lean from one to the other findings in each town to state generalities on the topic. It makes less sense to write a term-to-term comparison than individual, societal coherences attached to each case study in this context.

The originality of my research method, the newness of the topic, and the innovative tools used added to the boldness of doing it as an independent, brung me lots of support on my field investigations. As an outsider of the academic institution, I have set myself to avoid the usual gatekeepers and share as much as I can the results of my research online to an international network. Hopefully, my research will get the double value to incite other researchers to engage Taiwan, Israel, and Estonia in cross-border collaboration and to discuss my methodological proposition to use digital nomadism as a scientific research purpose.

Along the road, I have met many open-minded people willing to travel, discover different cultures than their own and enjoy the best side of globalization. While most institutions globally call for a reduction of the impact of the GAFAM on our societies, when others suggest a replication of their model by national states, and the most radical simply say to delete it, I must say that I would never have been able to deliver the following work ten years ago without Google, Airbnb, Facebook, Twitter, Meetup.

Suppose we certainly need a way to share wealthiness and opportunities inside and between nations. In that case, our generation also needs such tools to access international peace and productive collaboration.

PART 1 : RESEARCH PROBLEM

Suppose the smart-city standard model globally claims the consensual discourse about the citizen-centric approach of urban development. In that case, it neglects to spell out a realistic scenario of how collaborative decision-making, involving all stakeholders, is to be engendered across the city's public sphere. Indeed Smart Governance, Smart Citizenship, Citizen Participation, Citizen-focus, and broader social benefit of smart-city projects are often considered a necessary value to find in every urban project but not yet perceived as a vital component of the decision-making city scale.

In practice, each city develops an answer to participatory governance, according to a specific situation defined by the geographical, social, economic, and cultural context, the infrastructure state of development, and the resource at their disposal. A wide range of urban approaches, strategies, targets, and stakeholder interests define and influence the path to digital transformation to achieve the challenges of our times. Digital technologies, the spread of social media, neighbors' meetups, and city councils all refurbish the practices of urban planners to engage multiple stakeholders and communities in co-designing urban development. The sum of anonymous people, forming a social network, whose power lies in creating new interactions as much online as offline, expands the democratic process and the citizenship experience to unprecedented levels of possibilities.

My main goal is to develop an innovative, shared, and transferable model of citizen engagement in decision-making that better serves the needs of the city government and the inhabitants in the process of deciding what will be the future of their city. To assist the evolution of urban planning in a gathering process of all stakeholders, I am willing to explore the potential of inhabitants and local communities to lead a city's development through balanced network initiatives as a leader.

Problematic:

How does the digital transformation of cities improve the power of influence of the citizens on their local governments while making decisions on the future of their towns?

Hypotheses:

- Public investment in I.T. supports the digital transformation of citizenship and democracy.
- Civil society initiatives in favor of open-data and open-source software such as civic-hackers communities increase the educational level needed in the population to make it a success.
- Collecting data ethically on citizens and social networks allows the scientists to understand the social dynamics of a city better and build effective predicting models on the population.
- Such repositories of data and research are crucial resources to feed a startup ecosystem and develop an economy of knowledge and innovation.
- Stakeholders of different categories may have opposite interests. Still, it is necessary to engage them in consensual decision-making because none of them could reach enough power in a democracy to act alone.
- I am modeling computational simulations of the formation of public opinion to experience the collective dynamics of decision-making under the influence of multi-stakeholders with diverging interests.

1. Democracy: the "least bad" model of governance

Governance by the people for the people is the theoretical definition of our modern democratic regimes. However, reaching massive citizen engagement in permanent collective decision-making processes sounds to any city manager or political leader roughly like an unrealistic ideal. To better understand the political and philosophical frame of our public institutions, I had a look at the history of citizenship and democracy, two concepts that evolved a lot from Ancient Greece to nowadays and keep influencing the digital perspective of the most radical innovators.

As far as we commonly consider Antic Athens as the cradle of our modern political regime, it was very different from our contemporary context: Antic Greece was a slavery system where only privileged men could be citizens, while women, slaves, foreigners, and children, were kept far from political life. Suppose we can't consider that antiquity knew democracy as we live in. In that case, we can't assume that antiquity knew the capitalist economy as we do: having a business in ancient Athens had nothing to do with nowadays enterprises. It is also interesting to know that most Athenian philosophers were hostile to a people's government: Platon (428 BC—348 BC) argued against giving the power of decision-making to philosophers led by Absolute Truth. And Aristotle (384 BC—322 BC) considered elections as non-democratic because they imply selecting the best citizens instead of a government by the whole.

a. History of Democracy and Citizenship

Antic Athens—The origins

The first people to document, write and build political theories about the art of reaching a goal in society by discussing with peers were the Greeks of Antic Greece. "The great and new idea of people's sovereignty, composed of free and equal citizens" was the core principle for Cleisthenes reform in 508 BCE, considered as the foundation of Athenian democracy, which first gave citizenship a conditional status to civil rights in a society, and developed a political science attached to this way of governance. The background philosophy of democracy has been conceptualized by Platon, who considered that all humans raised in society are granted with a minimum of politiké techné (political technique or ability) which justifies that whatever artisan or shopkeeper of Athens engages in politics. Furthermore, humans possess the quality of philia (friendliness), which makes them cooperative by nature, and the diké (justice), these last two qualities being essential to the koinonia (community), according to Aristotle.

The Greeks were also considering paideia (elevation) as developing moral virtues, the sense of civic responsibilities, and the conscious identification to the community, its traditions, and values. The practice of the dicastéria (jury) and the Ecclésia (Assembly) raised the intellectual level of the average Athenian citizen, conscious that all citizens could be randomly assigned a governing position of a day on very diverse causes: civil, criminal, public, and private affairs. To maintain the fairness of this system, the Athenians invented ostracism: the right to exile for ten years someone overly influential without losing his goods, properties, and citizen status. And the graphé paranomon, when a man was accused and judged posteriorly to have given an unfortunate proposition to the Assembly.

Ancient Athens was a society without any media: the town crier's information in public affairs, small talks, and rumors. Thus oral reports and chats composed the governmental machinery. This situation forced the political leaders to have a direct relationship with their people, so they were directly controllable. Athens was a direct democracy, and this political regime led every citizen to have a good governance experience. Primary education to everybody, even slaves, was used to spread manipulating ideas in all the population.

Antic Rome—The power of conquest

The Roman empire (1st to 5th century ACE) didn't have the richness of invention of Antic Greece. Still, it ran Athenian ideas into the realistic and built institutions on it. At the opposite of Athenian citizenship, the Roman one was integrative and practically generalized: citizens' rights were given to many people, primarily for identification and protection. They gave them an obligation to respect Roman law. The law, the Respublica, and the Imperium institutionalize the military and the administrative orders established by the Senate and the People. The legal statements and the philosophic legitimations operate as a frame, a mark, and a perpetuation of the founding action of the civil community.

Every citizen has the right to vote, but the votes are organized by groups, not by heads. Most legal authorities are set by-elections, so an oligarch dimension remains. Three organizing features constitute the community: at the top, the king-priests, the senators, and the civil judges are charged to communicate with the gods and administer the Respublica under the invocation of Jupiter. In the middle, the Warriors defend the city and extend its glory under the prayer of Mars. On this basis, the farmers and the artisans supply the material needs under the invocation of Quirinus. Cesar Augustus, emperor because the public consensus wanted it, gathered diverse attributes: the administrative potestas (power) and the auctoritas (authority) made him master religious and political order. He also had the moral ability to judge what is suitable for the public. In his quality of imperator (commander), he is the supreme chief of the legions. Like princeps (leader), finally, he has the responsibility to engage in the economy and the culture, all that can contribute to the happiness and the honor of the city.

The success in the conquest of the Roman Empire will extend it to a scale that more and more fluxes go through and weaken the roman peace. People newly conquered do not have the time to adapt to their new political responsibilities and are at risk of subversion. The management of this vast territory asks for more and more intermediates, and the emperor can't be at the same time on the battlefields in faraway borders and at Rome to control the administrative network. In this situation, Christianity preaching developed until the emperor Constantin (272 ACE–337 ACE) ended anti-christian persecutions from 312 ACE and died baptized. He gave his name to the city Constantinople, which will become the Eastern Roman Byzantine Empire (from the 5th century A.D. to 1453 AD).

Middle-Age—The city of God

(Note from the writer: I focus on the evolution of citizenship and democracy in Europe)

Two events in the first Millenium in this area of civilization are undoubtedly the political success of two religions: Christianity (from the 1st century) and Islam (from the 7th century). Their vision of the world, relative but different, will deeply impress the minds and the habits of populations. They both root in Jewish sacral texts and affirms the superiority of a unique God, creator, and master of the law, the fall-down of the human lost by his sins, and the possibility of redemption in the condition to listen to the divine teaching. Monotheism introduces a big difference between Greek and Roman gods and myths. It allows the creation of communities of men not by legal contract but based on the common personal relationship with God.

Roughly from the 4th to the 18th century, the believer governor would aim to succeed in the higher goal to build the City of God by the believers' community, together with the City of Men and its tribulations on earth. Through the experience of living, studying, and practicing religious texts, the religious orders will give the rules to organize the spiritual becoming of the populations. In a feudal system, the King is the custodian of the common good and substitutes for the development of Christianity in place of civic goals. But in the centuries to come, the power rivalries between the Church and the Kings and Emperors lead to a division of powers and the creation of nations. This separation of political and religious powers is known as the main difference between Christianity and Islam context.

Christian philosophers are not indifferent to this change of paradigm: the political reflection of Thomas Aquinas (1224 AD—1274 AD) proved that human life, as part of the creation, had to be governed by reason, concerning human nature and the willingness of the community. Since so, if the Church is in charge to assure eternal salvation, the government is to ease life on earth. Marsilius of Padua (1275 AD—1342 AD) opposed the authority of the Pope. They advanced the definition of what should be a laic state inside Christianity, where the universality of the citizens has the responsibility to edict the laws and maintain them. He set the germ of the separation of the law and the political power. All humans have to conform to the rules, even the monarch, and the princes.

Republican revolutions—The power to the people

The political thought of citizenship will be radically renewed in the 18th century and imposed by two revolutions: the French and the American ones. This period is the foundation of new citizenship, still in constant gestation until nowadays. French philosopher Rousseau (1712 AD—1778 AD) will influence the rise of counter-powers and the claim of the superiority of "general willingness significantly." Rousseau embraced an ideal republic based on a social contract ensuring perfect equality between humans respecting laws of sovereign general willingness.

- **The American revolution:**

The rebellion of the British settlers from 1763 ACE will result in the foundation of the Republic of the United States in 1783 ACE in the name of natural equality, the liberty to undertake, and the right for everyone to use his property and the fruits of his work, as the right of the community to chose the judges and the institutions. Directly inspired by Montesquieu (1689 AD—1755 AD), the founding Fathers of the U.S. had constantly in mind to avoid excessive powers between the different scales of the federal system. They keep skeptical on the concept of a common will and shape the American Republic as an unavoidable division between individuals, definitely diverse in their desires and interests. The Americans, to limit the power, have broken the atom of sovereignty. The "American spirit" is a pragmatic combination of a pessimist perspective on human nature and the political limitation of power.

- **The French revolution:**

In a different context, the idea of a Nation strengthened by centuries of the kingdom is deeply implemented in the French revolution (1789 ACE). The King is precisely the target of the French republicans, but rather than abandon the concept of centralized power. They will lean on it to shape a national power sovereign, one and indivisible.

Anyone who is privileged and stands in his position self-excludes the nation. Anyone who abandons his privileges joins the whole of the people in the French nation, where no one can practice any authority on the others if not expressly emanated from the nation. For the French, the best way to escape the tyranny of particular interests is to grant a general mandate to an elective. In short, they substituted a Nation represented in institutional bodies to a whole people embodied in the King's persona. The liberty of every individual allows him to do "whatever don't harm others," and the law is the guardian of the limits to the freedom of everyone. On this point, the French revolution is at the antipodes of the American one, which put freedom of expression above every law.

20th century—An end to illusions

(Note from the writer: I focus on post-Totalitarianism evolutions of democracies)

In 1942, Schumpeter published Capitalism, socialism, and democracy and gave a powerful upswing to the consideration of democracy as a method, without an ideal goal, to build an efficient and peaceful political power led by strong but respected governments. Liberty and equality become nonessential compared to old definitions of democracies. The ideal goals anciently pursued are rejected: because they are goals, they are considered a menace.

In The Open Society and Its Enemies (1942), Karl Popper writes a solid attack on any form of totalitarianism and accuse the precedent philosophers, from Platon to Marx, to have promoted the advent of authoritarian governments in succumbing to the temptation to predict the purpose of humanity and its further phases of development. Popper considers democracy as the least bad model of governance, which nests processes forbidding the authorities to shirk its obligation to dialog. This scientific approach of the democratic argument, opposed to the idea of an abstract utopian goal to achieve, goes with the conscious warning by Popper of the ambitions of a scientific State.

The contemporary definition of democracy comes from Georges Burdeau (1905 AD–1988 AD): "The citizen is not the real individual, with his weakness, his selfishness, his blindness, and his enthusiasm. The human enlightened by reason, speaking under the necessities of this common reason, free from social-class bias and the inherent concerns to his economic condition, can give his opinion on public causes without being dominated by his interest. In short, a sort of saint laic who gained his qualification of a member of the sovereign nation by his disinterest."

b. Contemporary concepts of Democracy and Citizenship

How could a single word, in a period of 25 centuries, cover the same idea? Each period brings its proper enrichment to the previous concept and sometimes includes some regressions. The most recognized decline in contemporary democracies is the widespread indifference and ignorance of most voters. In some elections, the majority of voters do not even take care of voting. For a few experts in political sciences, this political apathy is not alarming. It has a rather good effect on the general political mood, counter-balancing the most radical voters who are the real danger of liberal democracies.

Consensus and general interest

Citizenship and democracy reflect society: a combination of contradictions and rules, conflicts and consensus, shared values, and confronted ideas. But the general interest is more than the sum of individual ones, and the inclusion based on the principle of equality can not erase all the unique particularities. The participation of the citizens in the political debate depends on the interest and the trust they have in the institutions. A democracy means initiative, spontaneity, and inventiveness from the people; it needs the willingness of the citizens to make it alive. Inward-looking attitudes generated by the widespread feeling of inequality in being heard by the decision-makers generate an overall political apathy and criticism. At which point the symbolic satisfaction of the consensus can balance political disaffection? When the decision made affects people directly in their values, a more significant political separation can appear. In practice, plenty of social groups can abandon the democratic method because they don't trust anymore to reach their primary goals democratically.

Citizen crisis and the mutation of citizenship

Information Technology brought significant changes in societies: it gave anyone a power never expected, simultaneously as a widespread intellectual passivity denying the classical democracy theory. The transformation of policymaking in a profession, and the growth of bureaucracy, went to the point that it opposed the interest of democracy: the inner stability combined with the monopoly led to prioritizing the organization's interests rather than its functioning for the people—inequalities of employment cumulates with inequalities of conditions of living, security, illness, indebtedness. Together with the loss of identity about family, social class, or nation, create generations with no historical identity. The feeling of living in a society disinterested by the public cause is correlated with the arising of incivility. On the other side, globalization encourages new solidarity networks outside of national interest. A renewed citizenship is experienced at a supranational level as a utility based on spontaneity and pragmatism. It tends to establish a distance with the national belonging but claim to recognize social and economic rights like work, education, housing, and health contractually.

Post-democracy after a democratic peak

At the same time, as the biggest dictatorships have disappeared and most nation-states worldwide are accepting democratic elections, the early adopters are less optimistic. Post-democracy designates the descending curb of the Democratic Parable, whose peak is set about 1980 in the western world. After thirty years of economic growth, where mass production and consumption supported by public spending was legitimated by prominent people's participation through decision-making structures, the multinational companies control the economy of the governments through their investment in public services. The privatization of public services resulted in a collapse of the trust in public agents and the resulting loss of leadership of the state in caring about the fields abandoned by private companies, coupled with the unprecedented power of the media in political communication, questions the democratic balance. As Colin Crouch says, "Under this post-democracy model, while elections exist and can change governments, the public electoral debate is a tightly controlled spectacle, managed by rival teams of professionals expert in the techniques of persuasion. The mass of citizens plays a passive, quiescent, even apathetic part. Politics is shaped in private by the interaction between elected governments and elites that overwhelmingly represent business interests."

Generational renewal in a distant citizenship

The upcoming citizens were born and raised in a context of political distrust where electives and parties are regularly taunted for not being able to resolve problems. At the same time, associations and grassroots movements have never been so actual as nowadays. The citizens can engage in politics through more and more diversified channels, from online to street activism. Nowadays, citizens act outside of any frame from the electives. The upcoming citizens globally have a higher level of education, women are almost equally present on the employment market and public representations, and people are very diverse in their religion and ethnic background. The growing mistrust in electives and political class leads to a foreign citizenship: where a lack of appetite for politics is doubled by a well-informed capacity to play an opposition role when necessary. If they do not trust anymore in the ones that govern them, the upcoming citizens widely ask for more democracy. We assist in a transformation of citizenship: more expressive and less dependent on traditional political intermediaries.

Astroturfing in public space and social networks

Former U.S. senator Lloyd Bentsen used the synthetic grass brand astroturfing in 1986 to qualify the fake grassroots initiatives orchestrated by professionals willing to benefit from the high credibility conferred to citizen movements in public opinion. This strategy of pretending to be or to defend citizen interests is growing on plenty of communication channels, hiding its real objectives from the public. A fundamental difference between astroturfers and volunteers is to be paid for an activist job. Thus some street protests can appear to the public and the media as spontaneous citizen mobilization but are organized by paid employees of communication agencies. In practice, astroturfers can act alone, more or less consciously, or in groups, for a company, a government, an association, or a political party. They can act as long-time permanent influencers or as short-lived opportunists in social influence. They can deploy massive lobbying campaigns or isolate actions like transferring a single message on the web. In doing so, astroturfing not only reduces the voice of actual citizens in public spaces it also negatively affects the trust we commonly have in regular people.

c. Digital perspectives for Democracy and Citizenship

In racing for public influence and a distance taken from traditional electoral bodies, a new political practice emerged by using Information and Communication Technologies. Digital Citizenship and Digital Democracy take advantage of the digital pervasiveness in both directions: from the citizens to their representatives and government to the people.

Digital Citizenship

Young people develop their civic identities between 15 to 22 years old. Three attributes: civic literacy, civic skills, and civic attachment shape the civic engagement of their adult political lives. Since teenagers spend up to 9 hours a day on the internet (2015 report), students should be encouraged to utilize technology with responsibility, and educators, parents, and school counselors should promote ethical digital citizenship.

Being a digital citizen refers to utilizing I.T. to engage in society, politics, and government. Creating blogs, using social networks, and participating in online journalism, the process of becoming a digital citizen goes beyond simple internet activity. In theory, digital technology can lower the barriers to entry for participation as a citizen within society. In developing countries, digital citizens are more sparse:

they consist of the people who utilize technology to overcome their localized obstacles, including development issues, corruption, and military conflict.

Digital Democracy

From the technology as a tool to serve a project to the technology to redefine social relationships, all devices and processes using I.T. to ease citizen engagement in governance can be considered digital democracy infrastructure. Interactive technologies are designed to answer the deficiency of representative governments, particularly in outreaching the pace of electoral phases, judged too slow and ineffective, and subvert political parties or groups of interests. Transparency and the constant participation of millions of citizens constitute the ideal of digital democracy. The multiplicity of the ways to increase online speaking outside of the official frame of public institutions is thus considered a means to transform it. This central role of social media to refashion citizenship raises the question of the democratic compatibility of the underlying algorithms. The concepts of filter bubble and echo chamber recently emerged to designate the intellectual isolation of the web users and radicalize their opinions, resulting in a fall-down of their capacity to understand those who do not share their views.

Innovation in voting

- Liquid democracy A form of government where the voter can delegate his vote to another voter of his choice borrowed its name from Liquid Society, a term from Zygmunt Bauman to describe post-modernity characterized by ephemerality and instability. The core principles of Liquid Democracy are the following. Each member can choose to endorse a passive individual or an active delegate role. Each delegate can determine the importance and the field of his implication. The representatives exercise their power in their name and in the name of the individuals who gave them delegation. And the delegates can delegate their voting power between them too. There are no political campaigns nor run for elections. Decisions are taken in public, but votes are kept in a secret ballot. Each individual can revise his voice at any time, changing his delegate if the first chosen do not act like expected or if his opinion on an issue has changed.

The singularity of liquid democracy is based on the fact that whichever militant who doesn't consider himself competent enough to make a decision can mandate one of his peers considered more capable. The major critique of the liquid democracy model is to create a new hierarchy of knowledge and responsibilities, far again from the ideal of enlightened active citizens. The accumulation of delegation by a few delegates could transform them into opinion leaders capable of influencing the decision process in the direction of their interests, a situation very similar to the defaulting traditional representative democracy. Furthermore, it could lead to a trade of the right to vote.

- Quadratic Voting, created by crypto-currency communities, the term quadratic refers to the possibility to buy supplementary votes for the cost of the square of the number of the votes bought. In this model, each voter is endowed with a budget of vote credits to influence the outcome of a range of decisions. Participants express how strongly they feel about an issue rather than just being in favor or opposed to it. The quadratic nature of the voting allows the voter to use his votes more efficiently than by spreading them across many issues. With a budget of 16 credits, a voter can apply one credit to 16 subjects. If he feels very concerned by a single point, he can apply four votes, at the cost of 16 credits, to this unique issue. In more populated communities, it's possible to select a random number of voters within the network for each voting proposal. This scenario would avoid speculation behaviors and prevent strategic alliances because it makes the voters' prediction uncertain.

The main guarantee from quadratic voting is that the cost of buying votes increases so rapidly that it makes it a very poor investment to try to influence the public decision by wealthiness. Finally, the central issue to the deployment of quadratic voting systems is that it could work only with a secured identity system. At the same time, most of the blockchain and crypto-currency users operate under pseudonymity or anonymity.

Beyond the libertarian-communitarian debate

Facing the post-democracy problems and the inability of both left- and right-wing politics to resolve them, Glen Weyl shares in Radical Markets: Uprooting Capitalism and Democracy for a Just Society (2018) the legitimacy of a market economy to organize society. By converting private property into collective leaseholds, the public goods could be owned by many people, creating radically expanded markets.

In this new model of society, a tax would be assessed based on individual ownership of public goods in the capacity to raise enough general income to eliminate other taxes on capital and revenue. A healthier relationship to property detached from material possessions but instead seeking to increase the value of commonwealth and strengthen community bonds. A visa between individuals program would tie together the interests of the wealthiest and poorest countries' working classes by sharing the gains from migration as a source of growing middle-class income. Citizens select migrants to sponsor with a personal connection of heritage, religion, language, or interests. Local communities regulate how many migrants their citizens can host. Many citizens in search of opportunities move to cities that are open to migration.

A Citizenship regime defines how citizens are produced through an ensemble of representational practices. Suppose digital technology is the pivotal medium through which governance and organizational change are to be achieved. In that case, it promises two essential functions to turn decision-making more open and inclusive: the record of detailed, measurable, real-time knowledge about the city and the delivery of accurate, timely, and comprehensive reports.

In this context, co-opting citizens becomes an essential element of the new way of governing cities. Digital technology plays an enabling mode on which to reconstruct citizenship: by engaging all citizens in decision-making for their town and promoting the exchange of ideas, knowledge, and skills.

While some contemporary philosophers, since the fall of the Berlin wall in 1989, still have in mind the concept of The end of history, establishing the advent of a universal and homogeneous State under Liberal Democracy regime, worldwide formation of communities, and their needs for better adapted organizational processes call for both Citizenship regime and democracy processes renewal.

2. Smart-City: Current trend in Urban planning

At the beginning of the smart-city concept, in the middle of the '90s, being smart meant being fully equipped with the city's modern infrastructure pushed by I.T. sector companies. The term extended later: being smart now includes transparency and reactiveness to a multicultural population whose citizen engagement is considered necessary ingredients for success.

Following a few early adopters, a broad mix of scientists, innovative industries, and public servants of the urban field took the turn to Smart-City developments about a decade ago. This new label matches both technical progress acceleration and the need for cities to be more visible in a very challenging market to attract investors, create new jobs and ensure long-term revenues for local finances. In 2015, the ITU —International Telecommunication Union finally found the following consensual definition of a smart city: "A smart, sustainable city is an innovative city which uses information and communication technologies and other means to improve quality of life, the efficiency of urban operation and services, and competitiveness, while ensuring that it meets the needs of present and future generations concerning economic, social and environmental aspects.".

a. Data to improve cities

The Smart-City movement holds a holistic ambition to transform the city in all its aspects by putting digital technology to improve the quality of life: real-time data gives the ability to predict events, understand how people's needs are changing, and respond with faster and lower-cost solutions. While new technology developers sometimes promise a self-achieving improvement of quality of life and security, a more pragmatic approach is to consider that becoming a smart city is not a goal but a means to an end. Technology is nothing but a way to optimize the infrastructure, resources, and spaces to respond more effectively to the needs and desires of inhabitants. In essence, technology has ever since the industrial era been a significant driver of visions about urban futures. These visions involved cities that would use technology to establish modern and healthy living conditions, where perfect democracies would stem from collective digital spaces. People's needs would be satisfied intuitively and instantly at a point that some smart city researchers currently acknowledge that the Smart-City movement is predominantly a strategic vision for the future rather than a reality.

Urban planning is all about finding compromises between cleaving opinions expressed by the population. Data usage and privacy are probably one of the most cleaving topics in western cities. There are blooming concerns about who owns the data, who gets the benefits generated from it, and how to regulate its use. It took some years for the average person to consider the meaning of intrinsic approval of data records on private online activities. Roughly two opposite opinions arise as answers to the question: if data is the new gold, why would I share mine for free? The first category of people thinks that they could get paid from their data sharing and have the right to choose which company can exploit it. The other type agrees on sharing private data as long as they receive free performing tools and apps as a service.

Knowledge economy:

In recent years, knowledge was recognized as a valuable and manageable asset capable of accrediting a competitive advantage to an enterprise, organization, or city.

The knowledge-based economy played a significant role in the emergence of the smart-city concept. The term knowledge economy refers to replacing labor-intensive activities with knowledge-intensive ones and increasing intangible capital compared to physical ones. McKinsey Global Institute, in a smart-city report from 2018, used an Adam Smith metaphor to explain the micro-to-macro scale causal effect that happens in a smart-city economy: "Centuries ago, Adam Smith observed that the actions of many self-interested parties combine to create larger benefits to society. Today a similar kind of "invisible hand" is at work in smart cities. When a resident looks at real-time traffic data and decides to set out at a less busy time, he avoids adding another car to the road that would worsen congestion for everyone. Millions of individual decisions and actions add up, making the city as a whole more productive and responsive."

Today's state-of-the-art technology is affordable, wireless, of increased performance, safety, and reliability, and functions on a real-time basis. Putting real-time information into the hands of individuals and companies empowers them to make better decisions and play a more active role in shaping the city's overall performance. However, smart technologies are already enabling the next wave of public investment. We need to collectively think about what kind of society we want to invest in.

Data ethic

Some cities are starting their transformations with inherent advantages such as wealth, density, and existing high-tech industries. Asian megacities, for example, with their young populations of digital natives and big urban problems to solve, are achieving exceptionally high adoption. But the cities which lack these ingredients can attract attention with a good vision, management, and a willingness to break with conventional ways of meeting the needs of residents. In particular, smaller cities in Europe gather a lot of family businesses indispensable to the countries' economy, sustainability, and cultural identity continuity. We need to take care of their needs, which are not the same as big metropolitan areas. Indeed, marketing competition between cities, motivated by potential private-public partnerships, under the condition of facilitating policies, seems to unlock innovative projects' achievement in infrastructure, e-governance, and citizens' participation.

When industries want data to improve new business models, Smart-City appears to the public sector as a way for investments to come in. Most of the time, self-declared by governments or clusters of businesses, smart-cities were first distributed in a balanced way between the USA, Europe, and Asia. At the same time, a dozen of South-American and African cities wanted to associate their name to this label. In 2008 Robert Hollands said humoristically, "Regarding cities like Kaboul or Oulan-Bator, it was impossible to know if the goal of getting "smart" was a pious hope, a public policy purpose, a diversion attempt or an announcement effect. Some researchers then noted the unsubstantial content of this self-satisfaction proclaims". Energy efficiency or transportation performance has nothing to do with the quality of life. It does not say which issue the society wants primarily to solve with these money gains or the moral purpose behind using data and digital tools.

Data-driven democracies ?

Traditionally, the delivery of urban infrastructure and services has been the concern of the public sector. But the urbanization dynamics evolve and call for a transition to a more collaborative approach, enabling broader participation in urban services. Technology providers can help boost resident's interests in their immediate living environment and involvement in the decision affecting their living standards. Open-Data and participative models of urban planning are supported by the private sector, ready-to-use by citizens. The purely technological smart-city risks being non-inclusive by design, but social technologies and a citizen-centric approach ensure that all inhabitants' real needs will be satisfied in the urban innovation process. Human-centered design is an approach to interactive systems development that aims to make systems usable and useful by focusing on the users, their needs, and requirements. It has been adapted in urban planning as it sounds obvious that stakeholders trigger social innovation by analyzing the collective interests of the society through a bottom-up approach.

Until recently, city leaders thought of smart technologies primarily as tools for becoming more efficient behind the scenes. But after a decade of trial and error, municipal leaders realize that intelligent city strategies start with people, not technology. Now smartphones have become the keys to the city: putting instant information directly into millions of residents' hands about traffic, health services, safety alerts, and community news. Voters can engage in a bidirectional conversation with public officials or candidates via social media and interactive mobile apps. Electives and public services can use technology to take the pulse of public opinion on a wide range of issues, using general feedback as the basis for making continuous improvements to the system. Furthermore, the inclusion of the people is necessary to provide the correct answer to the current needs. Still, it is also the guarantee that your development will be adopted the widest by the users targeted.

Technology push VS Market pull

A popular theory to describe forces at work in the digital transformation of society is inspired by management science. It's called the technology-push versus market-pull. In the smart-city field, too, this framework has proven relevance. At the same time, two main forces lead urban innovations: the new offers from I.T. companies push products and services towards a market of demanding consumers, urban inhabitants pulling innovation on their initiative. In practice, a very dynamic market of smart products lies behind the smart-city models, willing to monitor the urban environment and manage urban functionalities. Business development in a very competitive market and a run for innovation implies that new solutions are ushered into sales directly to customers' hands. The technology push refers to industrial production driven by supply due to fast-evolving science and technology, and these sales are made regardless of the expressed needs of the society. The market-pull refers to a highly demanding market of consumers, which can be the city themselves in infrastructure innovation or simply an app user if talking about new mapping or transportation software.

- **Technology-push:** The technological advancements of recent years have made feasible the development of a vast array of solutions and products that seek to enable the smart city. As a result, an increasing number of technology vendors and consultancies are looking for a niche in the intelligent city product market. The tech-push has surged the market with Web 2.0 platforms for large-scale collaboration, establishing knowledge exchange networks, the codification of vast databases, and their use in intelligent and innovative ways.
- **Market-pull:** Cities compete to attract high profiles of citizens and skilled workers, investors, tourists, and international events. Knowledge now circulates and is produced collectively. A city's people now have a more robust ability to create new ideas, products, strategies, and theories, either individually or in collaboration within social networks. The broad input of

knowledge, creativity, and collective intelligence of the population enhance innovativeness, the multi-perspective confrontation of the city's problems, and the delivery of new and improved services.

The most relevant factors of the smart-city paradigm to promote innovation and sustainability for the local economy are indeed the connectivity and the local social innovation. In this context, the technology-push and market-pull forces drive the advancement of urban futures to unprecedented levels. Several conceptual models of smart-cities have appeared under their influence of supply and demand. Technology with human capital development can give a city's constituents the power to innovate, create, participate in society and solve problems collectively for the common good.

A direct market—civil society deal?

Roughly all stakeholders in decision-making for a city are decided to bring better mobility, energy, and city services, moving ahead to a more performing and sustainable city. However, the Smart-City concept faces a double risk: first, to keep stuck at the marketing state, passing beside digital potential for territories, and second, to get out of the public sector's hand for the benefit of the private business only. Most economists ask to regulate new private actors of the Smart-City to ease their complementarity; this is also a practical management model we can observe in most public or remote startup hubs, where a coordinator usually tries to balance innovation and reach a circular dynamic in between innovation providers.

Suppose the free market economy and the right to undertake and benefit from selling products or services directly to consumers is a vital element of our contemporary democracies. In that case, this direct market-civil society deal is risky since it is highly volatile and unpredictable. No individual consumer usually considers the society as a whole when it chooses a product, and global coordination of social trends is not practicable in real-time. The direct market—civil society deal renews representativity, legitimacy, and responsibility of uncoordinated stakeholders in co-designing the public interest.

b. Stakeholders roles and needs

Stakeholders in the digital transformation of cities are plenty and diverse from one town to another: politics, industry, startups, citizens, architects. All of them are components of forces shaping the cities, which make urban issues complex to solve. Multi-stakeholder engagement often requires time to build an appropriate common language, find ways of working together, and communicate with the project. Even though all stakeholders don't have the same relevance regarding decision making, none of the actors will be able to achieve smart or sustainable cities without support from the other stakeholder groups. In the following, I am listing five categories of stakeholders with different interests that need consensus. Each of these categories is divided into sub-categories or types of stakeholders.

- **Public Sector :**

While cities face considerable population growth, increasing pressures, and economic burdens, to remain competitive and achieve sustainable developments, they must find ways to boost their efficiency and reduce costs although ensuring good quality of life for their inhabitants. The smart-city paradigm allows governing toward futuristic models of cities (post-carbon, waste, water, and energy-autonomous, impulsed by a circular economy), promoting virtuous stakeholders' behavior and awareness, improving bottom-up citizen-driven experimentations, and implementing innovative lifestyles in all services to residents. The value created by a smart city is inextricably linked to its capacity to pool, organize and release data from various urban systems and networks of people. These activities have historically been designed, managed, and operated "in silos." Intelligent devices generate profound change because it opens the door to an unprecedented amount of data on the infrastructures and the needs of the community and its inhabitants. In the use of digital technologies, cities are gradually shifting towards innovation, following or supporting the steps of the private sector toward sustainable enterprises, and encompassing a more interactive and responsive city administration, safer public spaces, and meeting the population's needs of all ages.

- o **Government (national):** Depending on countries of reference, the federal government organizes administration and ministries with various responsibilities to coordinate land use planning and housing programs at a country's level. They also master competencies such as transportation and national online/offline services like identity, visa.
- o **Government (local):** At a municipal level, electives from a city have more or less autonomy in urban planning. They usually master public spaces and housing plans of their locality to the limit of their financial capacity. At the condition, it does not interfere with national interests missions.
- o **Public Servant:** Workers in services are not electives but sometimes influential in decision-making or coordination when it goes to engage their service. They are in charge of all working features of a city: water, waste collection, energy, public worksites.

- **Private Business:**

Whatever the size, businesses, and enterprises directly involved in realizing infrastructures and implementing smart solutions like real estate developers, system integrators, competence centers, technology providers, play a decisive role in the transformation process for becoming a Smart-City. The expansion of Smart-City projects rely on technical and software infrastructures installed in tester consumers' homes, in new or existing residential homes, in public buildings, and collective housing: multi-fluid smart-meters, sensors, data displays, combined with energy management services. The challenge is to regenerate what already exists, to work on what was built. A project of the building is necessary to have high performances in energy efficiency and increased living comfort. Still, it is also essential that urban planning considers social needs such as commons, social cohesion, the possibility of self-realization, and emancipation of the individual. The clear majority of existing residential units are not fit to provide healthy comfort without using too much energy. New companies are better equipped but insufficient in numbers. As for the existing cities, a step-by-step approach is very much sustained by developing efficient tech solutions founded in comprehensive research programs. Affordability of all solutions is the key to a massive impact in the future years. Managing public social housing assets means having the possibility of identifying guidelines and developing projects on a consistent and extended system of residences. It means being able to influence the future of our cities and their inhabitants. By applying technical innovations in the city, startups learn how to overcome barriers, build new business models, and make technology both user-friendly and attractive. They often need to bypass bureaucracy, look for a first real business opportunity. Hence, they try to connect with "key account" companies, users, and the city. Global forums and their events are a common way to promote behavior changes by deploying temporary demonstration areas. Informative websites such as online newspapers and business magazines about urban development regularly engage with the smart city topic.

- **Corporate Company:** In the last ten years of economic disease, architects, engineers, and construction companies faced many and more revolutions to sustain growth and lead innovation in urban areas. All these innovations promote sustainability, efficiency, and security, technological advances in materials and products, according to a 4.0 industrial revolution toward industrialized building systems.
- **Startup & SMEs:** forward-looking software developers and technology enthusiasts who develop and use smart city services and applications.
- **Freelance:** They visit places and cities famous for innovation. They represent networks and new contacts. Also, business opportunities. Needs: They look for Benchmarks. They want to learn and find business opportunities.
- **Investor:** They support businesses and governments by sponsoring and investing money in projects. They secure investments of small and big savers by choosing profitable projects to invest in. Needs => All sizes of companies, investment platforms, and strong government relationships.

- **Research & Innovation:**

One of the critical elements for the success of the transition is to raise the awareness and understanding of the public about the system of the future and the diversity of technology and solutions. Academic research and the related generated know-how will allow cities to progress towards their full sustainability, increasing the system's flexibility in the short and long term and proposing new regulatory frameworks, business models, services, and applications that enable the mass behavioral shift towards a proactive relation of the prosumer to transition challenges. Integrating current research in applied solutions helps to understand the complexity better, and the proof of the practicability and commercial viability plays a critical role. Demonstration projects gathered in clusters and research laboratories allow for capitalizing valuable knowledge about market applications and commercial arrangements. R&I networks provide pragmatic environments to share experiences, validate good practice and compare results from different experimentations. It acts as a facilitator in this sense, connecting various stakeholders and enhancing the impact of solutions.

- **Academic research** plays a prominent role in creating new solutions that can lead to a healthier and more sustainable urban life. Scientists were encouraged by urbanization, globalization, and climate change to invent and experiment with new mechanisms, to develop solutions for intelligent cities from prototypes and models that bridge the gap between technical and socioeconomic.
- **Private research** is needed to bring together recent innovations and best practices of Smart-City solutions. Scientists in research facilities collect information, knowledge, and experiences in many projects and multi-disciplinary platforms and feed them into their simulation software or demonstration projects applicable and scalable.

- **Civil Society:**

The needs and concerns of the people are the point of departure for the community work. The interests of the people determine the issues that are taken up and dealt with. In this process, the people are supported and activated to make their issues a matter of public concern and achieve results for them. As urban transition pathways impact people's everyday life and thus depend on their choices regarding mobility, energy use, consumption, society needs to act accordingly. In this sense, community involvement in the city's future is the way we can get civic trust back in the politicians. Citizens are no longer just end-users and consumers but becoming prosumers, providing data and content, taking new roles in the smart and sustainable city. The social innovators in a Smart-City or Smart District must aim to promote new models of civic participation, with a constant eye to inclusion and social protection, that can effectively meet the social needs with an updated capacity. Social entrepreneurs, community-led initiatives, new partnership models in delivering business, all such approaches are contributing to creating new urban economies. Many of these developments are enabled by digital technologies through which a much vaster potential for economic transformation is made.

- ○ **Individual Citizen:** Citizen participation is an inherent need for urban regeneration and is entirely part of the smart governance tools. Talking about urban renewal means tackling the problems of social exclusion, which is always associated with physical and functional marginalization of the district, widespread poverty, lack of services, and unemployment
- ○ **Non-Profit (local)** is the scale where independent civil forces can meet temporarily to bring a bigger goal to succeed. Their core organizers provide information and advice to the people and regularly act by gathering or events that can eventually become very influential on a local scale.
- ○ **Non-Profit (international)** influences companies' behavior by influencing their social acceptance and that of politics and society in general.

- ● **Media Industry:**

The media industry plays a binary role in terms of ANT: it is an actor in itself, with its own goals and personal interests, and as a communicating device, it also plays the role of an intermediary between all the others. It gives them a place of choice in the formation of public opinion. Suppose we could be tempted to see the professional newspapers as less neutral because in the hands of few, then social media is supposed to give an equal voice to all users. But the reality is way more complex as more and more non-professional communicating tools are overwhelmed by fake news and propagandist messages. Furthermore, the algorithms are not neutral in the messages they deliver on your news feed, as the counter-effect of satisfying users' profile expectations tends to trap it into filter bubbles with an echo chamber effect.

In an omni-channel approach of media, I consider in my research the principal representative:

- ● Social medias (Facebook, Twitter, Youtube, Medium, LinkedIn, Instagram, Pinterest, Snapchat)
- ● Messaging Apps (WhatsApp, Telegram, Line, WeChat, Slack)
- ● Informational websites
- ● Email and Newsletters
- ● Print Communication (Books, Flyers, Brochures…)
- ● Newspaper Industry (Professional Journalism and Fanzines)
- ● Radio
- ● Television

Public-Private Partnerships in Smart-City Projects

A Smart-City can not be developed only with public money nor with private investments. In practice, a governmental authority (local or national) responsible for infrastructure delivery can act as a grantor and provide the right to deliver infrastructure services in a Private-Public Partnership contract. Simultaneously, public authorities become regulators, design the regulatory framework, issue authorizations and licenses to exploit public spaces. Private entities, investors are financially supporting the development and get paid by the final users. The joint-venture structure can be agreed upon when public infrastructure is not financed by a single institution but a bunch of investors. Typical founders of such projects include private companies: contractors, suppliers, and operators. Purchasers, companies of public utility deliver the product to final users and support the project as sponsors. Other investors such as institutional investors, public agencies, multilateral institutions might also help the initiative with different interests related to a reasonable rate of return or stimulation of local and regional development.

This most successful development model for the public infrastructure of urban areas seems to be characterized by a comprehensive, collaborative approach of strong and formal governing structures. This organization model can get into the details of the executive decisions related to the timeline of the project. Still, they are also often criticized, by political opponents with the support of the civil society, to indebt a population on several decades, accused of not mastering the public budgets sometimes and adequately not answering the real needs of the people but rather the personal egoistic ambitions of a few electives willing to stamp their footmark.

c. Key Success Factors

Given the newness of the topic and a scarcity of scientific research on smart cities and their users, political decision-makers and economics do not hold all the keys to understanding such urban developments' success or failure factors. Indeed, companies have to deal with market characteristics they can't directly control. Business performance is not an exact science, and subjective perceptions and decisions from business executives are often under-evaluated in economics. As a result, the industry is always looking for theories or methods which could help them understand what could lead them to success or failure.

Key Success Factors is a concept borrowed from management science, which can be perceived as the main elements required for an organization or project to achieve its mission or to be successful in a given market. This study aims to identify which factors can be considered essential to a Smart-City project's go-to-market strategy. This survey study emphasizes that qualitative methods relied on experts' experience in the field. An empirical analysis of Key Success Factors usually implies two major methodological issues: identifying the decision-makers point of view (=perceived success factors) and confronting them to reality (=actual success factors).

To get some insights from experienced field developers, I used my stay in Helsinki in spring 2019 to collect a survey from the RIL - Suomen Rakennusinsinöörien Liitto, the Finnish Association of Civil Engineers. The RIL was created in 1936 and now has more than 6,000 professionals in Finland. Collectively, they analyze Finnish urban development, lead studies on contemporary global issues and the latest trends in engineering and architecture, or share advice on the theories and practices for the Nordic urban development.

Profiling my respondents

- *Age:* My survey study is a sample of RIL members from 32 years old to 84, with an average age at 54 and median value between 49 and 52.

- *Gender:* 65% men and 35% women.

- *Residence:* 45% of respondents live in Helsinki, 25% in Espoo, a neighboring city of Helsinki, part of the Capital Region. 10% from Tampere, third Finnish city after Helsinki and Espoo. Then we have unique contributions from Joensuu, Kokkola, Nokia and Pori.

- *Seniority:* The oldest members of my sample (83 and 84 years old) have been members of the RIL respectively for 50 years and 62 years. And the three younger ones (32, 33, 33 years old) already have 10, 10 and 15 years of membership. I assume that urban developers enter the RIL at the beginning of their career and probably stay until the end of it.

- *Profession:* 35% of respondents are from the public sector, 25% designers, 15% real estate developers and 10% employed in a construction company. Then we have other professions depicted individually: NGO, Research & Development and Regional & Town Planning.

Success indicators in urban projects

A list of indicators was proposed to quote. Strong cohesion of stakeholders around the project gets 60% of the score while Not having significant opposition from the population receives 55%. As a second rank, Good appropriation by the users is quoted by 35% of the respondents, same as Long-term stability of the financial value and good resale for the first and the following buyers. Those last two indicators can be verified some years after delivering the buildings and the public spaces. Furthermore, almost 1 in 3 respondents consider Well progress in the building phase a key indicator of success. Surprisingly financial and commercial indicators haven't retained much interest from my respondents: only 15% quote Easy to find bankers and investors to finance the project, 10% Satisfying commercialization rate to final customers, and 5% Generous capital gain for investors and developers.

Strategic choice leading to success

Co-design of the future public spaces with neighbors has been selected by 60% of respondents and sets Citizen Engagement as the priority goal to succeed in urban projects. 45% confirm this tendency by quoting Organize workshops on urban topics to up-skill participants on urban issues and Communicate the project massively on digital and paper support. Implementing digital tools to consult the population and create maps didn't get that much success as it only reaches 35% of respondents.

Professional practice in urban development

Agility and possible reconsideration all along the project are considered as the best way to describe good professional practice for 60% of my sample. 30% quoted Patience and the fullness of time do more than force and fury.

Succeeding urban projects

As urban planning is often about finding compromises between opposite interests and opinions, all urban development projects have their complaints. Indeed communication and reaching all stakeholders is the most spread issue reported. Delivering relevant information for the people to understand the ongoing urbanization projects is the key. Time pressure can be hard to deal with, which is why an "Earlier is better" mindset can save your Smart-City project deployment.

But someone described as well what happens in hurrying real estate developments:

"The builder financially looks for the best solution and puts pressure on the planner in several stages. Interaction is difficult. The developer has too much power in decision-making, so it's hard to interact in a balanced way. It happened that the civil society could change a plan, for example, to cut too many commercial places, and people were happy to have been heard. But now the planning is moving fast to the implementation phase without extra rounds of hearings."

It is possible to make a city more attractive, more environment-friendly, and less wasteful of energy or water, facing several challenges at the same time: social, methodological, technical, organizational, and conceptual. Even if this contemporary utopia for our future cities sounds good, it can be helpful to bring in mind that Smart-City and democracy were not primarily related. We are collectively running, worldwide, into this model of living, but who asked for it? Mainly I.T. companies whose business models are based on data exploitation and governments sighted an excellent opportunity to bring private investments in public facilities.

Suppose no single stakeholder can be identified as more important than the others. In that case, all of them are necessary ingredients to succeed in Smart-City development. So how do we drive a collective decision-making process where all stakeholders engage as representatives of their interest? The disintermediation induced by the digital transformation helps overcome obstacles between their products and targeted customers, synchronizing with the call from the civil society for a more direct and participative model of democracy.

3. Theoretical Background - Data mining the city

While contemporary cities face a growing social and technical complexity, their managers see the ever-increasing necessity of scientific approaches to consider global transformations and evolving dynamics of urban areas. Rapid flows of people and information have profoundly changed our perception of space, time, lifestyles, community, and self. Cities are no longer perceived as geographical entities with distinct identities. The urban today has become a concentration of multiple socio-spatial systems with diverse cultural backgrounds and economic dynamics. The vital, cohesive force of the modern city incorporates technical solutions (urban infrastructures) and technologies (communication and media). In this context, social aspects (political, economic, and cultural) are considered contextual elements of the urban landscape, which need to be considered in decision-making for urban developments in globalized cities.

a. The city as an integrated socio-technical system

Relationships between stakeholders are not dialogical but interconnected. Developing and strengthening relationships in the business field is often considered as multiplying value creation, not only for the stakeholder directly involved but for the whole network. The moving interests of peers in a web of decision-makers make them sometimes cooperating, sometimes challenging, or even strongly opposing to influence a situation in the direction of their personal or group interests. Stakeholder Engagement is defined as the ability for an organization to establish collaborative relationships with a wide variety of participants—the stakeholder engagement theory proposed in 1984 byR. Edward Freeman suggests a four-step process through which an organization enhances its engagement capability (see Fig. 1).

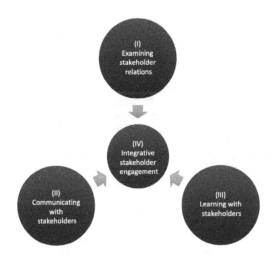

Fig. 1 - Framework for Stakeholder Engagement, from "Stakeholder Engagement: Clinical Research Cases" by R.E. Freeman and al. (2017)

The author considers that companies should not be exclusively concerned about satisfying shareholders' interests but widely the ones of the organization as a whole, including shareholders, employees, customers, suppliers, competitors, neighbors, and the community in general. Cooperation, the power of relationships, and the integration of all collaborators are of greater importance since they all strengthen value creation (see Fig2.). The latest management theories suggest that successful businesses are based on relationships rather than on transactional aspects. A wider community will create more value for the whole organization.

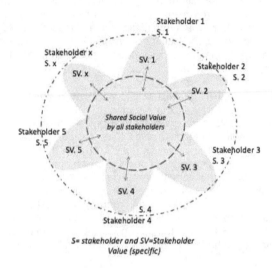

S= stakeholder and SV=Stakeholder
Value (specific)

Fig. 2 - Polyhedral model. Adapted by Leire San-Jose, Jose Luis Retolaza, and R. Edward Freeman in "*Stakeholder Engagement: Clinical Research Cases*" (2017)

Value creation among stakeholders is a continuous process in which they all add value to the organization's network. As the organization increases its value, it increases its chances of survival and its potential to reach more stakeholders. To collect the most value out of their collaborators, organizations need to generate a high degree of interaction between stakeholders. At the same time, they should strive to abandon opportunistic behaviors and power moves within their network. Value is created when the business focuses on creating value itself, the relationships and interconnections among stakeholders, or the nature of human complexity. Recent research makes a strong argument for studying how organizations can implement a strategic stakeholder management approach. Any practical implementation should build on pre-existing organizational routines to gain advanced knowledge and develop the best implementation tactics. Suppose it is not possible to record all connections and dynamics in a city context. In that case, my method for this thesis will be to collect information on representative stakeholders of each category and compare the results from one city to another.

In the context of digital acceleration, social scientists call for a renewal of their disciplines according to the new possibilities of research offered by technological progress. "The more the science and the technology extend, the more they allow us to draw physically, with an easiness and a precision always bigger, the social links," says Bruno Latour. Global systematic record induced by ICT on our cities offers researchers an unprecedented quantity and quality of data to explain humankind, to the point of reshaping social theories through social network experience.

The Actor-Network Theory

The Actor-Network Theory is a theoretical and methodological approach to social science. Everything in the social and the natural world is represented through constantly shifting networks of relationships. All the factors involved in a social situation are on the same level. Thus no external forces are interacting on the web at the present that would not be represented. Therefore, objects, ideas, processes, and other relevant factors are essential in creating social situations as humans are. This approach seems particularly adapted to my research on multi-stakeholder engagement in smart-city. The emergence of new techniques to develop urbanization, induced by the advent of further Information and Communication Technology. The method and the society define and shape together simultaneously, and the distinction between the two is dissolved. Thus, the simultaneous construction of tangible and intangible (the social) and the cohabitation of humans and non-humans in complex, relevant and egalitarian networks helps understanding how dynamics processes.

Michel Callon has shown in a foundational article that technical objects emerge by including the interests of a group of actors, humans and non-humans, and the associated hardware components. This theory redefines the social world by considering non-human artifacts which were traditionally highly distinguished by classical epistemology. In the Actor-Network Theory, both human and non-human objects can be symmetrically considered actors interacting in hybrid networks. Developing such an approach, Michel Callon is less interested in the philosophical correctness of his assumptions than in the practical analysis of the social process. In practice, all the socio-technic network components intertwine without hierarchy or distinction regarding their nature, and the technique emerges from a complex system of living actors, technical tools, and opportunities.

As a method to map urban development processes and visualize actors and networks through diagrams, the Actor-Network Theory deals with a city as a contingent, fragmentary and heterogeneous, yet the persistent product of interactions between humans, places, and infrastructures. An iterative urban development approach can overpass the perception of cities as merely economic, social, and cultural venues and treat them as complex, dynamic, and frontierless communicating systems. Any research on Smart-City should consider how cities' functionalities are shaped by human actions and non-human materials, which are influenced by the spatiality and history of the town itself. As contemporary urban planning is highly dependent on Information and Communication Technologies, as the renewal of democracies is, it seems evident that technological objects are nothing but passive in decision-making for a city's development. Objects play different social roles, at least one of the social intermediaries, and thus a catalyst for interaction between elements of the urban system across space and time.

Networks themselves are active elements linking urban actors, mappable on spatial and temporal layers and layers of decision-making in urban development processes. In political terms, urban development is anything that happens to a city in terms of maintenance, transformation, or any other change of its original state. In a context where physical spaces constantly intermingle with social constructions, places are no more considered neutral objects but rather as a more or less influential space of flows. As a result, the urban present is no longer attributed only to spatial forms, economic units, and cultural formations but also to integral, complex socio-material and socio-technical systems of interactions between human, social and technical elements. From an ANT point of view, each human person, a legal entity such as companies or associations, influential website or social network group page, each event and place in the city where people interact, all entities potentially influence the network of stakeholders by a complex set of intrinsic properties and extrinsic motivation to lead the decision-making according to individual interests. The distribution of roles within the regulatory framework is highly dependent on the human actors, individual or group, who assign, or are set at, a specific position in decision-making. Traditionally, the sense of personal interests can be categorized into three:

- **Top-Down urban planning actors** cover national authorities that conduct administrative tasks, govern strategic construction, site development, and infrastructure works, do surveying, and inspect and supervise actions in the field. And cities and municipalities, which have the legal means and right to develop their strategies, plans, programs, and local regulations regarding urban development.
- **Interest-Based transformations** gather influential business stakeholders and corporate bodies, powerful investors who use their economic and political dominance to buy precious real estate and market segments to serve their profitability.
- **Bottom-up participatory and urban design activities:** artists and cultural workers, NGOs, associations create an alternative strategic path for influencing the neighborhood's development. On a global scale, creative clusters forge a territory's reputation and attractiveness.

On another note, places in a city can't be considered neutral. Indeed, there are places where people interact spontaneously or through events, and this is where the opinion is formed.

- Neighborhood reunions
- Global promotional events (hackathon, meetups, forums…)
- Innovation and startup events
- Business clusters and entrepreneurial ecosystems
- Urban Infrastructure (Public Real-Estate, Transportation systems, Public Sport and Leisure areas)
- City Council or other Governmental Deliberative Assemblies
- Online (web forums and meeting apps)

b. A city science using Artificial Intelligence

If the idea to use data to improve cities isn't new: governing entities from the earliest civilizations gathered data about populations to provide services, build infrastructure, collect taxes and enforce the policy. In the '30s, surveys and statistics about the makeup of a place were already used to justify the redevelopment of underused areas. Today it's the quantity and the ubiquity of that data that is new. As digital systems multiply across the cities, they produce vast amounts of data that can help city managers tackle contemporary issues of the urban landscapes. Furthermore, the democratization of data through public APIs makes a clear difference in benefiting from data: formerly only accessible to a ruling elite, open data now allows independent developers to access huge datasets of millions of interactions throughout the city. Not only urban developers but many other people, from opposition activists to NGOs and ordinary citizens. All this information available gives new power to urban designers to rethink cities' use from a citizen-centric point of view and propose creative visions about the urban environments. The relationships of tools and space and computational models and simulations have to be taken into consideration in the changing landscape of the digital city. In this thesis, I collect big data with the Twitter public API and use the Python programming language to deliver advanced data analysis, social network analysis, and sentiment analysis. Finally, I am building different predictive models on citizen engagement in smart cities outside my datasets, using machine learning and agent-based modeling.

Pervasive computing and the global level of education to digital allowed us to get the data analysis out of the hands of a few experts, but rather lead studies with massive input from various stakeholders. Collaboration with participants of different backgrounds makes much sense to me: at the same time, it proof-tests my findings on the way, it extends my network of readers, followers, willing to give a hand. They will answer my surveys, comment on a report, share a message to their network. As I'm researching about citizen engagement in smart-city, I naturally tend to use citizen science methods in my research. All in one, I feel proud of delivering accessible analysis to the people I meet or get in touch with online. It gives me the satisfaction of growing the mainstream use of data as a common good, with the potential of empowering the people in their understanding of the societal transformation they experience daily. Incorporating social media scraping aside of surveys, one-to-one interviews, and collaborative workshops enriches my research by the voices of the people engaged in its process. It makes my work both more ethical, since I do not take the role of an expert lecturing others on what to do with their cities, and inclusive since I spread the idea of building collaborations between my case studies based on my work. Data is a raw material to develop and strengthen a vision of how the cities run in a digital era. It allows social scientists to get out of a personal perspective on a topic and support it with solid statistical models in the background. Data analysis and the resulting data visualizations boost fashion to spread ideas most impeccably. But data science is not only a new way to study old problems; it is also a way to explore contemporary issues that would never exist out of this new technical power. Data science is a significant mutation and promises a new look and an unprecedented understanding of the human world.

The data analysis community is very active on the web. It is easy to find handy machine learning tutorials to adapt existing algorithms to your needs with the support from developers' forums such as StackOverflow or Towards Data Science. Thus artificial intelligence has never been so accessible as now and widely popular to independent learners. As for building predictions out of my datasets, I have been particularly interested in the sub-branch of A.I. called machine learning. Machine learning algorithms improve automatically through experience by performing two types of work: automated classification and linear regression. Both are predictive models supported by statistical foundations. The learning task will be supervised when the user processes data regularly (e.g., sheets of record or a folder of pictures) and unsupervised learning when it randomly processes data of various types (sheets, images, texts). The steps of procedures are usually the same: you have a dataset at your disposal. It is composed of different variables whose one is your target variable. Let's say that you wish to predict the state of a data point (classification problem) or the value it will take on the next step (regression problem). You need to train your algorithm on existing data (the training dataset) before using it to predict a result from incomplete data (the testing dataset). Then you'll be able to evaluate the accuracy of your prediction by comparing it to actual values and refine your model until you have reached a satisfying performance. Refining your model includes different techniques such as normalizing input data, dropping irrelevant variables, reducing redundancy, and finding the most adapted algorithms to your task (see Fig. 3).

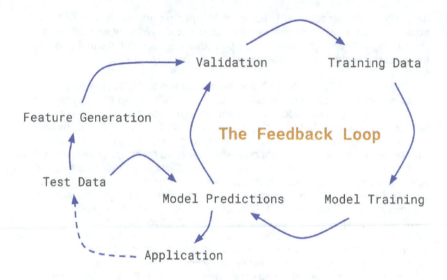

Fig. 3 - Supervised Machine Learning, the Feedback Loop.

This prediction technique from data has become increasingly popular in the city science field since cities are supported by an extensive digital infrastructure of sensors, databases, and smart applications. Even when a municipality does not invest in collecting data on its urban space, internet users worldwide keep track of records by using social networks or other online services. Web scraping techniques are automated data extraction from websites using collection software on a web browser. With very few exceptions, all that can be seen on your screen can be recorded manually by copy-pasting. So this manual task can be replaced by some bots doing it for you at an increased speed. It is usually recommended not to scrape any information under the copyright or overwhelm web servers in terms of ethics. As a matter of security, most web browsers and social networks kick out a user when it is detected that he overused their services in a short length of time.

c. Internet-Based Research

Internet-Mediated Research (IMR), Online research methods (ORMs), or simply Internet Research all designate how researchers can collect data and conduct scientific research via the internet. Many of these internet-based research methodologies are related to existing research methodologies but re-invented and re-imagined in the light of new technologies. Online questionnaires, online interviews, online content analysis, online focus groups are common sense. The field is relatively new and keeps evolving with the growth of social media and automation software, which offers new levels of analysis and opportunities to get in touch with the studied audience. There are two levels of research based on the internet:

- **Primary research** concerns using the internet to access the information available online, from resources such as library databases to online newspapers. Essentially, any approach that involves the analysis of data to produce new evidence would be considered primary research.
- **Secondary research** uses the internet to engage participants, make contact with people to spread research material such as surveys or any content of the interaction, collect world-to-mouth information, and book an in-person meeting

or a call interview.

In my research, I use both primary and secondary internet-based research. Primary at the step of writing a contextual monograph on my case study city, and secondary for the field investigation part. In practice, the internet gives me access to a wide range of material from different sources (academic publications, informational websites, Wikipedia) to settle an overall sense out of my investigation context, then make contact with locals by social networks or by sending them an email. I preferably use LinkedIn for direct contact and Facebook groups to spread my survey studies. Once the contact is made, I usually communicate with my target via a straightforward messaging app like WhatsApp or Line. The advantages of using the internet as a tool for administering questionnaires are numerous. First, the internet can dramatically increase the time- and cost-efficiency of a piece of research, as for distribution and conversion of data into a format ready for analysis. Second, it enables access to a vast and diverse group of participants. The best way to avoid bias while balancing the participation of very diverse groups of targets. Indeed, the most common prejudice against Internet-based research has a thick skin. Even nowadays, the internet-user population is often considered constituting an inherently biased sample of the people at large (in terms of sex, age, socioeconomic status). Thus data validity is often viewed as limited, if not invalid. The biased belief on the Internet-user population is mainly constituted by well-educated, high-earning, technologically proficient males who work in academic, computer, or other professional fields. While the evidence nowadays suggests that the Internet-user population represents a vast and diverse section of the general population that is rapidly moving beyond the once largely predominant technologically proficient professionals. And the collapsing of geographical or cultural boundaries enhances the possibilities for cross-cultural research, which in many cases may otherwise be infeasible due to time or funding constraints.

I can primarily argue that my surveys include the gender, the date of birth, and the district of residence for each participant, to look at a balanced sampling of the general population of the study. Then I have to say that my three case studies have the highest penetration rates in the world, which makes sense for global tech hubs. In Estonia, the internet penetration rate in 2019 was 90% of households. In Taiwan, the Internet penetration rate was calculated in 2018 at 92.6%. And in Israel, the Internet penetration rate was at 81,58% in 2017. note that most of Israel's country is composed of many small rural villages and settlements in the middle of desert areas. Still, my city of reference, Tel Aviv, is one of the most advanced tech hubs in the world. However, it is part of the researcher's responsibility to build a strategy for gathering participants that will constitute a balanced sample of the general population to give the best credibility to generalize results further. The samples obtained will rely heavily on the sampling methodology employed for both traditional and internet samples. Finally, I can argue that I focus on digital transformation studies, so I target the internet user rather than the marginal parts of the population which don't use it. I will get the majority of my research findings from people interested in digital transformation and future cities. In that sense, the broadest sample representativeness is not necessarily required.

Cross-sourcing data in a triangulation process

Triangulation refers to using multiple methods or data sources in qualitative research to develop a comprehensive understanding of phenomena (Patton, 1999). This is a way of maximizing the data quality, assuring the study's validity through the use of a variety of methods to collect data on the same topic, which involves different types of

samples and methods of data collection. The purpose of the triangulation process can be both to cross-validate datasets and capture different dimensions of phenomena. Denzin (1978) and Patton (1999) identified four types of triangulation:
- method triangulation
- investigator triangulation
- theory triangulation
- data source triangulation.

My sampling strategy of data collection consists of both a method triangulation and data source triangulation. My triangulation process has involved:
- documentary information (primary internet research, key stakeholder identification)
- direct observation (social network analysis, attending to events)
- other stakeholder observations (survey, workshops, and interviews)

Using four different sources of varying quantity and quality from internet-based data collection, I built a solid basis for my analysis (see Fig.4).

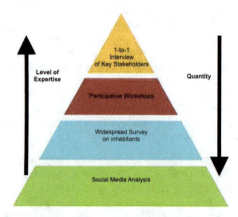

Fig. 4 - My data collection on targeted audience crosses four sources.

In the end, an iterative process of collecting and analyzing data by comparing existing and new data on stakeholder behavior. Specifically, to avoid being influenced by each stakeholder's view. Relations between stakeholders are interconnected, and my research results in multi-stakeholder and interconnected value creation. And that is my first argument for engaging critical stakeholders in participating in my study. By collecting contextual information in a crossed-source fashion, I put myself in the position of sharing an external point of view supported by collaborative data inputs. When I contact an elective or an executive in a big firm, they all get interested in sharing the time for an interview with me because they wish to get my feedback on their city or their market.

The invisible code that powers a city's use may have a more drastic influence than any physical invention in the last century. Each town has its networks of actors and agents influencing decision-making at a local urban planning level. Identifying stakeholders and relationships are keys to understand the phenomena of Smart-City.

4. Research Methodology - Pattern discovery in datasets

The primary seduction from big data comes from its capacity to integrate heterogeneous information about human behavior. What we expect from it is a new understanding of humanity. So far, we interpreted the cultural facts by the comprehension of the language or archeological artifacts. Data science gives us the possibility to discover hidden patterns in data. Once a pattern has been validated, it can be used as a referring point to classify, cluster, or predict similar information packages.

In the worldwide digital transformation of cities, local particularities emerge, depending on the temporary needs, the resources available, the contextual elements, and the cultural background. By deploying the same internet-based protocol of data collection in three culturally far contexts, I set the base of a comparative study of smart-city and civic technology.

a. Data analysis

Traditionally statistics can be descriptive or inferential. A descriptive statistic quantitatively describes or summarises features from a collection of information. For example, measures of central tendency such as the mean, median, and mode, and measures of variability such as the standard deviation, the minimum and maximum values of the variables, kurtosis, and skewness, are commonly used to describe datasets.

Exploratory data analysis (EDA)

EDA is an approach to analyzing data sets to summarize their main characteristics, often using statistical graphics or other visualization methods. It is for seeing what the data can tell us beyond the formal modeling or hypothesis testing task and possibly formulate hypotheses that could lead to new data collection and experiments. It also allows early patterns discovery, spot anomalies, and check simple assumptions such as the kind of model or distribution the data follows. EDA aims to reveal the underlying structure and model behind the raw dataset.

It is not a mere collection of techniques but rather a practical approach to dissecting a raw data set. Most EDA techniques are graphical with a few quantitative methods. The reason for heavy reliance on graphics is that the role of EDA is a comprehensive exploration with no precise goals to get ready to gain some new unsuspected insight into the data. Instead, it can be seen as a support to our natural pattern-recognition abilities with bare eyes.

EDA uses the techniques of :
- plotting raw data (histograms, scatter plots, ...)
- plotting simple statistics (mean plots, standard deviation plots, box plots, ...)
- positioning such plots so as to maximize our global understanding of the situation.

Data cleaning and transformation

EDA will often reveal some missing or irrelevant data points in your data sets. Both nulls and outliers usually mean to be deleted if possible or replaced by a mean value or 0 (numerical). Depending on the kind of model you wish to perform (classification or regression) and the variables at your disposal, you'll sometimes need to change the data type from categorical to numerical and split the dataset into distinct subsets of categorical and numerical variables to perform both analyses in parallel.

Correlation analysis

Data Correlation is a way to understand the relationship between multiple variables in your dataset. Using a correlation matrix, you can first look at the relationships between the variables of your dataset. Then, I'll identify if one or multiple attributes depend on others or if some features are associated with a causal relationship.

There are three types of correlations:
- **Positive Correlation:** means that if feature **A** increases, then feature **B** also increases, or if feature **A** decreases, then feature **B** also decreases. Both features move in tandem, and they have a linear relationship.
- **Negative Correlation:** means that if feature **A** increases, then feature **B** decreases and vice versa. They have a relation of opposition.
- **No Correlation:** No relationship between those two attributes.

By checking for correlation between variables, I will find the one feature having the highest relationships with most other ones. This will allow me to determine clusters of features to reduce redundancy in my dataset and select the most important features before training my machine learning models. Since all of my variables are numerical ones, I will also proceed with regression analysis to test their relationships.

Different coefficients can be used to measure the correlation intensity:
- **Pearson's correlation coefficient (r)** is a measure of linear correlation between two variables. To calculate r for two variables X and Y, one divides the covariance of X and Y by the product of their standard deviations.
- **Spearman's rank correlation coefficient (ρ)** measures the monotonic correlation between two variables. It is, therefore, better in catching nonlinear monotonic correlations than Pearson's r. To calculate ρ for two variables X and Y, one divides the covariance of the rank variables of X and Y by the product of their standard deviations.
- **Kendall's rank correlation coefficient (τ)** measures the ordinal association between two variables, similar to Spearman's rank correlation coefficient. To calculate τ for two variables X and Y, one determines the number of concordant and discordant pairs of observations. Then, τ is given by the number of concordant pairs minus the discordant pairs divided by the total number of teams.
- **Phik (φk)** is a new and practical correlation coefficient that works consistently between categorical, ordinal, and interval variables, captures nonlinear dependency, and reverts to the Pearson correlation coefficient in case of the bivariate normal input distribution.
- **Cramér's V** is an association measure for nominal random variables. The coefficient ranges from 0 to 1, with 0 indicating independence and 1 indicating perfect association. Unfortunately, the empirical estimators used for Cramér's V have been proved to be biased, even for large samples.

Correlations between variables are often visualized through a correlation matrix, choosing one of the coefficients. It allows the analyst to detect the highly correlated or uncorrelated variables and first answers about the early hypothesis or assumptions.

Regression analysis

In statistics, regression analysis estimates the relationship between a dependent variable and one or more independent variables. The most common form of regression analysis is linear regression. A researcher can find the line that most closely fits the data points according to a specific mathematical criterion. For example, the method of ordinary least squares computes the unique string that minimizes the sum of squared differences between the actual data and that line. This allows us to estimate the conditional expectation of the dependent variable when the independent variables take a given set of values.

Correlation and regression are both techniques to determine the level of relationship between two variables, but they do not work the same. Here is an interesting comparison of both (see Fig. 5).

Topic	Correlation	Regression
When to use	For a quick and simple summary of the direction and strength of pairwise relationships between two numeric variables.	To predict or optimize a numeric response Y from a numeric X..
Quantifies direction of relationship	Yes	Yes
Quantifies strength of relationship	Yes	Yes
X and Y interchangeable	Yes	No
Y Random	Yes	Yes
X Random	Yes	No
Prediction and Optimization	No	Yes
Equation	No	Yes
Extension to curvilinear fits	No	Yes
Cause and effect	No	Attempts to establish

Fig. 5 - Correlation and Regression method compared. *source: prism academy*

Machine learning

Machine learning algorithms build a model based on sample data to make predictions without being explicitly programmed. For example, ML models process statistical regression analysis when predicting a numerical value and statistical classification when predicting a class labell.

It usually asks for a few steps to reach the best performances: a feature selection, balanced datasets, train/test split, and performance comparison between different models. In my case, I'll be using Machine Learning algorithms to detect highly engaged citizens in smart-city. This refers to a classification task, so I'll be selecting four classification algorithms and compare their accuracies: Logistic Regression, K-Nearest Neighbours, Multi-Layer Perceptron, Support Vector Machines.

Logistic Regression: It is one of the most fundamental algorithms used to model relationships between a dependent variable and one or more independent variables. Similar to the linear regression model, but used on a discrete number of outcomes, the logistic regression uses a logistic function to model a binary dependent variable.

K-Nearest Neighbours: In statistical classification, the KNN algorithm is used to classify an object by a plurality vote of its neighbors. The thing being assigned to the class is most common among its k nearest neighbors. k is a positive integer, typically small. k-NN is a type of instance-based learning, where the function is approximated locally. The algorithm relies on distance for classification.

Multi-Layer Perceptron: MLPClassifier is an Artificial Neural Network model which optimizes the log-loss function. As ANN, it uses connected input/output units where each connection has a weight. During the learning phase, the network learns by adjusting the weights to predict the correct class label of the input data.

Support Vector Machines: A Support Vector Machine is a supervised classification technique that will find a hyperplane or a boundary between the two classes of data that maximizes the margin between the two classes. Many planes can separate the two classes, but only one plane can maximize the margin or distance between the classes.

Accuracy scores

Classification Accuracy is what we usually mean when we use the term accuracy. Probably the most straightforward and intuitive metric for classifier performance. It is the ratio of the number of correct predictions to the total number of input samples. It works well only if there are an equal number of samples belonging to each class.

F1 Score is the Harmonic Mean between precision and recall. The range for the F1 Score is [0, 1]. It tells you how accurate your classifier is (how many instances it classifies correctly), as well as how robust it is (it does not miss a significant number of cases).

Area Under Curve(AUC) is one of the most widely used metrics for evaluation. It is used for binary classification problems. *AUC* of a classifier is equal to the probability that the classifier will rank a randomly chosen positive example higher than a randomly chosen negative example.

Recall is the number of correct positive results divided by the number of all relevant samples (all samples that should have been identified as positive), which means the percent of truly positive instances classified as such.

Precision is the number of correct positive results divided by the number of positive results predicted by the classifier, which means the percent of positive classifications that are genuinely positive.

Mean Absolute Error (MAE) is the average difference between the Original Values and the Predicted Values. It gives us the measure of how far the predictions were from the actual output.

Mean Squared Error (MSE) is quite similar to Mean Absolute Error. The only difference is that MSE takes the average of the **square** of the difference between the original values and the predicted values. The advantage of MSE being that it is easier to compute the gradient.

Root Mean Squared Error (RMSE) is more appropriate to represent model performance than the MAE when the error distribution is expected to be Gaussian. It avoids the use of absolute value, which is highly undesirable in many mathematical computations.

R-squared (r2) is the percentage of the response variable variation explained by a linear model. The maximum value of R^2 is 1, but it may take a negative value.

Variance inflation factor (VIF) measures the amount of multicollinearity in a set of multiple regression variables. It is calculated for each independent variable. A high VIF indicates that the associated independent variable is highly collinear with the other variables in the model.

Inferential statistics

While it is assumed that the observed data set is sampled from a larger population, inferential statistics use the data to learn about the people that the sample of data is thought to represent, in my case, the highly engaged citizens of a Smart-City. With statistical inferences, it is possible to reach conclusions that extend beyond the actual dataset, to infer properties of an underlying distribution of probability. Inferential statistics is the counterpart of descriptive statistics, which do not assume the population outside the datasets.

Suppose the machine learning models are used to make predictions inside the dataset. In that case, probabilistic models are used to make predictions about extensive data, using the probability of an event to occur and statistical hypothesis testing.

Data Visualisation

Data visualization is a fundamental part of the data scientist's toolkit, as visualization is one of the most powerful ways to communicate and acquire new acknowledgment. By visualizing your results, you can also notice what you never expected to see.

A wide variety of tools exists for visualizing data. Mastering plot organization in *matplotlib* will make a real difference. Scikit-learn can help you generate quick and beautiful plots at different stages of your machine learning project.

b. Social network analysis

From the coding skills at my disposal and the presence or not of Key Stakeholders on this or that social network, I decided to realize my Social Network Analysis from Twitter. Even if my survey studies on the inhabitants commonly reveal that Twitter is a third category of importance (my respondents more often use Facebook, Linked In, Youtube, and Instagram), Twitter is the commonly used channel for digital diplomacy and official communication. After a bit of research, I found out that 131 foreign ministries and 107 foreign ministers maintain active accounts, encouraging their missions and ambassadors worldwide to become active on this social media. The 2018 Twiplomacy study of BCW (Burson Cohn & Wolfe) identified 951 Twitter accounts of heads of state and government, 372 personal and 579 institutional accounts, and the foreign ministers of 187 countries. So, 97 % of 193 UN member states have an official presence on the platform, with a combined audience of 485 million followers (see Fig. 6).

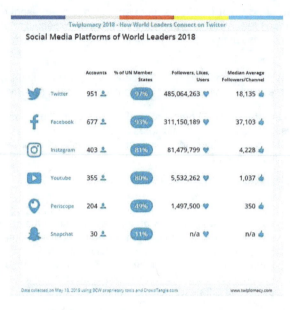

Fig. 6 - Social media platforms of world leaders

So, Twitter is a central social media platform for mining population-level data and accurate clustering of city-related tweets into topics to extract relevant insights. For each of the three cities composing my case studies: Taipei, Tel Aviv, and Tallinn, I collected:

- **Twitter Hashtags:** Scraping last Tweets mentioning the town's name in a specific hashtag is a way to inform what's talked about on Twitter about my case studies.
  #Taipei resulted in a list of 17,341 tweets, up to November 16th, 2013.
  #Telaviv resulted in a list of 17,628 tweets, up to September 30th, 2012.
  #Tallinn resulted in a list of 6,299 tweets, up to March 13th, 2008.

For each Twitter account of representative stakeholder category, I collected:

- **Followers:** Extracting all followers from an identified account is a way to make a targeted list of people interested in the stakeholder activities.
- **Followings:** Extracting a list of all the profiles followed by an account can better understand the sources of information and influences of any stakeholder identified.
- **Likes given:** Extracting every tweet liked by your stakeholder is a way to look at what it likes on Twitter. Each of those *Likes* are pieces of information they deemed valuable and worth remembering.
- **Tweets & Responses:** Downloading all the tweets & responses posted by your Stakeholder is the best way to look closer at their activities on the social network.

- **Likes received:** Extracting the last likes & retweets out of every tweet & response posted by your Stakeholder is a way to retrieve the most supporting followers online.

From raw datasets collected on social networks, two very different analysis are feasible:
- Lexical analysis on the content published by users
- Topological analysis of the connections between users.

Lexical Analysis—Natural Language Processing

Natural Language Processing is a subfield of linguistics and computer science working on computers with human languages to analyze sizeable natural language data. It allows visualization of the information contained in the network with bare eyes. Word embedding enables the capture of lexical, semantic, or even syntactic similarities between written interactions, which can be used for text categorization, determining influences or qualifying relationships between nodes and communities of a network, or detecting regular patterns in question answering.

NLP algorithms allow me to extract many features on lexical content, which will be used as many variables whose correlation will be tested. My analysis aims to identify profiling attributes from stakeholder categories and overall tendencies at the scale of a city. Usually, to embed text content from tweets, the conventional bag-of-words (BoWs) with a weighting model term frequency-inverse document frequency (TF-IDF) is enough. Based on word occurrence counts and sparse matrix results, and the K-means clustering algorithm, the most frequently used word clustering into topics includes variants of hierarchy, density, and centrality. Unlike pure clustering, topic modeling is a way of dimensionality reduction or feature extraction. A clustering algorithm can further follow it.

Sentiment Analysis

As a machine learning challenge on lexical content, sentiment analysis, or opinion mining, is one of the most popular insights extracted out of textual content, predominantly used in the context of analyzing reviews from customers of a new product for a specific brand or company. Also called opinion mining, it uses NLP techniques to identify affective states and subjective information from texts of very different scales and various topics. A list of socio-linguistic words such as emoticons, ellipses, prototypical words, hashtags can be studied at a topic level and provide behavior and feeling levels of understanding.

Topological Analysis—Graph Theory

Social network analysis refurbished the existing graph theory. It gave captivating applications in the digital world, as the study of the connection between things. Practically speaking, any network is composed of nodes and links. It can take an unlimited variety of shapes and sizes and can be fulfilled with additional properties, represented with directions, weights, clusters, and loops. The idea of effectively representing social networks from raw data has given its field of research called social network analysis. It provides various indicators to study from networks.

Some basic human-observation can provide the first insights :

- number of followers and the followers/followings ratio
- average likes, comments & RT per tweet
- average likes, comments & RT per account
- network associations between categories of stakeholders (public sector, private business, academics, civil society, medias)
- controversial messages, creating strong oppositions inside the network

Much deeper analysis can be done by using AI-programs on the datasets.
- Node-Level topology : centrality and community detection
- Network-Level structures : common patterns and local specificities
- semantic analysis

For each representative selected a priori, I will:
- graph the personal ego-network
- cross-check the ego-networks, looking for common relationships
- situate them in their corresponding city hashtag : which community do they belong to ? do they serve as bridge nodes or exposure nodes ?

A graph is a data structure used to represent and analyze connections between elements. The two main elements of charts are nodes (or vertices) and edges (or links) which connect two nodes (see Fig. 7). Even if two nodes are not directly related to each other, they will be joined by a sequence of edges (or path) which can be followed to go from one node to the other.

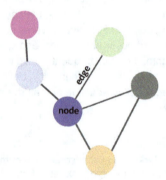

Fig. 7—A graph structure represent a network from its most basic elements: nodes and edges.

This graph representation can describe many relational systems: from the air traffic among different airports to the exchange of proteins between cells of a given tissue by the interaction of individuals in a group project. In social network analysis, nodes are users of the platform (in my case Twitter), and the edges represent any interaction (like, *follow, reply or mention*) between them. There are different types of graphs to represent different kinds of interactions. In my case, I am using an undirected graph with no weight on the edges as a matter of simplification (see Fig. 8). But the relation represented is those of the engagement of a node in the direction of another one.

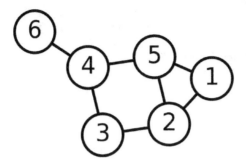

Fig. 8—Undirected graph with no attributes on nodes nor edges.

Generally speaking, whenever a graph can model a system, we say that this system is a network. Network science is the discipline whose goal is to understand the phenomena whose underlying structure is a graph, in my case, stakeholder interaction in a Smart-City. It consists of extracting features from networks by using different graph metrics and statistics. There are three levels of measures to make in a topological analysis of a network: node-level, edge-level, network-level.

Node-level analysis
It is necessary to determine a Root User (central node) to proceed with the node-level analysis, then consider followers and followings as directed edges, where bi-directional edges show mutual interest. From those two pieces of information, you can draw a first graph of the first-step neighborhood, corresponding to the edges between the relationships of the Root User.

Therefore, you can add a weighting coefficient to your graph. The more you can see a node's activities in the news feed (posts, retweets, likes), the node's most weighted. Similarly, the more you can see interactions between two nodes in the news feed, the most weighted is the edge between them. Finally, you will be able to deduct some behavioral characteristics from the positions of the nodes in the graph. The inter-related function allows you to describe the nature of a node's relationship with neighboring nodes, from attractiveness to repulsion, graduated by gravity forces inside the network. The intra-related position allows you to detect niche positions on the web or a specific community. It can reveal certain properties on the information flow, such as bridge nodes, serving as a link between two distinct communities, or exposure nodes which serve as an entrance window to new communities. In a community, the density level indicates higher interconnectivity between nodes. Modularity is the level of disconnection from one community with another. So it reveals the quality of community detection. On the contrary, a high number of outliers can show a lousy categorization.

Measures of Centrality

Indicators of centrality identify the most influential nodes within a graph. Centrality algorithm can also be a way to calculate the importance of any given node in a network. The three most common methods of measuring network centrality are:

- **Degree centrality** measures the number of connections a node has (see Fig.9).

Influential individuals may have many incoming connections (people who consider themselves tied to them) but fewer outgoing connections (their connections to others they reciprocate). A reciprocal connection is considered more robust. In this study, I am focusing on outgoing connections only.

Fig 9—Degree centrality : which node is the most important to the graph ?

- **Closeness centrality** measures one's closeness to all others in the network (see Fig. 10). A substantial closeness measure indicates that the individual can quickly reach others in the network through a minimal number of steps. It confers ease of quickly gathering or collecting information.

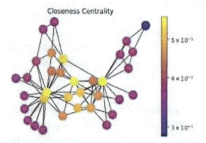

Fig 10—Yellow nodes are the ones with highest closeness centrality.

- **Betweenness centrality** measures the degree to which an agent stands in a central position across pivotal paths or vectors connecting the network (see Fig. 11). In a decision-making network, a bridge node with high betweenness can be considered a risk to compromise the flow of information.

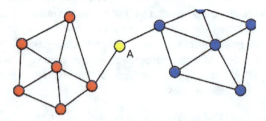

Fig 11—The node A (yellow) is the one with highest betweenness centrality.

- **Eigenvector centrality** is a measure of one's connection to those who are highly connected (see Fig. 12). A political advisor who councils many politicians would have a high Eigenvector score. Such a person plays a vital role behind the scenes to accrue great power and reach in a network while avoiding direct risk.

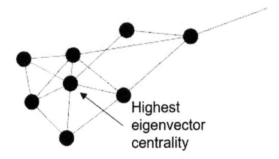

Fig 12—The node the closest to the most connected nodes has the highest eigenvector centrality.

- **Load centrality** is the fraction of all shortest paths that pass through a node. Load centrality is a betweenness-like measure defined through a hypothetical flow process.

Edge-level analysis

The second metric to take on a graph is at an edge level: each node is linked to at least one other, which means that some measures can be taken on this link. To prepare my data for a Machine Learning algorithm to predict links in my networks, I will focus on adapted metrics.

- **Common neighbours**: indicates the number of nodes in common between two nodes. Two strangers who have a friend in common are more likely to be introduced than those who don't have any friends in common.

- **Jaccard coefficient:** the ratio between the shared neighbors of the two nodes and all the neighbors of the two nodes.

- **Resource Allocation Index**: fraction of information that a node can send to another node through their shared neighbors. So if two nodes have nodes in common with a high degree, there will be a low ROI, vice versa if the neighbors have a low degree.

- **Preferential attachment:** the more connected a node is, the more likely it is to receive new links. This metric is the product of the nodes' degree.

Network-level analysis

The third level of calculation of a network's features is the network itself. A series of metrics can be taken at the ensemble level, which helps detect similarities between networks. I will also aggregate the node-level measures at this network level using mean, standard deviation, min, and max values to get some more features extracted from my networks. The number of tweets, the number of followers, and the maximum of likes collected on a publication evaluate the relationship between 'popularity' variables and the level of engagement.

- **Size** is a measure of the number of edges of the total of all edge weights. In my case, I chose not to represent any weight in my networks by the concern of simplicity. However, the attribute 'frequency' has been recorded to each link in the network and could be used for this purpose.

- **Density** is a measure of the number of connections in the network compared to the maximum number of links possible. A highly dense network may be challenging to change opinion as there are very tight connections amongst the agents. Most social networks are sparse, by the way, which means non-dense.

- **Transitivity** in a graph is the network's overall probability of having adjacent nodes interconnected, thus revealing the existence of tightly connected communities (or clusters, subgroups, cliques). It is calculated by the ratio between the observed number of closed triplets and the maximum possible number of closed triplets in the graph (see Fig. 13).

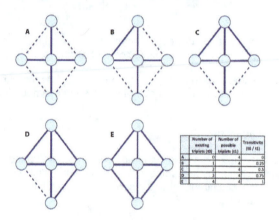

	Number of existing triplets (t0)	Number of possible triplets (t1)	Transitivity (t0 / t1)
A	0	4	0
B	1	4	0.25
C	2	4	0.5
D	3	4	0.75
E	4	4	1

Fig. 13—Network transitivity calculated on 5 different link combination between 5 nodes.

- **Edge connectivity** is an essential measure of a network's resilience. It is the minimum number of edges to remove to separate the remaining nodes into two or more isolated subgraphs. It is closely related to the network flow problems.

- **Diameter** (or distance) is the maximum eccentricity of any vertex in the graph. That is, it is the most maximum distance between any pair of vertices. To find the graph's diameter, first, find the shortest path between each pair of vertices. The most maximum length of any of these paths is the diameter of the graph.

- **Number of connected components** A graph is said to be connected if there is a path between every pair of vertices. So the number of related elements in a graph drops all the nodes in a dead-end or a single relationship with only one node of the graph. A graph is said to be connected when all the nodes of its network are. Otherwise, it is stated not connected.

- **Largest Subgraphs** are directly deducted from the connected components of a graph. It is the vastest number of related elements in a graph and so a connected graph by definition. The largest subgraph of a graph allows us to take some more measures as a connected ensemble, like the average clustering coefficient and the average shortest path length. It also helps speeding up some algorithms since it drops a significant number of non-relevant elements of a graph.

- **Clustering coefficient** is a measure of the number of triangles in a graph. It evaluates the tendency for nodes to cluster together or for edges to form triangles. In our context, they are measures of the extent to which the users interacting with one particular user tend to interact with each other as well.

Graph-based machine learning

Suppose we accept graphs as an elemental means of structuring and analyzing network data about the world. In that case, we shouldn't be surprised to see them being widely used in Machine Learning as a powerful tool that can enable intuitive properties and power many valuable features.
The main inferences to do with machine learning on graphs are of three kind :
- node classification
- link prediction
- association between networks.

These predictive models can have direct applications in community detection, probability of network growth, and detection of similarities between graphs.

Community detection

The tendency of nodes in a graph to spontaneously form clusters of internally dense linkage (at this moment termed community) is a remarkable and almost universal property of networks of all kinds: biological or social. Thus community detection algorithms are a central part of the research and development of machine learning on graphs. A specific family of algorithms called agglomerative work collects (or merges) nodes that optimize the local modularity (see Fig. 14).

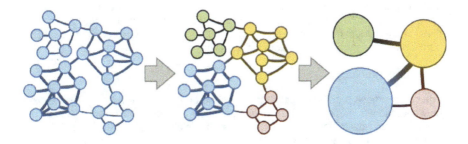

Fig. 14 —Steps of a community detection and agglomeration process.

Another process for detecting communities is the Label Propagation algorithm (LPA) which consists of an iterative algorithm. We assign labels to unlabelled points by propagating labels through the dataset. For LPA to work, we have to assume that an edge connecting two nodes carries a notion of similarity. It means that people tend to communicate with other people having similar interests. Assume that we have a network of nodes, most of them being unlabelled, but a few being labeled red or green (see Fig. 15). So the question is, can we predict the color of the remaining nodes? We can walk randomly in the graph, starting from node four until we meet any labeled node. When we hit a labeled node, we stop the walk. Based on all the possible random walks starting from node 4, we can see that most walks end in a red node. So, we can color node 4 in red. This is the basic intuition behind LPA.

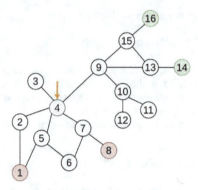

Fig 15—The node 4 has more probability to turn red than green based on closeness with coloured nodes.

To test the different methods for community detection on my graphs, I will cross the result of four different algorithms :
- Greedy Modularity algorithm
- Louvain Algorithm
- Maximal Cliques
- Label Propagation.

There are many ways of detecting communities in a network. Still, the most popular method is to use the modularity metric. Modularity measures relative density in a network: a community has a high density with other nodes within its hub but low density with those outsides. Modularity gives a score of how fractious a network is and can partition the web and return individual communities. Very dense networks are often more difficult to split, but most real-life networks are sparse and disconnected. Most community detection algorithms start with selecting the best partition of the network like the Louvain algorithm does in my case.

Link prediction

The other famous problem in graph theory is the one of link prediction. Given a fixed network, can we predict what new edges are likely to form in this network? Given a pair of nodes, how to assess whether they are possible to connect (see Fig 16)? A series of measures can be taken on the network to detect the probability of edges to be formed between two unconnected nodes.

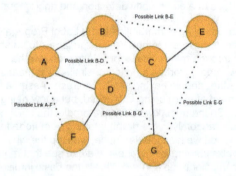

Fig 16—Considering existing edges, what chances as each non-edge to be formed ?

We will use the four edge-level measures described above: shared neighbors, Jaccard coefficient, resource allocation index, preferential attachment, to train a classification machine learning algorithm and reach the best performance in predicting which non-edge is likely to be formed based on how closely are their attributes to those taken on existing edges. Since there are much more non-edges than edges in my graphs, like in most of them, the first step will consist of balancing the datasets of edges and non-edges by using a downsampling technique.

c. Agent-Based Modelling

The phenomenological approach used for my research asks me to profile critical stakeholders from the cross of diverse sources of information: personal research on the web, survey study on inhabitants, participative workshops with the most engaged of them, one-to-one interviews of local experts, and personal attendance to events during the time of my field research.

Modelling the collective dynamics of a Smart-City

The social sciences seek to understand how individuals behave and how the interaction of many individuals leads to large-scale outcomes. This means understanding how the final results of interactions can be more than the sum of the parts. It's often said that "Architecture as the art of shaping public spaces, is the most political art of all." Indeed, political systems are composed of citizens, voters, politicians, parties, legislatures, and governments. These political actors interact with each other and dynamically alter their final decision according to the results of their interactions. The same phenomenon is observed in the interaction between stakeholders in decision-making for urban planning. In my research, I don't try to determine the final consensual decision of a defined project but to identify which parameters' combinations influence public opinion formation. So, I'll use a computational simulation technique called Agent-Based Modeling to observe the evolution of artificial societies featuring the rules I'ld have extracted from my data analysis.

ABM uses concepts and tools from both social and computer science. It represents a methodological approach that could ultimately allow essential developments: 1 — the rigorous testing, refinement, and extension of existing theories that have proved to be challenging to formulate and to evaluate by using standard statistical and mathematical tools; and 2 — a deeper understanding of fundamental causal mechanisms in multi-agent systems, whose study is currently separated by artificial disciplinary boundaries. ABM is a methodology that integrates into a simulation the specific properties of the agents. The rules governing their interactions observe how such micro-specifications can generate the macro-level phenomenon of interest (see Fig. 17, 18, 19).

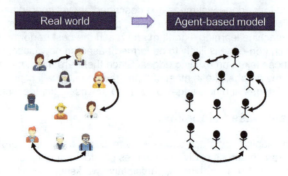

Fig. 17 - Each Agent with its characteristics and interaction rule is translated into a model

Fig. 18 - A simulation of large-scale phenomena is produced from the smaller-scale empirical research results

Fig. 19 - The large-scale simulation is conceptualized to a macro-level phenomena of interest.

ABM assumes that complex collective patterns can emerge from the repeated execution of individual behaviors once lower-level unique properties and rules are specified in a simulation. It is precisely suited for studying systems exhibiting the following two properties:

- The system is composed of interacting agents
- Properties arising from the agents' interactions cannot be deduced simply by aggregating the properties of the agents.

When the interaction of the agents is contingent on experience, especially when the agents continually adapt to that experience, mathematical analysis is very limited in its ability. ABM might be the only practical method of analysis to derive the dynamic consequences of evolving properties of agents along with time sequences. So, the three critical components of ABM are agents, environment, and time.

- **Agents are entities in the model with attributes, states of mind, and behavior rules** that affect how individuals interact with others and the environment. They are usually heterogeneous in characteristics and conditions. Each agent has different emotions, preferences, and spatial locations but usually follows the same regular rules of interaction and exposure. Their feelings and opinions change in the interaction with their neighbors and in the direction of media messages. So potentially in events and clusters or other places promoting city transformations and new forms of behavior.
- **Environment determines who interacts with and how.**
- **Time determines the sequence of interactions amongst the agents.** With the ease of computing power nowadays, synchronous updating of states across agents and the entire system is achievable and recommended for the simulation model. In practice, most models typically start with a distributively random system state and focus on the final results taken from when the outcome of interest has stabilized or when the model has reached equilibrium.

The simulation starts with a rigorously specified set of hypotheses regarding a proposed system of interest but does not prove theorems with generality. It begins with assumptions about agents and their interactions. It then uses computer simulation to generate scenarios that can reveal the emotional consequences of the variation of some independent parameters. Thus, simulation differs from standard deduction and induction in both its implementation and goals but allows increased understanding of systems through controlled computational experiments.

Building an ABM in 7 steps:

1—What are your world's dimensions? Group formation models are often multi-dimensional to represent complex social spheres. Still, dimensions only apply to models where interactions between agents are governed by space. Even if my study consists of a spatially rooted problem (Urban Development), the network model retained to illustrate the unlimited possibilities of connexions and interactions between stakeholders has no dimensions.

2—How do agents meet? Will interactions be governed randomly or according to a rule (or a bit of both)? Do they interact only with neighbors or with any other agent in the simulation? Agents can entirely avoid interactions (because of their unpopularity) or interact with more than one agent? In my case, **a scale-free network appears like the most relevant** to illustrate the context of decision-making in urban planning, where interactions are governed by rules (current regulation and laws) but also randomly (mainly for counter-power exercised in NGOs and Civil Movements) and by a combination of both (especially for business motivated interactions of private sector stakeholders in a liberal economy context). **The agents can interact with any other agents. They can interact with more than one agent simultaneously** (round), even if they are more likely to interact with friends than enemies. Behavioral patterns, emotions, and opinions can change by interaction with others and the satisfaction derived from the previous position.

3—How do agents behave ? When agents meet, what do they do? Do the agents' behavior approximates the type of social behavior of interest? In my case, **agents try to influence each other as long as they have reached a form of final**

consensus on the decision to take, marked by a threshold: the "Irreversibility" state, beyond which it becomes impossible to turn back on other options.

4—What is the payoff? Generally, the agents will get out money, happiness, or social bonds from interaction with others. In my case, as for many ABMs that feature interactive decision-making, payoffs are determined by considering an agent's decisions and those of that agent's partner(s). Indeed, **the gain of any agent of my model will consist in benefiting from a final consensual decision that will be the closest to its interests.**

5—How do agents change? In many models, agents learn from their previous payoffs and adjust their behavior in future rounds. Some agents will "die" (move out of the network, often when the gain is too low) or reproduce (will be joined by agents with the same characteristics, usually when the payoff is high). When agents gather in groups, their influence on some other agents can increase or decrease. In my case, the change in behavior or opinion will be driven by temporary views, groups of affinity, the spatial or ideologic proximity with a decision to take. This let me think that a minority of agents will be constant in their opinion. At the same time, a majority of them will change often. Moreover, the results of my survey study "Grassroots Movements: The motivation of American, Taiwanese and Russian Civic-Hackers compared" suggests that, at least in civil movements, the engagement of agents in decision-making will be dependent on cultural and political heritage, management choices from the leaders and the personal look for money.

6—How long does your world last? In some cases, models should run until they have reached some forms of equilibrium. In other cases, models should run for a length that approximates some phenomenon of interest. In my case, the stakeholder engagement model in decision-making should never arrive at an end because **democracy is a continuous process of collective decision-making.** But simulation models will be delimited by computer storage and CPU speed. The need for a conclusion in my thesis leads suggests I **identify regular cycles (patterns) in the influence of actors on the others.**

7—What do you want to learn from your world? ABM is a theory-building and hypothesis-testing paradigm including dependent and independent variables. The experiment customizes the independent variables (or "parameters"). In contrast, dependent variables are measured throughout the model or at the conclusion. Adding more independent variables into the model or using new variables to test the generalizability of a phenomenon is often called "robustness analysis" and can reveal surprising new effects or non-linearities. In my case, **I want to examine the best scenario for participative decision-making on urban planning, where all stakeholders' opinions have been taken into consideration,** resulting in a consensus that will generate the lesser opposition in the short time and the lowest critic *a posteriori* in a long time.

5. Protocol Validation: Warm-up on side studies

In the early stage of my doctorate research, I have been training my protocol on different warm-up tours. Indeed I chose a somewhat practical way of proceeding with my academic research, and I needed some trials to refine my methods. Both to frame better the questions of my surveys than to get used to online recruiting participants. It also helped me in improving my English speaking and starting to build relationships abroad.

a. A sound out of my LinkedIn network

At the same time that the French government, led by Emmanuel Macron, was organizing his "Great National Debate" in late 2018, I was mailing the ampler part of my french LinkedIn network to ask them to participate in my first survey studies on "Stakeholder engagement in Smart-City." From the beginning of my urban studies, my topic has always been "How do people influence their urban environment ?". I spread this survey by email and collected 158 respondents.

What are the profiles of the respondents ?

- *Gender and Age:* Balanced ratio between man (54%) and woman (46%) from all ages: the oldest just celebrated his 83 years old while the 2 youngest were 20.
  Roughly 27% of respondents are in their 20's, 18% in their 30's, 17% in their 40's, 12% in their 50's and 7% are more than 60 years old.

- *City of birth and city of residence:* Born in a range of different French towns (some abroad): 13% was born in Paris while 7% was born in Perpignan. The predominance of Perpignan at this scale is not representative of France but instead of my network (I was born in Perpignan and started my career there). Now 25% of the respondents live in Paris while 12% live in Perpignan

- *Professional situation:* The majority (42%) are private-sector employees, 20% are freelance or liberal professions. Then 10% each for entrepreneurs, public sector employees, and unemployed. Only 5% retired (not surprising for a LinkedIn contacts-based study). They define their current occupation in the majority as Project Manager (23%), Consultant (21%), or General Direction (18%). So I can tell that **my respondents are more executive than non-executive.** Teachers or trainers, Sales, R&D and chargé d'affaires are each between 10% and 5%.

- *Background education:* On the one hand, it's interesting here to confirm the executive position of my respondents regarding their study level: 66.5% of Master's Degree, 11.4% of Bachelor Degree. On the other hand, the education background is very diversified: 27.8% of engineering, 17.7% of social sciences, 12.7% of economics, 12% of business studies, 11.4% of business administration, 10.1% of marketing, 5.7% of political sciences, then Law, Art, Architecture, and Literature studies each gets less than 5%.

What is their way of living ?

- *Housing, marital status, holidays:* 72% live in urban areas, 17% in the suburbs, and 11% in rural areas. Living in a couple for 33%of them, in a couple with kids for 30% or alone for 25%, flat sharing for 6%. A large majority

(89%) visit another city twice a year.

- *Internet use*: 98% of my respondents use the internet several times a day for "everything," which means working, searching, hobbies, networking, listening to music, watching movies, resting.

- *Social network and newsletters:* My sample's two most popular social networks are Facebook (84%) and LinkedIn (77%). Then comes Youtube (60%) and Instagram (48%). And finally, Twitter (35%). They use it for professional reasons (83%), for recreation (75%), and to keep in touch with friends (63%). 84% of the respondents subscribe to a newsletter, but only 34 % feel well informed of specific news by this way. Indeed, most (39%) do not have the time to read the newsletter they subscribed to.

- *Volunteering:* A perfect 50/50 share between members and non-members of non-profit associations! While 96% say, they do not have any membership in a political party.

What level of urban knowledge do they have ?

- *Urban information:* Three out of four (75%) say feeling well informed on urban news. Of course, they get informed on the internet for 95% of them, but offline conversation such as word-to-mouth is the second most crucial channel for 61%. Far ahead of the press, books, conferences, and education.

- *Interest for urban topics:* Most of the respondents (89%) say they are interested in urbanism issues. 57% for more than five years, 25% for one to five years. They are interested personally or professionally, but only 10% do it through a non-profit association.

- *Willing to engage in local urban planning:* 89% of them distinguish between belonging to a political party and taking part in urban planning choices. They consider the freedom to make personal choices about the urban environment and the right to citizenship at a very local level as issues important to them and not satisfied by being a political party member. 79% had never participated in blocking an urban project, but 81% think they could do it for different motivations: the destruction of a historical heritage or natural space, non-respect for ecology or environmental sustainability, non-respect for the well-being of inhabitants.

How to engage in future planning of their cities ?

- *Collaborative Processes on urban development:* 27% already participated in a co-design workshop, 46% already went to an informative conference, and 32% attended a neighborhood meeting. However, 38% had never participated in such an event. Those who have been to and did not appreciate it say: "It takes time, it's less fun than going to the coffee with the same discussions, it's neither very constructive nor effective. It was not interactive, very top-down organized and not adapted to allow everyone to express their thoughts."The participants who kept a good feeling on it are less expressive and say that it was informative and a good way for democracy. Finally, 56% would agree to go to an event of participative urbanism once a year, 23% once a month, and 21% would not go.

- *What prevents you from engaging more?*: 71% of the respondents say they are running out of time. The same proportion says that a mobile or web application would help them engage more often in their local urbanism. Empowerment, to get followed by tangible results, transparency with government, and a real impact of their engagement would be the most motivating.

- *How do they define a "Smart" city:* A city which respects humans while delivering more efficient services for transportation and jobs. Governed by more inspiring elected representatives but less involved. A municipality using data to reduce costs that would be transparent, inclusive, and offers a good quality of life. A reassuring and secured city where everyone feels good. Not polluted but ecological, that respects nature, linked with the countryside.

- *Could they leave their living place?* Almost 1 in 2 respondents already left his city or neighborhood because it no longer matched their lifestyle. The reasons are too individual to report here. Still, the people are leaving their cities for studying, working, or going out, but also for neighborhood disagreement, dirt, insecurity, or lack of integration.

- *What would you like the least in future cities?* Most of the answers are about noise, pollution, technocracy, technology-saturated, big brother watching, dependent on digital tools, standardized, overcrowding, and loneliness.

- *Taking part in future planning of the city:* **87% of the respondents would be interested in participating in planning for their cities' future.** Moreover, 85% would be interested in providing an interactive model of their city, which allows them to access simulations of buildings and demolitions or the development of public spaces. But 3D models are not the only way to engage people in decision-making: they also suggest using social networks, referendums, organizing meetings, games like Minecraft, electronic voting, cultural exposition, and education.

Finally, it seems like the French people would love to engage more in urban planning, and digital tools based on the internet are approached like the easiest way to do it with the least waste of time and other inconvenience.

b. 100 Civic Technologies worldwide

Citizens worldwide are keener and keener on using social networks and digital tools in their daily lives to get informed and organize themselves on news, social movements, and civic issues. I wondered what kind of web-based services could help local communities get a better catch on their regional urban planning and started to look at civic-tech providers. I collected feedback from 100 of them worldwide, both by survey study and a one-to-one call interview. Suppose the emerging market of civic technology is becoming very popular. In that case, we lack information about this market, its leaders, and background strategies to change the old-school political game. So I decided to conduct this study on Civic-Tech and publish my results to give potential users, tech developers, and local governments a better view on who is doing what actually on civic engagement through technology, and where in the world? This analysis gives a pretty complete overview of what it was in 2019. My most read article so far and attracted some interest from the field actors in my research.

I picked up approximately 400 civic-tech providers' names on_civictechno.fr (French repertory of civic-tech providers)_angels.co (US repertory of startups) and_linkedin.com (worldwide social network for professionals). I contacted them by email to ask if they wanted to participate in a case study on civic-tech.

I finally collected 100 participants for my study with peer-to-peer calls and survey answers. Most of them are based in the EU and USA, which may be significant for the Civic-Tech and the Digital Democracy market, but needs to be taken with caution because I used French and USA-based directories. Despite this skew process due to a lack of information at my disposal on Asia, Africa, Latin America, and Russia potential civic-tech developers, I had some interesting contacts in Uruguay, Nigeria, Mali, Cameroun, Georgia, India, New Zealand, and Australia (see Fig. 20).

Fig. 20 - My Civic-Tech Case Studies are principally based in EU and US (that makes sense considering directories used and also the state of democracy and internet development)

Who is developing Civic-Tech?

- *Age:* The average age of the founder or leading representative is 33 years old, and the median age is 32. Since the average and median age are almost similar, we can call this distribution *symmetrical*.

- *Background experience:* About their background career or studies, engineering is the most widespread answer, followed by Business School, Business Administration, Computer Science, and Political Sciences at a similar rate. Software Development, Managers, Entrepreneurs and Designers are the least represented.

- *Political engagement:* These findings confirm that some political research says that the people engaging politically online tend to be the same as those who have been engaging offline. Indeed, **most civic-tech founders (61.9%) were already engaged in civic engagement, activism, or political parties.**

What are their organizations?

- *Headquarter:* 12 of 100 of my respondents are based in Paris, 5 in San Francisco, and 4 in Washington DC. 3 in Brussels, 3 in Boston, 3 in

Bucharest, and 3 in New York City. The rest is distributed worldwide, with a high concentration in Europe and the United States of America.

- *Date of creation:* About 50% of them were created in the last three years, and only 25% have more than five years of existence (see Fig. 21). So we can confirm another common hypothesis which says that **civic-tech is a young market**. The bad news about it is that it's still unstable and unregulated. Still, the good news is that it will continue evolving and innovating for the years to come.

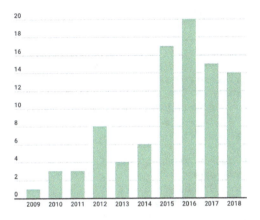

Fig. 21 - Numbers of civic-tech organizations created year-per-year from 2009.

- *Workforce:* To evaluate the size and the workforce of each organization, I'm combining three essential characteristics: how many people are working, full-time or part-time, with an employee or volunteer status?
  I can easily assume the fact that full-time workforces are paid for their work. Indeed, full-time employees are 45% of the organizations engaged in this study. It sounds like an excellent economic health status indicator! 34% of the part-time workers are a majority of volunteers and some contractors, interns, and associates.

Marginally Code For All organization claims 25,000 volunteers involved through 230 local communities around the world. Code for Romania is part of them and declared 600 volunteers for its only community. They prove that volunteer engagement is vital for some of them.

How do they define themselves ?

- *Do you recognize yourself in the term Civic-Tech?* from 1: 100% Civic-Tech to 5: I don't like this term. The results let us know that +70% of them feel very close to the Civic-Tech label (see Fig. 22). In the 15% who do not recognize civic-tech, we can find one artist, one advocate, one activist who works on civic engagement with tech without defining them like civic-tech.

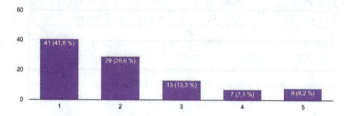

Fig. 22 - How do you recognize yourself in the term "civic-tech"? 1–100% to 5-Not at all

- *How do you consider citizen engagement ?* Political Science researchers make a big difference between methods based on aggregative processes and deliberative processes. The respondents could position themselves on a scale from 1 to 5, where *1 = Statistical aggregation of individual interest* and *five = Confronting points of view leading to a choice*. No one answered one, and the majority is a tie between 3 and 4, skewed right (to the 5), which means 90% of them validate the deliberative process.

- *What is your vision for public services?* This question wanted to check how civic-tech actors represent themselves in the relationship between the state and the citizens. They had the choice from 1: Necessarily from a government to citizens to 5: Could be delivered from the private sector to citizens (see Fig. 23). Here again, we are not in the presence of ultra-liberal profiles willing to delete the state: the modal value is balanced between *government to citizens* and *business to citizens*, skewed left, which means that Civic-Tech developers are still attached the concept of the state and somehow to centralized governance.

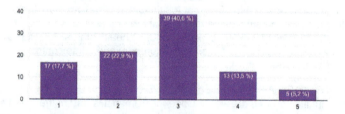

Fig.23 - What is your vision for public services? 1-Gov to citizen 5-Business to citizen

How do they perceive their impact ?

+80% of them feel like they already impact public services, and +77% say they participate in increasing local government efficiency (lower spending or lower resource consumption). In peer-to-peer call interviews, the answer was more subtle: real impact is hard to measure. They are aware of sometimes representing an over-cost short-term but think they can help streamline spending or give better service with the same budget in the middle/long-term. Some others specify that they facilitate information flow between electives and people, fighting against fake news, web obscurantism, and abstention at elections.

How are they entering their market ?

I have been able to identify four strategies to enter the market of civic technologies:
- 31 % provide services to governments, candidates in elections, professional intermediaries, and community leaders. They talk for the most about digitizing governments and equip team organizers with more efficient tools.
- 27 % focus on citizen empowerment and direct democracy tools, such as daily voting app, sometimes with secure ID validation processes.
- 22 % work on data collection, analysis, and visualization to better understand the people, help individuals get a more knowledgeable opinion, and go on real-time transparent policies, using both printed press and digital.
- 20 % is above all common supporting goods, social causes, and development initiatives in the most vulnerable communities.

Any secret feature to success ?

Is there any chance to get effective results according to functionality choices? So far, there is no correlation between the presence or absence of specific functionalities and success in adoption by the final users.

It's clear that civic engagement is, first of all, a human management issue, and humans do not seem predictable as computers are. I have classified my results into three categories of success: Successful, not sure yet, Unsuccessful. 66 % claim successful performance on at least one civic engagement action, 20 % in early-stage or beta-testing don't know yet, and 13 % feel unsuccessful in waking up democracy. Despite the lack of precise rules to adopt in civic-tech strategies leading to success, 2 in 3 respondents are pleased with their work, and it's the prime indicator to predict that they will continue to do it. Something that seems helpful to specify here is that success looks uncorrelated with workforce size because I find equivalent proportions of a single developer and more prominent teams in each category.

- *Composition of ownership:* 1 in 3 respondents is self-funding his own business with customer sales, no subsidies, no external investors.
  10% each for those who get external investors, subsidies or not, but get money income from their customers.
  7% for those who have received a public grant but no external investors and now balancing with customer sales. The ones who get subsidies but no customers yet are 3,5% with or without external investors.
  10% have no customers and no subsidies but external investors.
  23% of respondents say they have no customers, no external investors and no subsidies.

What could be the worst and the best scenario for them?

Aside from two of them, which referred to the best situation where they could crash for having too many users, the most representative fears come from the disinterest of the public, the government, or the partners (27%) and not selling enough, no more philanthropists or lower public budget (25%). The anxiety of not finding the excellent product or not being useful is present too (12%) as far as significant political changes (10%). Data closeness and opacity in governance (7%), being hacked, stolen, censured, or crushed by the GAFAM (7%).

On the contrary, as the best thing that could happen to their organization, 22% would strike a great deal with the public sector. 17% expect more users, 12% would attend funds availability, 10% hope for a profound societal change, and 8% dream of a monopoly on their market. Technology advent and everyday use are 5% each. 17% would need better communication and 15% stronger trust in their solutions to achieve this ideal scenario, 14% more investments, and 12% more sales. An extended network (8%) to get support from government and representatives in the public sector (12%) and strong partnership with industry or more giant companies (8%). A more knowledgeable and emphasized workforce would also be welcome (10%).

Finally, we can say that Civic-Tech is a young market conducted by young educated leaders, sensitized to political issues. Based in democratic countries, they often hire employees to drive the social and digital transformation of politics. They do not seem to be keen on ultra-automatization, bots, and algorithm-driven decision-making processes in society. Quite the contrary, they are committed to human beings' sensitivity and the concept of local government.

c. Motivation of volunteer civic-hackers

Because of some results from my two previous preliminary studies, revealing that a vast crowd of volunteers supports the most significant civic technology movements, I wanted to know more about the motivation of volunteer civic-hackers. I used that opportunity to try my first cross-cultural comparison and chose three case studies with very different backgrounds on democracy and citizenship. So, this study has two goals:

- Enlighten the role of each web-based community in its cultural context and observe how citizens around the world take part in the digital transformation of civil society.
- Understand the people involved in these bottom-up political movements, defining them like civic hackers, and what they expect from it.

I chose to write a contextual monograph for each, as I will do for my case studies of cities, and then present the results to the survey (same for all). Self-fulfillment, personal goal achieving, up-skilling, wish of reward. Do Americans, Taiwanese and Russian volunteers share the same motivation to engage in emerging civil society transformations?

Language barrier:

The most delicate part of this comparative study was to find a way to translate the western concept of Grassroots Movements into other political cultures and languages. Fortunately, my research on web-based communities engaged in the digital transformation of society in Asia quickly drove me to g0v zero, based in Taiwan. Most participants speak English and use it to manipulate these political concepts easily. Considering Russian, I met the founder of a Russian company helping Russian NGOs with IT and innovative ways of civic engagement. He translated my survey from English to Russian and delivered it to its network.

1. Code for America

A non-partisan, non-political organization founded in 2009 by Jennifer Pahlka addresses the widening gap between the public and private sectors in their effective use of technology.

CFA began by enlisting technology and design professionals to work with city governments in the United States to build open-source applications and promote openness, participation, and efficiency in government. They define themselves as "a network of people doing government work for the people, by the people, in the digital age."

In practice, they work with residents and governments in solving community problems. For this, CFA provides government services that are simple, effective, and easy to use, working at scale to help all Americans, starting with the people who need them most.

Running through 76 brigades in many US cities, Code for America gives each brigade its autonomy in acting on a local level in its base city. They all have their website, Facebook, Meetup, Twitter, or Github accounts. All this put together, the CFA network is about 25.000 volunteers across the USA.

From my point of view, there seem to be four hierarchical levels: volunteers, brigades, head of brigades, and board of directors. This organization allows true autonomy at local levels and centralized management for critical strategic decisions and public representation. In practice, it has been easy for me to get in touch with the direction board, who redirected me to the head of brigades, who gave me access to local brigade leaders to reach a vast audience of volunteers.

American Volunteers :

- *Profile:* Average age of respondents is 38 years old, and the median value is 35. While CFA says to be a majority woman-led organization in its diversity report, my gender division is 70% men and 27% women.

- *City of residence:* As you can see on the map below, the hometown of my respondents are well distributed in the USA and conforms to the brigade's extensive presence. I can notice a few respondents: 7 Oakland, 5 Orlando, 3 Asheville, 3 Austin, 3 Boston, 3 Burlington, and 3 San Diego.

- *Volunteering:* On my results, new volunteers' traction looks growing from 2009 (CFA creation) to 2019 with two peaks in 2014–2015 and 2017–2018 (see Fig. 24). Since then, 62% have had continuous participation while 38% had an interrupted one. It takes 53% of them more than 1 hour a week and 23% more than 1 hour a month. Only 5% engage more than 1 hour a year. The 18% of volunteers the most involved spend more than 1 hour a day participating in CFA development.

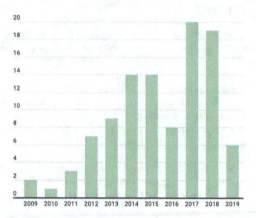

Fig. 24 - When did you start participating in CFA ?

- *Motivation:* The most motivating for a large majority of CFA volunteers (63%) is Self-Fulfillment: feeling good about what I do. 20% are motivated by knowing that I'm contributing to the success of CFA, and 9% seek Advancement in my career/profession/company by volunteering. Good to add that 87% of respondents were self-placed in the motivated half, 26% of which felt Incredibly motivated, and no one feels Motivated.

- *Influence of the community:* While 70% of respondents feel responsible for their co-volunteers motivation, only 14% say not to touch it (16% neutral). The result was roughly confirmed by team-working feeling. We get 67% of people who answered that I feel part of a community or could never achieve my actual goals without the other co-volunteers. On the contrary, 12% say to instead be in individualistic free-ride, and 21% enjoy working by a team on some goals achieved.

- *Influence of leaders on their motivation*: on a scale of five where 1= definitely and 5= not at all, 37% answers 1, 30% answers 2, 17% answers 3, 11,5% answers 4, and 4,4% answers 5. The role of a leader to bring the people in achieving goals seems to be essential for CFA volunteers.

- *Goals to achieve:* 66% checked Networking with others inside and outside of the organization, 64% checked Advancing my skills/knowledge to learn as much as I can, 54% contained Just doing the best job I can, 23% checked Strengthening my relationship with leaders and executives, 20% checked Taking on additional responsibilities and 6% checked Tackle routine by regular rotation on tasks to do.

- *Reward system:* CFA volunteers mainly say not looking for money gain (37%) or having other income sources (36%), being satisfied with non-cash fringe benefits perceived by participation (12%), but 9% wish to be, one day, rewarded for participation. According to this, 66% say they would not engage more if they could perceive some crypto-currency reward for their involvement. But all the same, the other 34% would engage more with this kind of compensation. Indeed, suppose 37% already participate as much as possible. In that case, 46% limit their participation because they need to get some "bread and butter job" elsewhere. Ultimately, in the case of a deployed crypto-currency reward system, the average and middle time of engagement per person would stay to 1 hour a week. And it's exciting to see that it could make the organization gain a 7% full-time workforce and increase from 1% to 10% the number of people working less than 1 hour a year. Having a look at "why" answers, it appears that most of the people do not trust or do not use any crypto-currencies actually and consider that it would harm the organization's philosophy.

2. G0v

G0v is a Taiwanese citizen initiative created in December 2012 by Wu and some friends, unsatisfied with their government's asymmetrical and non-transparent attitude on its economic power-up plan. They introduce themselves as " An online community that advocates transparency of information, also known as open data, focusing on developing information platforms and tools for the citizens to participate in society. Based on the spirit of open source, g0v cares about freedom of speech and open data, writing code to provide citizens with easy-to-use information service. Passionate coders, designers, activists, educators, writers, and citizens from across Taiwan, we hope to build a better Taiwan for its citizens. The transparency of information can help citizens to have a better understanding of how the government works, to understand the issues faster, and to avoid media monopoly, so they can monitor the government more efficiently, become involved in actions and finally deepen the quality of democracy."

The origin myth behind g0v begins with inevitable complaints on web chats. A recurring phrase was 'Why is nobody doing…?', as in 'Why isn't g0v tracking the new legislation by the government?' The legendary response is: 'Don't ask why nobody is doing this—because you are that "nobody"!' Since then, g0vers have self-identified as 'nobodies' (沒有人). If you have an idea, do it—there is no need to ask and no one to get permission. This approach shaped a culture of bottom-up initiatives over the past seven years, where g0v.tw has demonstrated a way to combine online and offline activism. Following the model established by the Free Software community over the past two decades, they transformed social media into a platform for social production, with a fully open and decentralized cultural & technological framework.

In practice, g0v doesn't have a leader or spokesperson. Participants decide what to work on and are at the heart of the communal culture. Using Liquid Democracy techniques, the g0v community makes decisions on important issues and strategic direction. That's why it's sometimes hard to pin down individuals. As there have been many researchers wanting to study g0v by doing interviews or surveys, it depends on every g0ver's willingness to fill it out. One g0v Hackathon happens in Taiwan every two months, each time bringing together 80–130 people. They're running the 35th since December 2012. They manage to gather an impressive network of people: 139.000 followers on the g0v Facebook page, 12.985 members on the g0v Facebook group, and up to 5.000 members on the g0v slack workspace. Despite personal access to these platforms, it has been pretty hard to reach out to respondents to my survey. g0v practices decentralized management and decentralized communication.

Taiwanese Volunteers :

- *Profile:* Average age is 33 years old, middle-aged is 34, and most widespread age is 35—the unbalanced ratio between man (73%) and woman (20%).

- *City of residence:* 77% of respondents live in the Taipei area, which is a highly robust network, 13% from other cities of Taiwan, 6% from Japan, and 1 American (lives in Boston).

- *Volunteering:* Half of the respondents started to be involved in the g0v movement before 2015. The traction peak seems to be in 2013-2014, with another growth bounce in 2016. Since first participation, most of the g0vers (60%) had an interrupted relationship with the community they mainly used to engage for more than 1 hour a month (for 37% of them), more than 1 hour a week (33% of them) and more than 1 hour a day (13% of them).

- *Motivation:* There's a clear priority on self-fulfillment to explain Taiwanese volunteers' motivation: almost 3 in 4 g0vers join the movement "to feel good about what they do." Knowing that they contribute to the success of their organization is the second choice with 13%, and Advancement in career/ profession is the third choice with a small score of 7%. And while one on two respondents rates its motivation at two on a scale from 1-Incredibly motivated to 5-Not motivated at all, it's ultimately 97% of them feeling more motivated than non (from 1 to 3 on a five-point rating scale).

- *Influence of the community:* Whereas Taiwanese respondents stay moderated about the effect of "leaders or potential executives" on their motivation (20% says to be influenced by the leader), roughly one on 2 filled a rate of 2 on 5 points where one means "definitely influenced by leader" and five means "not at all." About co-volunteers motivation, 57% feel responsible for it, 30% are neutral, and 13% don't feel accountable for the others motivation. At the same time, 43% feel like being part of a community, and 20% recognize they could never achieve their actual goals without the other co-volunteers. Finally, 13% feel an individualistic free-ride and 23% enjoy working by a team on some plans.

- *Goals to achieve:* In this question about personal goals to achieve by participating in civic-hacking at g0v, it was possible to fill in as many answers as wanted. 60% of respondents said, "Advancing skills or knowledge as much as possible," roughly the same as "Networking with others in and outside of the organization" (57%). The third objective would be "to do the best job as I can" for 47% of them and "Taking on additional responsibilities" for 23%.

- *Reward system:* g0vers mainly says "not looking for monetary gain" or "having other income sources" (33% for each). The final third is shared between "being satisfied with non-cash fringe benefits perceived" (23%) and "Do not spend as much time volunteering" to need money from it (10%). Good to notice that these choices are confirmed consciously because no one answered "wishing to be, one day, rewarded for involvement." But finally, almost 1 in 2 said limiting participation because they need to get a "bread and butter job" elsewhere. So only one in 3 would participate more if possible to get some cryptocurrency as a reward. Except for the people who confirms that they are not participating as a volunteer in g0v movement for money and are OK with self-fulfillment only for this type of hobby-work, some others shared exciting thought about this choice like the crypto-currency would probably not generate enough to replace the "Bread and Butter job" and civic-engagement may be less stable too, so more risky to pay invoices and family live. It appears like the most interested in getting some "extra (crypto) money" are the junior workers and recently graduated software developers. The most enthusiastic suggests that it would be fun to gamify participation with points collection or badges. Finally, engagement time with reward compared to actual engagement is not increased: 3% could take this opportunity to work on g0v all working hours, but twice (7%) would engage less than 1 hour a year if so. It seems. However, global engagement time would go up from an actual middle value at 1-hour participation a month to a median value at 1-hour participation a week with a crypto-currency reward system.

3. Teplitsa

A public education project aimed to develop cooperation between the non-profit sector and IT specialists was founded in 2012 by Alexey Sidorenko. Teplitsa encompasses an information website, a series of educational events, and a software development team with associated products like Leyka, a free and open-source fundraising plugin that helped at least 35 organizations with approximately $1,292,000 US 2018. They are more invested mainly in ecological and social challenges of Russian society and, among other projects, assist in innovating civic engagement for Russian NGOs.

Through connections of civic activists, CSO workers, and socially aware IT, media, and creative businesses, Teplitsa strengthens civil society with technology's intelligent use. They have nearly 18.000 followers on their educational youtube channel, 20.000 followers on their Facebook page. They don't use slack, but their Telegram channel has 1.500 members.

Teplitsa is a middle-size non-profit organization whose management is centralized around its leader. They organize regional Hackathons with 40–70 participants every month to foster civic tech communities in the Russian regions and promote socially aware applications.

Russian Volunteers :

- *Profile:* The age average of respondents is 33 years old, and the median value is 32 years old (that means 50% are more than 32, 50% are less than 32). And despite a shorter sample of respondents, it covers from 17 to 55 years old. Gender division is 71% men and 29% women.

- *City of residence:* As you can see on the map below, the town of the home of my Russian respondents are not spread all over Russia, but relatively close to the southern border, with a few 18% concentration in the Moscow area.

- *Volunteering:* We can consider that it's a young sample of Civic-Hackers because 73% of them started participating in Teplitsa events after March 2017. Since then, only 29% had a continuous engagement, so it looks like participating in civic-hacking events in Russia is still an infrequent hobby. Indeed, more than one in two (53%) spent more than 1 hour a month participating, whereas 18% more than 1 hour a day, 18% more than 1 hour a week, and 10% more than 1 hour a year.

- *Motivation:* The most critical issue is "Self-fulfillment: feeling good about what I do," with 47% choices. Then 24% "Advancement in my career/profession/ company by volunteering" and 12% "Knowing that I'm contributing to the success of my organization." And the actual level of motivation is either neutral or relatively modest for Russian civic-hackers: 53% of them say to be in a middle position on the five-point scale but oriented towards the motivated side.

- *Influence of the community:* While only 35% of respondents feel responsible for their co-volunteers motivation, the majority, 41%, stays neutral, and 24% says not to handle it. But almost 1 in 2 respondents said leaders or potential executives influence their motivation: 47% of respondents filled the higher score on the five-point scale. Result roughly confirmed by team-working feeling as we get the majority 35% people answered "rather be in individualistic free-ride" ex-aequo with 35% who answered "enjoy working by a team on some goals achieving" against 17% "I feel part of a community" and 11% " I could never achieve my actual goals without the other co-volunteers."

- *Goals to achieve:* In this question about personal goals to achieve by participating, it was possible to fill in as many answers as wanted. 71% chose "Advancing my skills/knowledge to learn as much as I can" as a priority goal, 53% "Networking with others in and outside of the organization," and 35% "Strengthening my relationship with leaders and executives." While "Doing the best job I can" retain a small 18% interest.

- *Reward system:* Russian Civic-Hackers mainly say "having other income sources" (41%) and "not looking for monetary gain" (29%). The reason for "not spending as much time volunteering" is also persuasive for not gaining money in return for 18% of them. Only 6% "wish to be, one day, rewarded for engagement." Suppose 56% limits his participation because of the need for a "bread and butter job" elsewhere. In that case, 65% will participate more if possible to get some cryptocurrency as a reward. Ultimately, in the case of a deployed crypto-currency reward system, the average and middle time of engagement per person would move from 1 hour a month to 1 hour per day, which would also become the most spread value for engagement time in our sample.

Cross-cultural comparison of volunteer civic-hackers

The first common finding is about gender equity. This study can't exclude the usual geek stereotype. There are commonly more men than women in American, Russian, and Taiwanese civic-hackers(about 70%). Then, because civil practice's digital transformation is a recent trend, the most successful year in attracting new participants is commonly between 2016–2017–2018.

Most respondents commonly answered that their primary motivation is Self-fulfillment: to feel good about what I do, followed by Knowing that I'm contributing to the success of my organization and Advancement in my career/profession by volunteering.

They commonly feel more responsible for co-volunteer motivation than they don't. Americans, Taiwanese, and Russians said that leaders or potential executives influence their cause.

Also, 67% of Americans and 63% of Taiwanese feel part of a community or said they could never achieve their goals without the other co-volunteers.

Then, the first and second goals to achieve are the same for the three geographical origins: "Advancing my skills/knowledge to learn as much as I can" and "Networking with others in and outside of the organization." But if both Taiwanese and Americans filled up "Just doing the best job, I can" as the third priority. The Russians would prefer either to "Strengthen relationship with leaders and executives."

On another note, we also have quite the exact proportions of volunteers who are comfortable with spending time on some tasks that do not give them money as a reward. Indeed almost one on three "Is not looking for monetary gain" and another one on three "Have other income sources." Commonly 1 in 2 volunteers could not engage more because of the need for a "bread and butter job" elsewhere.

Taiwanese g0vers look to be very concentrated in Taipei Area, Taiwan's capital (77% of them), while CFA and Teplitsa participants are mainly spread all around the country.

While 62% of American volunteers say to have a continuous engagement from first participation, 40% Taiwanese and 30% Russians say the same.

The most spread value in time spent is 1 hour a week for Americans, balanced between 1 hour a week and 1 hour a month for Taiwanese, and 1 hour a month for Russians.

CFA network seems to feel much more responsible for other co-volunteers motivation 69%, than Russian 35% (while Taiwanese 57%). Result roughly confirmed by team-working feeling: we get 70% Russian answers in the couple "rather be in individualistic free-ride" or "enjoy working by a team on some goals achieving." In comparison, both 65% of Taiwanese and American chose the opposite couple answers "I feel part of a community" or " I could never achieve my actual goals without the other co-volunteers."

Reminding me what Teplitsa staff said about the Civic-Hackers participating in their events, who do not probably know Teplitsa's name, I could argue that it's a credible hypothesis to explain this lack of cohesion the participants and lack of long-term engagement. I could suggest to Russian Civic-Hackers to implement some team building to test if they can get more support from their participants in creating a community culture. It could, at the same time, help to balance the continuous/ interrupted engagement in the direction of an increased fidelity, set the unselfish "Knowing that I'm contributing to the success of my organization" at second choice, just like the two other communities g0v and CFA, and give a better satisfaction in "just doing the best job I can" as a unique priority, actually ranked at fourth goal by Russians (18%) against big third goal by Taiwanese (47%) and Americans (54%).

But it's a choice of management strategy because I can see another exciting result where Russian respondents distinguish themselves from the two others: the rate of leaders' influence on their motivation. Indeed, 47% of Russians put the higher score of 1 on 5 points, while 37% Americans and 20% Taiwanese did.

At the end of the survey, I'm moving forward with the hypothesis that crypto-currencies systems could be a future way to motivate citizenship. I've not planned yet to develop this kind of service (I would love to be part of a startup working on it, just to say), but I try with my studies to make the people think about the next steps and move ahead. Rewarding citizens for engagement is an old political idea, probably as senior as politics itself, that has perhaps always been practiced in some way. And from time to time, I can hear it in smart-city or civic startup brainstorming, when they look for a way to get more participation in their platform or tools for democracy. So, I was curious to sound out my samples of volunteers on this topic. It just happened that this is probably one of the most breaking comparisons of this study: twice more Russians (65%) than Taiwanese (27%) and Americans (34%)

could engage more if their organization was deploying a crypto-currency reward system.

And it could make Russian civic hackers jump a big gap forward in civil society transformation as they would gain a 40% workforce that could engage more than 1 hour a day in return for a crypto-currency reward (see Fig. 25). We can imagine that this disruptive result depends on historical background and cultural heritage for the relationship with monetary gain and citizenship in nowadays democracy..

How much time would you be disposed to spend, if rewarded with crypto money ?

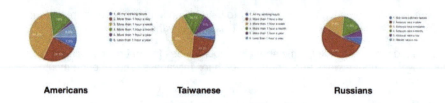

| Americans | Taiwanese | Russians |

Fig. 25 - Russian Civic-Hackers workforces would gain 40% more people engaged more than 1 hour a day if rewarded by crypto money.

In worldwide civic-hacking as in other selfless dedications, there seems to be some invariable human sensitivity like seeking self-fulfillment in life, meeting new people, and the motivation to advance personal skills continuously. But the way people take into living depends on cultural and political heritages as contemporary management choices from the leaders. Of course, the need for money is structured to do good and look for a positive impact on the people around us. Trust in the future and the new technologies can also influence our actual choices and have consequences in some decades, so we need to communicate sincerely with others to move ahead in a better world.

6. Presentation of case studies in Taiwan, Israel, and Estonia.

I was looking for comparable cases of digital transformation of cities with three different cultural backgrounds in Asia, the Middle East, and North-Eastern Europe. I was targeting advanced free-market economies, leaders in smart-city with citizen engagement features. I was also looking for startup-friendly ecosystems, with a particular interest in civic-hacking and open data, or any civil initiative on IT. The English-speaking level of the population would be a plus since I wanted to address my survey and interviews in English. Still, an open-web policy was indeed a priority to run my tools of research. The underlying topic of my research can be called e-Democracy, so I was inclined to visit the most advanced ones in the regions of the world I was interested in. By comparing different rankings such as Smart-Cities Index, Startup City Ranking, Democracy Index, Cities in Motion. All in one, I chose Taipei (Taiwan), Tel Aviv (Israel), and Tallinn (Estonia) as case studies. Digging into their respective history, I found many points in common, opportunities of their time which now makes sense to understand why those three appeared as the top choices for my research. Taiwan, Israel, and Estonia are commonly three small countries, recently independent. Their modern economy arose in the '90s after strategic choices of development in tech, science, and education, due to a lack of other natural resources than the human one to exploit autonomously. All three lately became independent after centuries (Millenium) of domination, feeling of existence by virtuous nationalism of the 19th, slowly building a nation in the 20th, achieved in the 21st by hyper-development of the economy from IT / internet. The fast transition to democracies sustained by free-market economies was urged by the necessity to support their existence as independent nations on the sidelines of robust authoritarian regimes at the border. Nowadays, two of them keep struggling to make themselves recognized by the international community. Taiwan built itself on an island in the Chinese Sea and is not recognized anymore as a nation (the United Nations General Assembly voted to expel Taiwan, Republic of China, in 1971 in favor of integration of Mainland China, People's Republic of China), Israel built itself on a piece of desert stuck in the middle of the Arab League (whom 15 of the 22 countries did not recognize its legitimate existence, and actively promote a boycott of trades with Israel). Estonia was freed from Russian powers at the fall of the Soviet Union. At the same time, nowadays, Russia keeps considering the Baltic states as an area "of privileged interest" and proposed recently to make them Russian protectorates. Those three democracies commonly face propagandist and nationalist attacks from hackers or diplomats of the neighboring country. All three got the military and financial support of the USA (and sometimes EU), which remains at the moment but moved recently in a re-organization of its international policy. Those three have already been investigated many times as individual cases, set in perspective with the geopolitical powers around them. Still, they have never been taken together in a comparative analysis. I will be looking for common strategic choices or opportunities that could lead me to a deeper understanding of the smart-city phenomena and the evolutions of democracy and citizenship. The steps of modern development must be understood as the product of complex systems based on new global cultural values expressed in evolving contexts of exclusive groups of people and societies. By living 3 to 4 months in each of my case studies, I joined events all along with my stay, in-person March 2020, then online, and contacted many people on the internet. I have collected contextual information about my case studies: actors, networks, places, and events. An extensive list of critical stakeholders identified has been cut from this version of the book. Still, it can be found on my online medium blog.

Three distinct cultural backgrounds

In the last three decades, Taiwan, Israel, and Estonia emerged as global hubs for Tech Innovation, with higher production than most older developed nations. How have these newborn states gone from besieged territories to highly advanced economies under democratic regimes? How can a global phenomenon such as the advent of Information Technologies, aiming to turn cities into smart cities and revive the apathetic democracies by empowering its citizens with digital tools, allows us to make relevant assumptions from these case studies globally?

While archaeology reveals prehistoric findings of various origins in Taiwan, Israel, and Estonia, attesting early human settlements and cross-roads of multiple ethnic migrations along time, while each of these territories commonly hosted the cradle of an indigenous people with typical cultural artifacts, it has lost its independence of will under the domination of the solid military powers of their neighbors of the time.

The Ancient Israelis had about 1000 years of an identified existence when they lost their political independence by the invasion of the Roman Republic in the Kingdom of Jerusalem in 70 BCE, forcing most Jewish people into exile.

The Estonians distinguished themselves from their proto-Finn origins about 900 BCE. They showed traces of a distinct tribal dialect and understanding of true identity. Their name is mentioned in Roman records of the 1st century and the Greek of the 2nd before their influence significantly weakened during the noisy European migration period of the 3rd to the 6th century.

The racial diversity of the Taiwanese and the 20 identified aborigine languages and ethnic groups on the island attest to a long-term integration of various migration waves from diverse Austronesian peoples for millennia. Never united in a single kingdom-like organization, they kept living in tribes until the first foreign occupation of the 17th century.

In the following centuries, Jerusalem has passed from one middle-eastern domination to another: the Roman Empire followed by the Byzantine one and the early Islamic conquest. Taken by the crusaders' army of the European Christians in 1099 CE, it went back to Muslim rule by the power of the first sultans of Egypt and Syria in 1187 CE. The Mamluk Sultanate left the Ottoman Empire from 1515 CE, which ran the city until its fall at the beginning of the 20th century.

From the 5th century, the slavicization of North-Western Russia affected the early middle age of Eastern Baltic Europe, at the same time with the Scandinavian Vikings from the north and the Germanic from the west. In 1208 the Livonian crusade resulted in creating the Danish Duchy of Estonia, which was sold to the Teutonic Order in 1346. The Livonian War (1558-1583) against the Tsardom of Russia marks the end of the crusaders' rule. It replaces Estonian domination by the Swedish Empire. In 1710, the Russian Empire took the Swedish Baltic provinces and ruled Estonia until the 20th century.

In the Far East, when the Dutch and the Spanish settlers took occupation of the island of Taiwan in 1624, it has already been used as a trading post by Chinese and Japanese merchants for quite a long time. When the Chinese Emperor pushed out the colonial administration in 1662, the Chinese dynasties ruled the island of Taiwan until Qing's defeat in 1895 at the First Sino-Japanese War. The Japanese rule in Taiwan will run until the Japanese surrender after the American bombing at the end of WW2. At the same time, the National Government of the Republic of China will lose Mainland China against the communist army in 1948 and exile in Taiwan. Willing to fight back the People's Republic of China, the nationalist regime dragged the Taiwanese people into martial law from 1949 to 1987.

Three different nationalist pathways

If the nationalist movements of the late 19th centuries in Central and Eastern Europe have commonly been a support to the liberation from foreign rulers in Estonia, a core inspiration for the zionists in the migration back of Jewish people to Israel, and the reason for Taiwan to serve as a back base to anti-communist China in post-WW2, it led those three into uncomfortable bordering states which keep struggling nowadays for their existence as a legitimate independent political entity.

After WW1 and the Russian Revolution of 1917, an Autonomous Governorate of Estonia was formed, whose Tallinn is the designated capital city. The declaration of Independence of the Republic of Estonia on 24 February 1918 was followed the next day by the Estonian War of Independence, which ended with recognizing the Estonian independence in 1920. Therefore Estonia leads a decade of public infrastructure and cultural institutions development before being hurt by the Great Depression of 1930 and establishing an anti-communist right-wing authoritarian regime in 1934. WW2 will result in the breakdown of Europe between West and East, Estonia falling under Soviet Regime occupation for almost fifty years. At the fall of the Soviet Union in 1991, Estonia recovered its independence, built a liberal democracy, and developed a highly advanced capitalist economy. However, the Russian government keeps exerting a repeated pressure on Estonia nowadays, calling it a "zone of privileged interest" in its foreign policies and political discourses, which receive varying support from the 40% of Russian-speaking Estonian citizens.

After 400 years of Ottoman rule in the Middle East, the British Empire won the Battle of Jerusalem in 1917. It began thirty years of Mandate for Palestine. At the end of WW2, in reaction to decolonization movements and the immigration waves of Jews fleeing worldwide pogroms, the United Nations General Assembly approved a plan to partition Palestine into two states: one Jewish and one Arabic. The state of Israel was established in 1948. Still, the fight for Jerusalem escalated and continued into the first Arab-Israeli War for nineteen years, leading to massive displacement of Arab and Jewish populations and the division between Jordan and Israel. After the Six-Day War won by Israel Defense Forces, the reunited status of Jerusalem remains a highly controversial issue. Suppose Israel achieved an exemplary inclusion of migrations from the four corners of the globe and raised among the world's most advanced scientific and technological hubs. In that case, it keeps struggling with regular military attacks and a boycott in trade from its neighboring countries, in solidarity with the Arabic League countries to the Palestinian populations which lost their lands in the win of the State of Israel.

In Far East Asia, the Republic of China was sovereign from 1912 to 1949. At the end of WW2, the communist took power in Mainland China, and the anti-communist army occupied Taiwan to prepare a reconquest of the power. While the exiled government continued to represent China on the international scene during the Cold War (1947-1991) with the support of the USA, it has progressively been de-recognized from 1971 by the United Nations needing to build relationships with actual China. From 1987, Taiwan engaged in a peaceful transition to democracy and a thriving free-market economy. Suppose the island is independent de facto, monitoring its frontiers, having its proper defense forces, pressing its currency, and fully integrated with international trade. In that case, the Chinese Communist Party ruling the government of the People's Republic of China keeps increasing its pressures on the international scene to recall its partners that the island of Taiwan is Chinese territory. The recent escalation of tensions in the China-US relations intensifies the trade war between these two challenging superpowers, hurts the Taiwanese economy, and raises uncertainty on the status of Taiwan.

Three geopolitical context

Recognizing the power of Washington and Beijing in determining Taiwan's future is essential to understand the geopolitical reality behind the Taiwanese model of democracy. What happened in Hong Kong in 2020 increased the Taiwanese concern about the assumed expansion of China in the area. The normalization of the political project of Israel is highly dependent on the slowly evolving relationships with the Arabic world. If Saudi Arabia delivered repeated pro-Israel messages in April 2020 over two popular series during Ramadan, followed by the end of the boycott of Israel the same year in Bahrain, UAE, Soudan, and Morocco, four countries of the Arab League, Palestinian support movements in May 2021 have weakened the legitimacy of Israel globally, even in the USA. In Estonia, after the series of hackers' attacks of 2007 as a Russian nationalist retaliatory to the displacement of a statue of a Soviet soldier, NATO established its cyber defense center in Tallinn. But the US military forces in the Baltic sea have also been moved recently, allowing Latvian leaders the opportunity to express their concern about Russian ambitions in the area and recall the importance of USA defense on their side, when Vladimir Poutine was paving the way to extend its eligibility until 2036. The USA commonly played a significant role in Taiwan, Israel, and Estonia, making them dependent on both American markets and US military forces. Being number one means having as many challengers as ambitious game players. None of China, Russia, and the Islamic states cover its hostility against the American hegemony and the will to take back power in its area.

All three states express concerns about the expansionist ambitions of nationalist authoritarian neighbors. Cyber-attacks, propaganda, and fake news on social networks are as many attempts to intimidate the governments and influence the peoples during elections or daily topical discussions. While Taiwanese youth face regular intrusion of Chinese nationalists on web forums and social networks, telling them they are a declining society in a dead-end, Chinese propagandists approach the older people in the traditional places of worship in Taiwan. The Israeli TV news channels broadcast warnings from the state to young soldiers and the audience to be careful with online messaging, reminding them Israeli enemies collect open-source intelligence through fake profiles on social networks. In Estonia, Russian TV channels and web media influence 40% of the population born Russian-speaking is a severe concern. Estonia considers banning the Russian state-controlled international television network RT (Russia Today). It has already launched its own Russian-speaking TV channel ETV+ to deliver a European democratic point of view on the actuality.

The enemies of democracy use similar strategies to undermine free economies: blocking the country's partners, organizing a boycott of trade, and negotiating with its partners not to trade with the other. Strengthening a communication of the historic ruling of the area and asserting it will take it back. European countries and the USA receive threats from China when they trade with Taiwan—supporting Israel wherever in the world awakes a worrying criticism worldwide, making it challenging to distinguish anti-zionism from antisemitism. The Russian energy and freight transport companies can be aggressively dominant in their competition over the Eastern Baltic Sea. The politically fragmented, economically open, and ethnically mixed domestic political environment creates several opportunities for enormous power constraints among small democracies. When business is the main challenge, the democracies are highly conditioned to their capacity to make money to maintain the level of satisfaction of their population high and sustain the willingness of the people to trust in the consensus rule. While the emerging economies are more and more tempted to boost their economic growth by using authoritarian politics, the USA started to get more concerned about its internal economy than its foreign partners. And they progressively collect their military forces back, allowing their enemies to bet on the decline of the Western culture.

Three economic miracles

The informal economic term to qualify the unexpected fast-speed economic growth has been applied commonly to Taiwan, Israel, and Estonia. Also called one of the four Asian Tigers, Taiwan's economy is ranked as the 7th largest in Asia and 22nd most prominent globally, also the largest economy outside the United Nations. With a GDP per capita of more than 30.000 USD, Taiwan is the most technologically advanced computer microchip maker globally, making its high-tech industry vital in the global economy. Since the '90s, Taiwan has been a hub for hardware development and manufacturing. The Taiwanese ecosystem can now bet on the rising economies of the fastest growing neighborhood of the planet: the South-Eastern Asian countries to keep its industry going. As of 2018, telecommunication, financial services, and utility services are the three highest individuals paid sectors in Taiwan. The whole service sector makes up 73% of the economy. In the lack of natural resources, Taiwan followed the Japanese model of development. It invested a lot into education and health, the key to a robust human resource economy. It does not create as many startups as in Singapore, Hong Kong, or Seoul. Still, Taiwan hosts many startup services and incubators and Taipei Angels and Taiwan Venture Capital Association investors.

The economy of Israel is a highly developed free-market economy, primarily knowledge-based. Major economic sectors are high-tech and industrial manufacturing and a GDP per Capita of about 40.000 USD. With an impressive track record for creating profit-driven technologies, Israel has the second-largest number of startups globally after the USA and the third-largest number of companies in the Nasdaq. Despite geopolitical tensions and regular armed conflict, Israel has become the first choice for many of the world's leading entrepreneurs, investors, and industry giants. In 1991 the government opportunely created 24 technological incubators to use the high skills in science and technology of the migration wave from ex-soviet Union countries. The global technological acceleration of the '90s has benefited Israel who became a center for global innovation. Israel fulfills a lack of natural resources by human resources. It leads to much technological innovation, medical and pharmaceutics, food and agriculture technology, security, and support services. Venture capital in Israel benefited from the financial reform of 2005 to become a significant industry for the economy of innovation, participating in the Israeli reputation of Silicon Wadi (wordplay with Silicon Valley).

Known as a highly liberal economy, Estonia was ranked 12th of 162 in Economic Freedom 2008. In 2011, Estonia became the first ex-Soviet republic to join the Eurozone and one of the fastest-growing economies in the EU. Since its second independence, the country has rapidly developed its IT sector, becoming one of the world's most digitally advanced societies, having 15 companies listed on the main list of Nasdaq Tallinn. A very competitive flat tax system and active attractiveness from the state to simplify foreign talent acquisition have made Estonia a home for tech startups. Its first unicorn Skype contributed to developing the local technical skills and created a very dense community of investors willing to grow more local success.

Very important to the economy. The startup community is being actively heard by the government, which does its best to satisfy the needs of entrepreneurs. The primary industries of the Estonian economy are engineering, electronics, wood and wood products, textiles, information technology, and telecommunications. Banking in Estonia enacted effective bankruptcy legislation, and so privately owned banks emerged as well-managed market leaders.

The Estonian government has been at the forefront of supporting the ecosystem, both on the investment side and through agile governance, which makes it operate much like a startup, experimenting with legislation to see what works and what does not. Compared to other major tech hubs in Europe, such as London, Tallinn maintains a much lower cost of living, allowing startups to pay their employees competitively.

Three demanding states supporting entrepreneurs' offer

In the three cases, the first customer, in crucial need of innovation, was the state: the public sector ordered a deep refurbishment or reconstruction of main infrastructures and public services. This state transformation created many opportunities for local entrepreneurs to develop companies dedicated to filling the demand in innovation, new technology, scientific research, and education. This dynamic has set the basis of a service economy with the best technicality levels and financial support to innovation. Secondly, the government helps companies reach global markets since they tend to communicate together on their achievement. It helps them access public facilities, find their product/market fit and share meeting opportunities. Estonia, Israel, and Taiwan markets are too small to be self-sufficient. If their enterprises want to grow up to crucial stability scales, they need to look for customers abroad. This element forces them to shape their business in the fashion of a global market from the beginning. In the academics of Israel, most professors are experienced entrepreneurs. Usually, they have a double degree in their primary discipline and business administration. They pass on their practical experience directly to the students. They are considered primarily responsible for spurring the country's high tech boom and rapid economic development of Israel.

Multinational companies enter the national market through R & D labs. They do not relocate companies; they host startups to get them right on their products and skills. As a consequence, there are over 250 R&D centers in Israel owned by multinational companies. Similarly, people with political knowledge will look for an executive role in a company or create a startup. The government and the municipality are involved and support all significant initiatives to ease the potential growth by creating a link between entrepreneurs and the population and by driving and coordinating companies in the concern to centralize governance and ensure the security of the territory.

Those three countries also use national branding as soft power to attract more foreigners to live and work there. A strategy is necessary for survival since the limited resources are seen as a crucial aspect affecting their independence. Small nations are less resistant to external pressure and more sensitive to the external economic environment because foreign trade plays a significant role in their economies. Thus they need to focus on the niche aspects of their expertise to make a difference and stand out from other countries. Estonia focuses on promoting and exporting its e-State solutions and attractiveness for entrepreneurs. Taiwan makes itself famous by being a forerunner in Asia on human rights, resisting Chinese influence over the region. Suppose Taiwan regularly speaks about changing its name Republic of China, by the Republic of Taiwan. In that case, this is depending on them and the international community to accept this change in the context of Chinese pressures.

However, China Airlines is the state-owned flight company of Taiwan. It should change its name for Taiwan Airlines much more quickly. Israel has made itself popular as a startup nation, now attracting worldwide entrepreneurs to push its state forward in the definition of a post-zionist era.

Effective nation branding helps to increase awareness of a small country and increase its prestige. Image and reputation are thus becoming strategic values in the state's foreign policy. Economic success supported by entrepreneurs' hubs is a solid value in diplomacy when politicians have to negotiate their commitment with other nation-states at the global level. We had the recent example in the international run for the covid-19 vaccine. With its dense network of science and technology labs, Israel has been the first to vaccinate its population and then had a significant surplus of vaccines. The state of Israel used the excess vaccine for diplomacy: it notably negotiated with Czech Republic, Honduras, and Guatemala, all of them agreed to strengthen their diplomatic presence in Jerusalem, the internationally contested city of Israel.

Three definitions of citizen engagement

Taiwanese people, like most Asians, do not often engage in political counter-forces. They vote for the professional politician with the best project for the country but, more importantly, with the most chance to achieve it. They keep it practical: diplomas, references, and confirmed skills to manage their city or country, and they make a statement at the end of the term. Most people consider it not their job or have more important things to do than engage in activist movements daily to influence the political agenda. They appreciate the government as much as it increases the economy and helps them make money. In Taiwan, this reality is shaded by the strategy to become an Asian leader in human rights and social issues. So the voters of the progressive party balance their government's valuation to look for progress on social policies. However, in terms of civic engagement, even if Taipei is the home of the famous g0v civic-hackers community, the city office Smart-Taipei had no more success when it tried to launch its mission by using a platform for citizen engagement. It did not work at all. They finally changed their strategy to contact the people by organizing events in the public space.

In Israel, and also in the whole Middle-East but for other reasons, the civil society is not very engaged in government actions either. Even if the television population does not lack words to criticize the government and the religion, self-organization with peers is sufficient to satisfy social needs in everyday life, which do not call for the need to establish official civil movements. Furthermore, they all served in the army or volunteering jobs after high school. They know that the political situation is complex and conscious about surrounding enemies. The liberalization of the economy goes with inflation, so everyone is trying to make money out of their skills and network. In a sense, social causes are of national interest and need to find their business model like any other business. Social issues in Israel are, for a majority, related to the security breach from the Israeli-Palestinian conflict and the poverty of the population in some urban areas and countryside villages. Aside from the prosperous liberal economy of finance and tech, a part of the population is kept away from the high standard of living. Third sector activities are more concerned about promoting peace, justice, and political neutrality, assisting poverty and migration, defending civil rights such as work visas, and a right to citizenship for the children born in Israel from non-Jewish migrant workers.

In Estonia, the job market and economic growth offer attractive opportunities for young people to know what to do with their brains and hands. Once graduates, the youth often starts a career soon. Even those with the most radical temptation to change society know they will have a better impact inside a successful startup or a hierarchical position in some well-paid job. In Estonia, like in all the Nordic countries, the trust in government is very high. Most electives usually respect full transparency and have no corruption nor suspected fraud. They are often recognized as full members of society, with reasonable salaries and a regularly renewed political class. The low hierarchy by design tends to limit the need for intermediary bodies between two stakeholders. It is pretty easy for all entrepreneurs or social workers to directly reach the upper decision-makers searching for the best solution to common issues. In that context, an online platform for civic engagement thought as a counter-power to the government would not make any sense. Non-profits are instead composed of networks of experts who want to contribute back to society. It is pretty hard to reach them in the long term because they are already busy. Still, they also have very qualified skills in their topic of reference, making their organization more trustable from a public sector perspective. In Estonia, the perspective "civil society VS public sector" does not make sense since their government is the best defender of citizens' rights. They look neither for decentralized governance because they already are.

Three versions of smart-city models

Taiwan has emerged as a multi-cultural society exemplary in the human rights and corruption issues, unemployment rate, and openness mindset. They managed to strengthen traditional Chinese and aboriginal cultures to become advanced high-tech industries, making Taiwan a model for Asian democracies. Taipei City is often considered one of the most advanced smart cities in the Asia Pacific. It is granted for its integrated transportation system and technology manufacturing. Their city-as-a-platform model allows urban innovation in a real urban context and actively modernizes the democratic regime with wide open-data portals. Aside from the high real estate price, the quality of life is pleasant for middle-class revenues: restaurants and leisure are very affordable, and the public health system. Public Libraries are open on an extensive time range, accessible to anyone for free, and offer international books and magazines on all topics. You can have access to all kinds of cultural offers and meet expatriates from all parts of the world and Taiwanese people quickly. All types of shopping options, restaurants, business networks, meetups, and parties are available. After the abolishment of martial law, civil initiatives and community groups rapidly emerged. Citizens wanted to participate in urban planning instead of accepting directives from the top. But the economic stagnation of Taiwan in the late 1990s contributed to a neoliberal twist, in which this belief of "People owning the city" is looking for a second breath.

In Tel Aviv, the organic metaphor often explains the Smart-City Model: a human body without a heart or a brain could not work. Applied to urban governance, it justifies centralized data-driven decision-making. But the Tel Aviv model is both committed to central management and very agile. All public servants benefit from much autonomy at all levels of their shared mission. The Mediterranean Jewish culture encourages disintermediation rather than a formal hierarchy, resulting in an ongoing dialogue between everyone in the look for the success of the innovative ecosystem. Israeli mindset is to improvise things without asking permission. "In Israel, a long-term plan is a plan for the end of the week." The urban planning of Tel Aviv can look like a patchwork: the city just achieved 100 years old and already hosted about 1 M inhabitants. The bikeways lack continuity, and public transportation is awful: buses do not have a dedicated line, and the unexpected attractiveness of the city makes its streets unadapted to such traffic jams. Half of the startups hosted by the municipality are working on solving this issue, and tramway lines are under construction. Life is not cheap, especially when you don't speak Hebrew and fall in the tourist offer or the one for high-revenue expatriates of the tech society. The resident card or an Aliyah is a need to access public services and facilities. Life can be challenging for the locals too, but the gap between the international wealthiness flowing and small local revenues are redistributed at the condition to embrace a long-term settling plan in Israel. A city in transition, though, which tackles the hardness of life with a chilly lifestyle.

At the fall of the Soviet Union in Estonia, the lack of financial resources to build public institutions and the good scientist and IT level in the population resulted in a very liberal economy with entrepreneurs-friendly tax and law regulations. It also resulted in blind confidence in the government that citizens agreed from the beginning to share all their private data to improve public services. An economy supported by IT innovation and state services improved by data are the two big goals of democracies nowadays. Estonia is already 10 or 20 years ahead of many nation-states worldwide. They use this opportunity to develop consultancy services abroad and share their experience in the state's digital transformation through many European Union working groups. Two main lessons emerged from the Estonian model: take care of politics first and then proceed with economic reform. It is essential to follow the reformist agenda despite the short-term pain it can cause.

Three smart-devices for e-Citizenship

Smart-devices for e-Citizenship usually result from a mix of gov-tech and civic-tech, reflecting both the government strategy to smart-city and the willingness of the inhabitants to use it.

In Taipei, the EasyCard was first developed to give the citizens integrated access to all transportation systems of the island: metro, bus, train. It later extended to no-ticket car parking and taxi services, a shared bike float and electric scooters across the city, and other public facilities such as a public library, public hot springs. It finally can be used as a debit card in the network of 24/7 small supermarkets covering last-minute necessities all over the country. The EasyCard device has been the cornerstone of integrating the public transportation service in a strategy for environmental protection and modernization of public spaces to allow more pedestrian areas. The willingness of Taipei inhabitants to transition to a more sustainable way of moving across the city has been supported by a range of measures that have been implemented: e-Car charging stations have been deployed, as well as a network of shared plug-and-play batteries for electric scooters. A massive bike2work campaign offered free coffee and snacks to bike users on designated road sections each Friday. It was serving about 540 coffees a week and up to 3265 a month. Moving from one point of the city to another the most efficiently as possible is at the core of the Taipei model of Smart-City, which received an award at the 2017 Intelligent Transport System World Congress as the most advanced Smart-City in the Asia Pacific.

In Tel Aviv, the smart-city strategy is different. The tourism industry and the attractiveness of high-profiled bankers, tech developers, and entrepreneurs call for various cultural services and leisure activities that a large part of the population can't afford easily. Tel Aviv municipality developed its DigiTel resident card to share access to the best Tel-Avian benefits with all its residents. By collecting data on each resident, the city of Tel Aviv closely follows the needs of its population by neighborhood, range of age, lifestyle, or socio-professional category. It offers them tailored services to make their life more enjoyable, from alerting residents to working sites in their neighborhood to sending reminders for school registration and other location-specific services to young parents, dog owners, new neighbors, retired people. Tel Aviv municipality uses the DigiTel platform to send direct invitations to yoga classes on the rooftop of the city hall or a tournament of beach tennis. It organizes birthday-like parties for newly arrived children. It sends you a refund for a sunbed on the beach or a famous Opera piece. Owning a dog is such a popular thing for TelAvivians that the DigiTel resident card has its declination for dogs so that the municipality can invite dog owners to dedicated events in parks and dog playgrounds. The digital infrastructure worth Tel Aviv price of the Best Smart-City 2014 in the Smart-City World Congress of Barcelona.

In Tallinn, with the first large-scale governmental deployment of a blockchain-like infrastructure, all digital services which can be imagined are accessible to each Estonian citizen with an e-ID card. And the state is very arranging in sharing access to foreigners through diverse dispositions such as e-Resident card, digital nomad visa, or resident card. Publishing the balance sheet of your company, paying taxes, sending a bank transfer, 815 e-services representing 99,5 % of all public services can be done remotely. In the context of a growing concern with private data leak and the loss of state sovereignty in favor of the GAFAM, the Estonian model of e-Government is one of the first at our disposal, which proves its efficiency and is already implemented to secure all citizens personal data while sharing it transparently between public institutions and facilities. Public transportation in Tallinn has become accessible for most inhabitants since 2013. The next step is now a cross-border e-Ticketing service between Estonia and Finland. More and more people travel between the two capitals using public transport. Tallinn has been awarded many times in the digital innovation field and received a Smart-City award from UNESCO in 2019.

Comparative Survey Study

I collected 122 answers in each case study. In Taipei, I had 42 in Chinese and 80 in English, In Tel Aviv, 78 in Hebrew and 44 in English, Tallinn, 31 in Estonian, and 91 in English. I proposed that respondents share their emails to be updated on the next steps of my research. 66 of 122 shared it in Taipei, 33 in Tel Aviv, and 71 in Tallinn.

- Gender representation: I have a majority of women respondents (57%) in Taipei, but men are the most numerous in Tel Aviv (65%) and in Tallinn (59%).
- Age: I collected a wide range of birthdates for each city, from 1952 to 1999 in Taipei, making my respondents 68 to 21 years old. In Tel Aviv, it goes from 1936 to 1999, so the oldest participant of my samples is Tel Avivian, and he is 83 years old. The youngest respondent of Tel Aviv is 21, but the youngest of my samples is from Tallinn, and he is 18 since the birthdates collected there are between 1954 and 2002. The oldest respondent from Tallinn is 66 years old.
- Arrival date in the city: The migration policy of Tel Aviv is somewhat visible here since 78% of my panel of respondents arrived in the town less than ten years ago, against 40% in Taipei and 55% in Tallinn. But the attractiveness of Tel Aviv is not new either, and the oldest arrival of my three samples is in Tel Aviv in the late '50s. Taipei has attracted more respondents in the '80s and the '90s but less in 2000. Differently, Tallinn has been more attractive from the '90s and 2000s than in the '80s. Tel Aviv follows a stable growth in attractiveness over the decades.
- The Engagement feeling: The most common answer to engagement feeling is "Not engaged at all" in the three cities. 16,7% of respondents in Taipei, 30% in Tel Aviv, and 34% in Tallinn. And commonly, the not engaged side of the panel is dominant, with 65,3% in Taipei, 83% in Tel Aviv, and 84% in Tallinn.
- Source of information: Social media is the most selected source to provide information to make any opinion in the three cities, but word-to-mouth takes second

place in Tel Aviv while third in Taipei and Tallinn after informational websites.
- Influencer: The National Government is the first influencer in decision-making in Taipei and Tallinn, but it is second in Tel Aviv behind Individual Citizens. Citizens are 2nd influencer in Taipei but the only 8th influencer in Tallinn after the academics and businesses.
- Relationship with stakeholder categories: The respondents commonly express neutral relationships with all categories: public sector, private sector, academic research, and civil society. However, Tel Avivians says the highest lousy relationship with the government (22%) and the highest positive ones toward the other categories. In Tallinn, the relationship with civil society remains neutral. Still, in Taipei, it is the category with the highest positive feedback.
- Meeting places: Meeting people online is commonly the first place to share an opinion. Business clusters and innovation hubs come second. Tel Aviv meeting people in the neighborhood arrive 3rd while 4th in Tallinn and 5th in Taipei.
- Opinion sharing in public: is commonly neutral, oriented on the side to a capacity to express it.
- Opinion change in contact with others: is commonly neutral. Still, Taipei is the only one skewed to the direction of a capacity to change it. At the same time, Tel Aviv and Tallinn follow a normal distribution.
- Engagement wish: Taipei gets the highest score to engage more in decision-making for the city, with 85% of people answering YES. Tel Aviv receives 78%, with a gap between Hebrew speakers and English ones willing to engage, while Tallinn gets 72%.
- Engagement channel: Online survey studies and mobile voting apps are commonly the two first channels selected to engage more often in Taipei, Tel Aviv, and Tallinn. Community projects or participative workshops arrives typically in the 3rd position.
- Time to spend: In terms of availability to citizen engagement, 1 hour a week is commonly the most selected answer, with 46% of respondents in Taipei, 36% in Tel Aviv, and 49% in Tallinn. As a second position, 1 hour a month is a standard answer to the three case studies. Both solutions accumulated collect more than 60% of each sample.

Twitter datasets

#Taipei: I collected the last 17,341 tweets mentioning #Taipei, riding up to 16 November 2013. #TelAviv: I collected 17,628 tweets mentioning #Telaviv, riding up to 30 September 2012. #Tallinn: I collected 6,299 tweets mentioning #Tallinn, riding up to 13 March 2008.
The imbalance in the datasets reflects the global popularity of the city on the social platform. Tallinn is a smaller and less populated city which attracts less tourism.

Public Sector representatives:

- **Ko Wen-Je** has been the mayor of Taipei since 2014, former doctor at the National Hospital.
- **Ron Huldai** has been mayor of Tel Aviv since 1998, former military with a career in business.
- **Startup Estonia** is the main public Estonian brand communicating on Twitter.
Mihhail Kõlvart the recently elected Mayor of Tallinn does not use twitter.

Corporate company representatives:

- **AsusTeK Computer** is Taipei-based multinational computer and phone hardware and electronics company, world's 5th-largest PC vendor by 2017 unit sales.
- **Check Point Software** is a multinational provider of hardware and software for IT security based in Tel Aviv with 70 offices worldwide.
- **Bolt** is the latest Estonian unicorn, valued at 1 billion USD.

Startup business representatives:

- **Gogoro Scooter** is a Taiwanese startup of electric scooters and battery infrastructure.
- **Moovit** is an Tel Aviv-based mobility as a service provider and journey planner app.
- **AdCash** is one of the many promising startups in Tallinn.

Academic research representatives:

- **Academia Sinica** is the national academy of Taiwan which supports research activities in a wide variety of disciplines.
- **Tel Aviv University** is the most famous university in Tel Aviv.
- **Tallinn University of Technology** is the most famous education institution in Estonia.

Civil Society representatives:

- **g0v.tw** is the civic-hackers movement in Taiwan which develops open data and open-source software repositories for citizen engagement.
- **Hasadna** is a non-profit opening data repositories to Israeli and Jewish worldwide.
- **CleanTech forEst** is one of the few non-profit NGO, dedicated to protecting the Estonian forest.

Media Industry representatives:

- **Taiwan News** was the first English-speaking daily newspaper in Taiwan, now both paper and digital, it is published in Chinese and in English.
- **Israel Hayom** is a national daily newspaper headquartered in Tel Aviv.
- **Postimees** is the first Estonian daily newspaper with a digital media platform.

PART 2: Data Analysis and Computational Models

I have been tempted to implement some artificial intelligence algorithms to get the most out of my datasets. Not only helping in terms of data analysis and in building inferences outside of my actual datasets, these computational models, once trained on my case studies, would be ready to run on other ones, making them prototypes for a data app on citizen engagement in smart-city.

I built five artificial intelligence models presented below: three machine learning algorithms and two agent-based models. The first one is a ranking model for cities based on their civic engagement. It detects highly engaged citizens from the survey data with an accuracy of more than 95%. The second one is a predictive model for public opinion based on Twitter content. It can detect a sentiment attached to any message published on the platform. The third one is also based on Twitter but focuses on the shape of the network: who is connected with who and to which probability new connections form. It predicts the most influential users of a city's network from graph-based machine learning. The fourth and the fifth ones are an agent-based model, a distributed artificial intelligence to simulate complex systems of interactive agents. My first agent-based model is a computer simulation of the formation of public opinion based on citizen engagement attributes extracted from the survey study and its data analysis through the machine learning model. It allows us to observe and collect more data about forming the opinion of neutral citizens under the influence of highly engaged ones. The final model is the most integrated. It uses information from the datasets and the machine learning models of the survey study, the lexical and the topological analysis of Twitter, to simulate how opinions spread across a social network. I did these two simulations to compare inferences on a population representing each of my case study cities and any random one.

7. A Ranking Model for Citizen Engagement in Smart-City.

I collected 366 answers (122 respondents each in Taipei, Tel Aviv, Tallinn), making contact with inhabitants online (Facebook, Linked In, and messaging apps) and in-person in events related to my field of interest (urban innovation and startups).

In this chapter, I am first conducting a complete data analysis on my survey study, using Python programming language, to get an in-depth look at the features and insights that can be extracted. Then, I create a profile of highly engaged citizens and train different machine learning algorithms to detect them in the datasets. Finally, once the algorithms are prepared, I can test their performance to see highly engaged citizens in records they haven't previously been confronted with. The prediction from the machine is compared to the actual dataset, so a level of accuracy is calculated to retain the algorithm with the best performance. This allows me to rank cities on their citizen engagement dynamic and potentially explain why one or the other has more or less highly engaged citizens by recalling some of the cultural specificities observed in the individual monograph.

This data analysis goes with its problem, very close to the whole thesis and hypothesis to test. It is conducted in Python tools, whose outline is represented in the infographic below (see Fig. 26)

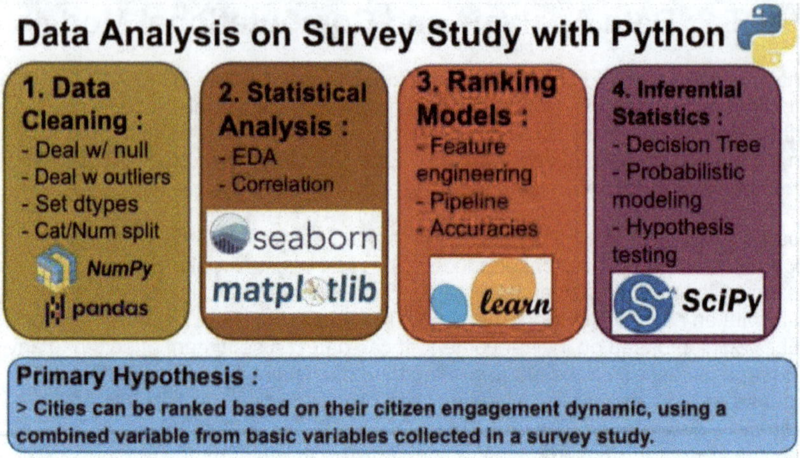

Data Analysis on Survey Study with Python

1. Data Cleaning :
- Deal w/ null
- Deal w outliers
- Set dtypes
- Cat/Num split

NumPy
pandas

2. Statistical Analysis :
- EDA
- Correlation

seaborn
matpl tlib

3. Ranking Models :
- Feature engineering
- Pipeline
- Accuracies

learn

4. Inferential Statistics :
- Decision Tree
- Probabilistic modeling
- Hypothesis testing

SciPy

Primary Hypothesis :
> Cities can be ranked based on their citizen engagement dynamic, using a combined variable from basic variables collected in a survey study.

Fig. 26 - Overview of the technical tools used for this study.

Problematic:

In contemporary democratic regimes, citizen engagement is widely considered by city professionals, from both public and private sectors, as a key to successful urban transformations. Accordingly, Smart-City promoters tend to emphasize their citizen-centric models worldwide. But we lack methods and insights about how to engage inhabitants in decision-making for the future of their cities. The widely used management models are highly determined by a design-thinking way which we are not sure about the influence on society at scale. In practice, we can even say that most digital engagement of citizens is mainly a communication campaign that fails to produce any satisfying result. However, we are experiencing a pessimistic citizen crisis in most modern democracies of the World, with a loss of trust in public agents and media, political apathy, and disinterest for elections by a majority of the voters. In this context, there is a crucial need to revive the citizens' feeling that their opinion is taken into consideration when building the future of their cities. I assume that highly engaged citizens are identifiable from random samples of a population, presenting specific behaviors.

In this study, I am answering the following questions: Which typical attributes differentiate highly engaged citizens from others? Is it possible to use these profiling features to rank cities on their citizen engagement dynamic?

Hypothesis:

- ○ Civic engagement is a mindset, and the engaged citizens wish to engage more.
- ○ The citizens feeling the most engaged, share their opinion in public more easily.
- ○ The citizens feeling the most engaged, change their opinion in contact with others.
- ○ Gender and age do not correlate with the engagement feeling.

Methodology:

Since my research methodology consists of cross-cultural comparisons, I will use the

results of my machine learning to rank models to classify from the least to the most dynamic city and look for attributes in detail that could help me strengthen local specificities observed by bare eyes. I am defining a highly engaged citizen as someone who:
- has an engagement feeling of 5/10 at least
- uses social media and the internet as a source of information to make their opinion
- uses at least two social media
- uses at least two messaging app
- meets other citizens online
- rather share its opinion in public (at least 3/5)
- rather change its opinion in contact to others (at least 3/5)
- wish to engage more
- through multiple engagement channels (at least 2/5)
- at a moderate to a high frequency (at least 1h a month).

This combination of variables allows me to create a new boolean variable to classify highly engaged citizens out of my general population. I will use this newly created variable as the target (independent variable) in my machine learning algorithms. So I'll ask my model to predict if this or that citizen can be considered highly engaged depending on their answers to the survey. This method also allows me to create an engagement score to rank citizens from the lowest to the highest engagement level. To do so, each of the conditions above will deliver 1 point to the citizen. In the end, highly engaged citizens will have a score of 10 on 10.

After having validated the accuracy of using a combined variable to classify highly engaged citizens out of a survey study on random inhabitants, I will use inferential statistics to proof test my last hypothesis "I can use my definition of a highly engaged citizen to detect citizen engagement in Smart-City from a random population of inhabitants."

This last step of my study will consist of generalizing my results by using statistical inferences. Building inferences on a general population from a sample usually consists of testing hypotheses using probabilistic techniques. However, hypothesis testing can be a tricky exercise since the method consists of writing a Null Hypothesis and its symmetrical contrary to the Alternative Hypothesis to evaluate the level of certainty for one or the other hypothesis to happen. In my case, the inference to test would be:

1. NULL HYPOTHESIS: We can't use the combined variable highly engaged citizens to identify this class of citizens inside a random population of inhabitants.
2. ALTERNATIVE HYPOTHESIS: We can use the combined variable of highly engaged citizens to identify this class of citizens inside a random population of inhabitants.

Setting up a statistical test includes several subjective choices, and their results are easy to misinterpret. A more informative and practical approach for comparing groups is one based on estimation rather than testing. It is driven by Bayesian probability rather than frequentism. Rather than testing whether two groups are different, we instead pursue an estimate of how different they are.

a. Descriptive Statistics—Distributions and relationships

Data cleaning and data transformation

Some cleaning and transformation will need to be done to make further analysis on raw data:

- **There are a few nulls** (4) in the variable engagement_wish. I will replace it with 1 which means "No" to the question "Do you wish to engage more ?"

- **There are a few outliers** in the date of birth (3) and arrival date (3) in the city of reference. That was predictable since some people want to keep it private. Others have had some difficulty in the mobile version of Google Forms to choose a specific year on the calendar. I will only keep the birth dates which makes my respondents being between 18 and 90 years old.

- **All my dataset is composed of categorical variables,** recorded as ordinal integers. Most ML models and algorithms work on numerical variables, so to proceed with the most calculation, I will store each variable in its numerical and categorical versions.

- **Split categorical and numerical in different sub-sets** to ease its manipulation (see Fig. 27).

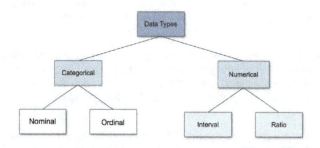

Fig. 27 - Data types are usually distinguished between categorical and numerical.

Exploratory Data Analysis

- *Engagement feeling:* from 1- not engaged at all to 10- very engaged, my sample globally expresses a somewhat not engaged feeling with a mean of 3.61 and a standard deviation of 2.43 (see Fig. 28). The Taipei sample expresses a more neutral engagement feeling than Tallinn and Tel Aviv. Tallinn is the one with fewer citizens feeling engaged (see Fig. 29).

- *Sources of information:* They globally use at least three sources of information to shape their opinion, with a mean of 3.44 and a standard deviation of 1.61 (see Fig. 30). All three cities are instead customarily distributed (see Fig. 31).

- *Social media:* They globally use at least two social media, with a mean of 2.48 and a standard deviation of 1.30 (see Fig. 32). Tel Aviv's social media use decreases linearly from 1 to 5. It increases from 1 to a dropping point of 3 in Tallinn and between 3 and 4 in Taipei (see Fig. 33).

- *Messaging app:* They use at least one messaging app globally, with a mean of 1.55 and a standard deviation of 0.88.

- *Total Influencers:* A big majority of my sample (78,4%) say to have between 1 and 3 influencers out of 9 when decision-making (see Fig. 34). If the decreasing line between 1 and 3 is more soft in Taipei and Tallinn, the decrease in Tel Aviv is clearly sloping (see Fig. 35).

- *Meeting places:* They globally and individually respect the same distribution of at least 2 meeting places, with a mean of 2.17 and a standard deviation of 1.25 (see Fig. 36 and 37).
- *Opinion share:* from 1 - I don't express my opinion in public to 5 - I can really express my opinion in public, my samples globally express a moderate opinion share, skewed right, with a mean of 3.21 and standard deviation of 1.25 (see Fig. 38). Same for individual (See Fig. 39)
- *Opinion change:* from 1 - I never change my opinion to 5 - I always change my opinion, my samples globally express a moderate change with a mean of 3.06 and a standard deviation of 0.80 (see Fig. 40). Individual samples respect the same tendency (see fig. 41).

- *Engagement wishes:* when 0 means No and 1 means Yes, my sample globally expresses the wish to engage more, with a mean of 0.77 and standard dev of 0.42.
- *Engagement frequency:* from 0 - Less than one hour a year to 5 - More than one hour a day, my sample agrees to engage about one hour a week to one hour a month, with a mean of 2.50 and a standard dev of 1.14 (see Fig. 42). Tallinn has the highest number of respondents agreeing to engage 1 hour a day and 1 hour a month, but Taipei has a bigger combination of 1 hour a week and 1 hour a month (see Fig. 43).
- *Engagement channels:* They globally agree to engage through at least 2 engagement channels, with a mean of 2.37 and a standard deviation of 1.25.

- *Gender:* My respondents are 44% of women and 56% of men.
- *Age:* My respondents are in their 30s skewed left, with a mean at 36 and a standard dev of 13 (see Fig. 44.)

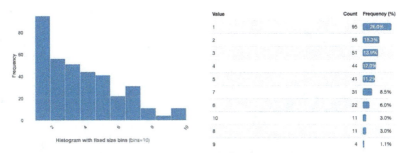

Fig. 28 - Frequency of engagement feeling (1: not engaged at all, 10: very engaged)

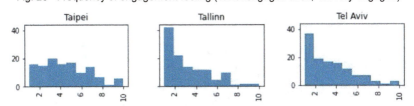

Fig. 29 - Frequency of engagement feeling values compared between cities.

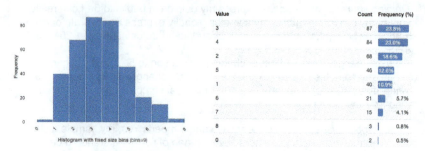

Fig. 30 - Frequency of total sources of information to shape its opinion.

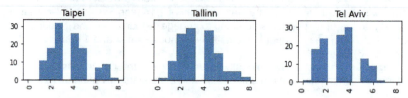

Fig. 31 - Frequency of total sources of information compared between cities.

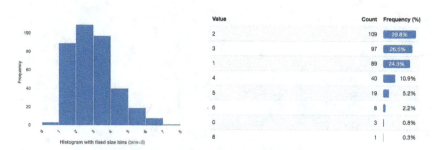

Fig. 32 - Frequency of total social media uses

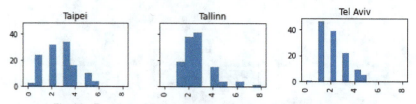

Fig. 33 - Frequency of total social media use compared between cities.

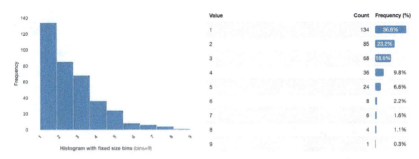

Fig. 34 - Frequency of total influencers

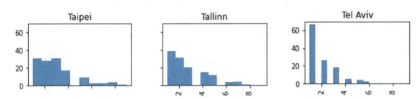

Fig. 35 - Frequency of total influencers compared between cities.

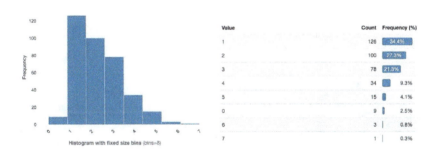

Fig. 36 - Frequency of total meeting places

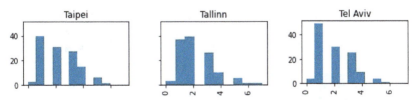

Fig. 37 - Frequency of total meeting places compared by cities.

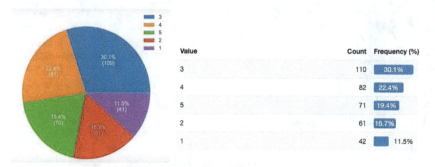

Fig. 38 - Distribution of Opinion Share (1: do not share, 5: share very easily)

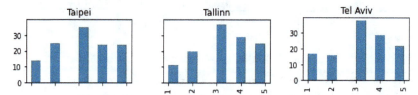

Fig. 39 - Distribution of Opinion Share compared between cities.

Fig. 40 - Frequency of Opinion Change (1: Do not change, 5: Change very easily)

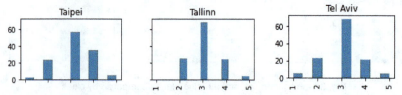

Fig. 41 - Distribution of Opinion Change compared between cities.

Value	Count	Frequency (%)
One hour a week	146	39.9%
One hour a month	105	28.7%
One hour a day	43	11.7%
One hour a year	34	9.3%
Less than one hour a year	26	7.1%
More than one hour a day	12	3.3%

Fig. 42 - Distribution of engagement frequency they agree to.

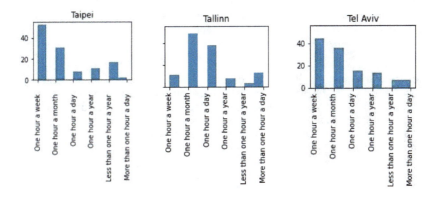

Fig. 43 - Distribution of engagement frequency agreed by cities.

- Age

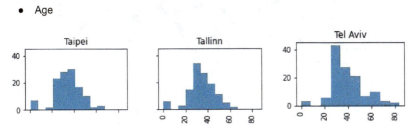

Fig. 44 - Distribution of ages compared between cities.

Correlation analysis

I have compared the intensity of correlation between variables using three coefficients: Pearson's r, Spearman's ρ, and Kendall's τ are represented on the following three matrices (see Fig. 45). It is not readable in detail at this size, but we can see the three respects the same distribution of correlations. I chose Pearson's r coefficient to go further.

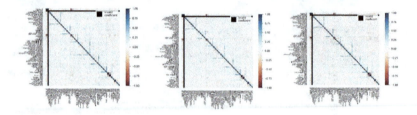

Fig. 45 - Pearson's r, Spearman's ρ and Kendall's τ matrixes indicate similar correlation

Because of the many variables in my dataset, overall matrices do not produce any interpretable visuals. I will split my variable between hypothesis ones and other attributes. The first will be visually interpreted (see Fig. 46), and the correlation intensity will be calculated with Pearson's r scores. The second will produce lots of peers (see Fig. 47), out of which I will filter the ones having the most significant correlated scores to check if some more hypotheses can appear.

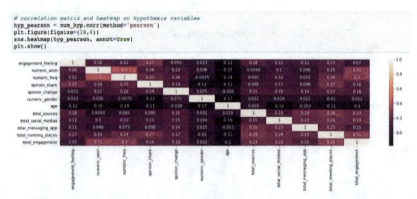

Fig. 46 - Pearson's correlation coefficient matrix on hypothesis variables.

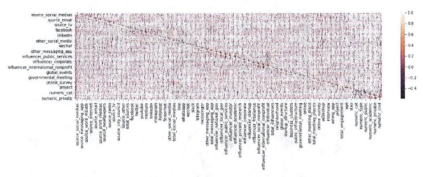

Fig. 47 - Pearson's correlation matrix on my whole variables. Unreadable.

There are too many variables to read the correlation matrix, so I will filter out the correlation coefficients I'm interested in: coefficients more significant than 0.50 express strongly correlated variables. Coefficients lower than 0.001 equally express sense from strongly non-correlated variables.

Negative correlations

- *Whatsapp / Line* have a negative correlation score of -0.59. Indeed depending on the city, the people prefer one or the other messaging app. Taiwan : Line, Tel Aviv : Whatsapp.

Positive correlations

- *Total Engagement / Voting Apps* has a positive correlation score of 0.51.
- *Total Engagement / Online Survey* has a positive correlation score of 0.53.
- *Total Engagement / Interview* has a positive correlation score of 0.54.
- *Total Engagement / Workshop* has a positive correlation score of 0.55.
It means that the citizens agreeing on the most engagement channels are those which agree using one of these.

- *Total Meeting Places / Startup Structures* has a positive correlation score of 0.56.
- *Total Meeting Places / Global Events* has a positive correlation score of 0.59.
It means that the citizens meeting others in the most different places are also the ones visiting Startup Structures or joining global events.

- *Total Social Medias / Youtube* has a positive correlation score of 0.56.
- *Total Social Medias / Instagram* has a positive correlation score of 0.59.
It means that the citizens using more social media are also those who use those two.

- *Total Messaging App / Messenger* has a positive correlation score of 0.52.
It means that the citizens using more messaging apps are also using Messenger.

A new correlation matrix of correlated variables aside from my primary hypothesis has been plotted. It is more visually accurate (see Fig. 48).

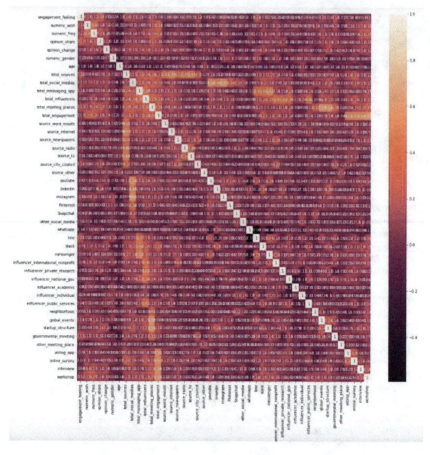

Fig. 48 - Pearson's correlation matrix on correlated variables aside of my hypothesis

These correlation matrices (Fig. 46 and 48) are more readable than the overall ones (Fig. 45 and 47). Still, it doesn't reach any clear proof of my hypothesis. One explanation could be that my variables have been recorded with varying scales. Furthermore, varying scales can affect the performance of predicting machine learning algorithms I will be using in the second part of this study.

To prevent any trouble, I will normalize the variables of my hypotheses and re-check the correlation.

I will also categorize my variables in three classes of values: Low, Medium, and High, to check if this manual clustering can help me reach more proof of relationships between variables of my interest. But first, let's take a look at the most exciting non-correlations of my dataset.

Strong non-correlations

Variables being strongly non-correlated express a very low probability of being in a relationship together. There are a lot, so I present only the ones the most meaningful to me.

- *Age / Voting apps* are uncorrelated (0.0003). It means that the age of the citizen has no relationship with the willingness to use a voting app as an engagement channel. This is meaningful information in terms of breaking a cliché.

- *Newspapers / Snapchat* are uncorrelated (0.0005). The use of Snapchat has no relationship with the use of Newspapers as source of information.
- *Newspapers / Governmental Meetings* are uncorrelated (0.0009). The use of newspapers as a source of information has no relationship with attending Governmental Meetings.

- *Whatsapp / Internet* are uncorrelated (0.0009). It means that the use of the messaging app Whatsapp has no relationship with the use of the Internet as a source of information.
- *Whatsapp / Total Meeting Places* are uncorrelated (0.001). The use of Whatsapp messaging app has no relationship with the total number of Meeting places visited.

- *Engagement Wish / Influencer Individual Citizen* (-0.0008). Being influenced by individual citizens when forming its opinion has no influence on the willingness to engage more or not.

- *Engagement Feeling / Meeting Place Neighbourhood* (-0.0001) ! The engagement feeling has no relationship with the use to meet other citizens in our neighbourhood !

Normalising variables

Normalisation is a scaling technique in which values are shifted and rescaled so that they end up ranging between 0 and 1. It is also known as Min-Max scaling.
- When the value of X is the minimum value in the column it will be changed to 0.
- When the value of X is the maximum value in the column it will be changed to 1.
- When the value of X is between the minimum and the maximum value, it will be assigned a proportional value between 0 and 1.

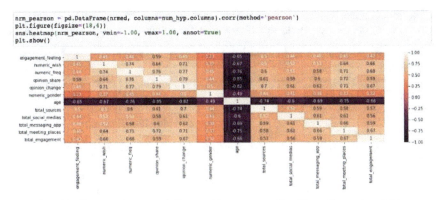

```
nrm_pearson = pd.DataFrame(nrmed, columns=num_hyp.columns).corr(method='pearson')
plt.figure(figsize=(18,4))
sns.heatmap(nrm_pearson, vmin=-1.00, vmax=1.00, annot=True)
plt.show()
```

Fig. 49 - Pearson's r correlation matrix on normalised hypotheses' variables

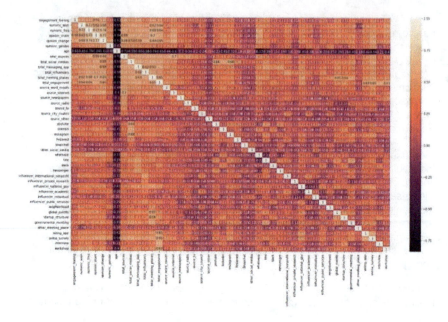

Fig. 50 - Pearson's r correlation matrix on normalised detected variables

Normalization has been an effective way to increase the correlation coefficients between my hypothesis variables and the ones seen by filtering. All correlated variables reveal a higher correlation score. To finally test my hypothesis, I will use the categorization technique.

Categorising variables

The categorization is a data transformation technique that will fit my data in sets of classes. My ordinal numerical variables will be turned into categorical ones.

- *Engagement Feeling (1 to 10)* is encoded as 1, 2, 3: Low, 4, 5, 6, 7: Medium, 8, 9, 10: High.
- *Engagement Frequency* is encoded as "Less than one hour a year" and "One hour a year": Low, "One hour a month": Medium, "One hour a week" and "One hour a day": High.
- *Opinion Share (1 to 5)* is encoded as 1, 2: Low, 3: Medium, 4, 5: High.
- *Opinion Change (1 to 5)* is encoded as 1, 2: Low, 3: Medium, 4, 5: High.
- *Age (18 to 84)* is encoded as 20s, 30s: Youngest, 40s, 50s: Mid-Aged, 60s, 70s, 80s: Oldest.
- *Length of stay (0 to 61)* is encoded as "Less than 1, 5, 10 years": Shortest, "Less than 15, 20, 25, 30, 35, 40, 45 years": Mid-Length, "Less than 50, 55, 60, 65 years": Longest.

After categorizing the variables of my hypothesis and calculating the mean for the supposedly dependent numerical variable, I reach proofs of validation to my view.

Hypothesis validation

Hypothesis 1 is validated: the citizens feeling the most engaged wish to engage more. Those willing to engage more have the highest engagement feeling (see Fig. 51 and 52).

cat_feel	engagement_wish_mean	engagement_wish	engagement_feeling_mean
High	0.961538	No	2.891566
Low	0.717822	Yes	3.830389

Fig. 51 - Hypothesis 1 is validated using the categorisation technique.

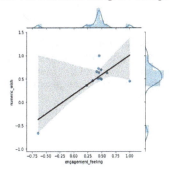

Fig. 52 - A linear regression confirms the validation of hypothesis 1.

Hypothesis 2 is validated: The citizens feeling the most engaged share their opinion in public more quickly. The citizens sharing their opinion in public more easily feel more engaged. This pair of variables is the one receiving the best correlation (see Fig. 52 and 53).

cat_feel	opinion_share_mean	cat_share	engagement_feeling_mean
High	3.884615	High	4.411765
Low	2.960396	Low	2.757282

Fig. 52 - Hypothesis 2 is validated using the categorisation technique.

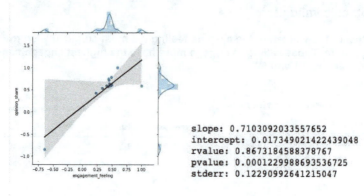

slope: 0.7103092033557652
intercept: 0.017349021422439048
rvalue: 0.8673184588378767
pvalue: 0.0001229988693536725
stderr: 0.12290992641215047

Fig. 53 - A linear regression confirms the validation of hypothesis 2.

Hypothesis 3 is validated: The citizens feeling the most engaged tend to change their opinion in contact with others (see Fig. 54). Suppose the Opinion Change and Engagement Feeling do not express a strong correlation. In that case, the Opinion Share and Opinion Change are correlated to each other (see Fig. 55).

cat_feel	opinion_change_mean	cat_change	engagement_feeling_mean
High	3.153846	High	3.797872
Low	3.044554	Low	3.294872

Fig. 54 - The opinion change and the engagement feeling are lightly correlated.

cat_change	opinion_share_mean
High	3.372340
Low	2.820513

Fig. 55 - Opinion Change and Opinion Share are strongly correlated.

Hypothesis 4 is validated: Gender has no relationship with the engagement feeling (see fig. 56 and 57)

gender	engagement_feeling_mean	cat_feel	gender_polarity
Man	3.568627	High	0.423077
Woman	3.679012	Low	0.435644

Fig. 56 - Hypothesis 4 is validated using the categorisation technique.

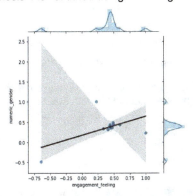

Fig. 57 - A linear regression confirms the validation of hypothesis 4.

Hypothesis 4bis is unvalidated: age has a negative correlation with engagement feeling. It means that younger citizens feel more engaged than the older (see Fig. 58 and 59).

recat_age	engagement_feeling_mean	cat_feel	age_mean
Oldest	2.842105	High	29.192308
Youngest	3.680365	Low	36.668317

Fig. 58 - Hypothesis 4bis is unvalidated with the categorisation technique.

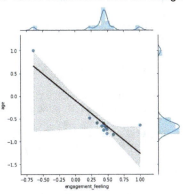

Fig. 59 - Older ages has the lowest engagement feeling

I have been tempted to double-proof this counter-intuitive insight by the length of stay. Indeed, it seems like the citizens who have stayed the longest in the city feel the least engaged, and the citizens having a high engagement feeling have the shortest length of stay in the city (see Fig. 60).

recat_stay	engagement_feeling_mean	cat_feel	length_stay_mean
Longest	2.923077	High	13.153846
shortest	3.469945	Low	15.410891

Fig. 60 - The longest length of stay expresses the lowest engagement feeling.

I have been tempted to dig in another counter-intuitive insight found earlier: does the voting app enthusiasm have a relationship with age? No correlation can be found (see fig. 61)

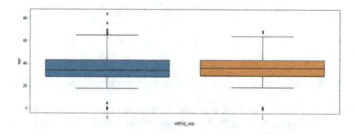

Fig. 61 - No correlation can be found between age and voting app enthusiasm.

b. Machine Learning—Classification algorithms

Machine Learning is computer algorithms that improve automatically by experience. My end goal is to build a ranking model able to predict if a citizen is highly engaged in decision-making for its city or not. So far, I am defining a citizen highly engaged in Smart-City as someone who:
- has an engagement feeling of 5/10 at least
- uses social media and the internet as a source of information to make their opinion
- uses at least two social media
- uses at least two messaging app
- meets other citizens online
- share its opinion in public (at least 3/5)
- change its opinion in contact to others (at least 3/5)
- wish to engage more
- through multiple engagement channels (at least 2/5)
- at a moderate to a high frequency (at least 1h a month).

Using my definition of a highly engaged citizen, I found 16 respondents out of 366, representing 4,4 % of my sample - 8 in Taipei, 6 in Tallinn, and 2 in Tel Aviv.

Feature Engineering

Feature engineering consists of selecting the subset of features that are the most relevant to your model construction. The chosen variables can significantly influence the performance of machine learning tasks: irrelevant or redundant features can negatively impact a model.

- Highly correlated features are, in essence, providing the same information.
- Some features provide little information, for example, when most records have the same value.
- Features that have little to no statistical relationship with the target variable are also avoidable.

Thus feature selection is a process where you automatically select the variables which contribute the most to predict the variable you are interested in. It asks to define the X-y axes. The purpose of my machine learning model is to automatically detect highly engaged citizens from a combination of questions answered by a survey study. So the boolean variable "Highly Engaged" where 0 means: "No" and one means "Yes" will be the y axis of my model (independent variables). The features will be selected and combined into an X-axis (dependent variables).

Optimal Number of Features

Using a Recursive Feature Elimination with Cross-Validation, coupled with a Stratified K-fold on a *Random Forest Classifier*, I found an optimal number of features for my model at 3. As you can see in fig. 62, the performance of a classifier is evaluated by the number of features selected. It is visible that with three features, the accuracy was about 97% which is pretty satisfying.

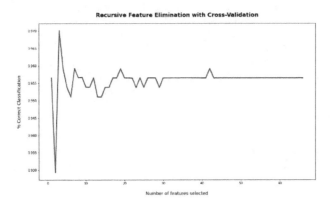

Fig. 62 - Recursive feature elimination with cross-validation

Feature Importance

Once the model is trained on the dataset, it is possible to evaluate the feature importance of the performance achieved (see Fig. 63). It allows us to understand the effects the features have on the classification task and determine which variables are most critical to the model performance.

111

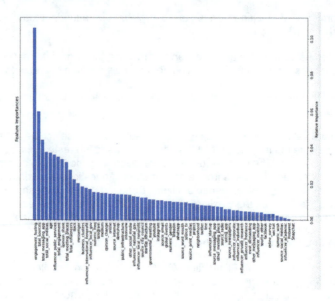

Fig. 63 - Features importance on the performance of the Random Forest Classifier.

The features having the most significant impact on the classifier algorithm are visible. I can choose to remove the fewer ones manually or use a mathematical technique called principal component analysis to reduce the number of dimensions in an optimal combination. Since the results from fig. 63 are counter-intuitive I tried the first two other feature importance rankings with an Extra-Trees Classifier and a Decision Tree Classifier (see Fig. 64).

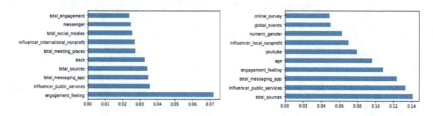

Fig. 64 - Features importance by Extra-Trees Classifier (left) and Decision Tree Classifier (right).

These two different rankings confirm the first one: the essential features to achieve the best-automated classification performance are not the variables of my hypothesis. All in one:
- Engagement Feeling
- Total Sources
- Total Messaging App
are the three most important features to my classification model.

Balancing the datasets

The distribution of highly engaged citizens (16) compared to others (350) is very unbalanced. To train the best machine learning model, I will use an over-sampling technique to balance it.

The Synthetic Minority Over-sampling Technique (SMOTE) is a kind of data augmentation that synthesizes new samples from the existing ones. I will use it to oversample the minority class. SMOTE is not a simple duplication of existing data records from the minority class: it creates new samples using the K-Nearest Neighbour algorithm. This approach can create as many synthetic samples as needed, bringing further relevant information to the dataset. As a result, we will have a new dataset of 700 respondents, where 350 respondents are highly engaged, and 350 respondents are not (see Fig. 65).

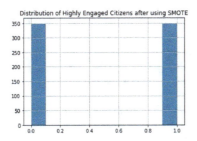

Fig. 65 - The class balance of y variable is perfect 50:50

Train/test split

Since my dataset is now balanced, I will split it in two: a 1/3 split called *train set* will be used to train my algorithms before using the other 2/3 split called *test set* to deploy the trained model (see Fig. 66).

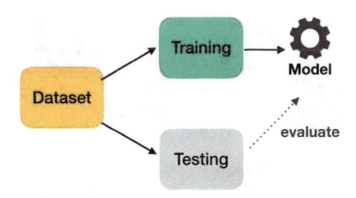

Fig. 66 - Typical dataset split into train and test sets

Comparison of four algorithms

There are many classification algorithms available, and it is not possible to tell if one is better than the other before testing it. To get a broad overview of the relevance of

my machine learning model, I will try and evaluate four different classifiers (see Fig. 67).
- Logistic Regression
- K-Nearest Neighbours
- Multi-Layer Perceptron
- Support Vector Machines

The performance of respective algorithms will be evaluated by crossing the results from a confusion matrix for each of them (see Fig. 68) and different accuracy scores (see Fig. 69). A description of each algorithm and accuracy score is available in chapter 4 of part 1 of this thesis.

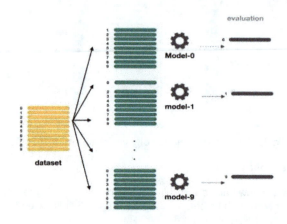

Fig. 67 - Different classifiers will proceed the same dataset.

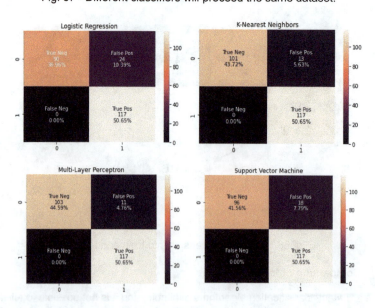

Fig. 68 - The confusion matrices show the number of errors of each model.

Accuracy scores

	accuracy	f1	auc	recall	precision	mae	mse	rmse	r2	vif
Logistic Regression	0.896104	0.906977	0.894737	1.0	0.829787	0.103896	0.103896	0.322329	0.584345	2.405844
KNN Classifier	0.943723	0.947368	0.942982	1.0	0.900000	0.056277	0.056277	0.237228	0.774854	4.441558
Multi-Layer Perceptron	0.952381	0.955102	0.951754	1.0	0.914062	0.047619	0.047619	0.218218	0.809492	5.249115
Support Vector Machines	0.922078	0.928571	0.921053	1.0	0.866667	0.077922	0.077922	0.279145	0.688259	3.207792

Fig. 69 - Accuracy scores from the four selected models.

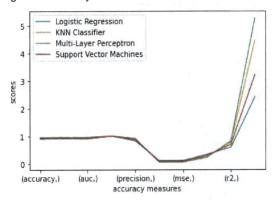

Fig. 70 - Accuracies compared for my four ML Classification models.

All in one, it looks like the artificial neural network algorithm called Multi-Layer Perceptron achieved the best results in all accuracy scores, and it has the lowest error rates (see Fig. 70).

c. Statistical Inferences—Generalising the ranking model

In this third part of the study, I'll use probabilistic models and the analysis of variance to test the potential scalability of my ranking model. Statistical inference requires some assumptions to be correct. If these assumptions are right and the analysis of variance conclusive, I will be able to prove the ability of my ranking model to predict inferences correctly on all similar datasets.

Probabilistic Model

Estimating probabilities with a probabilistic model is to formulate my problem: I am investigating citizens of a city searching for highly engaged citizens. I know that the overall population of a city can be classified into highly engaged citizens and non-highly engaged citizens. Still, I don't know how many of each are in the population. By survey study on a random sample, I found 4,4 % of highly engaged citizens. Assuming that highly engaged and non-highly engaged citizens had an equal chance to appear in my sample, I infer a similar percentage of highly engaged citizens in the whole population. I want to test this assumption. This means answering the following questions: How can I be sure that my sample represents the entire population? How can I incorporate prior beliefs about highly engaged citizens into this estimation?

A Bayesian inference method can handle these doubts but asks to assume that:
 - The chances to reach a highly engaged citizen are independent of each other.
 - Any citizen can potentially be highly engaged and match my definition.

Since I am not spreading my survey in some niche of engaged citizens and that no bias would reserve this class to a niche population, I can assume that the probability of picking highly engaged citizens or not follows a binomial distribution. In probability theory, the binomial distribution with parameters n and p is the discrete distribution of the number of successes in a sequence of n independent experiments. Each experiment owns a boolean-valued outcome: success (with probability p) and failure (with probability $q = 1-p$). In my problem, p is the ultimate objective: I want to figure out the probability of meeting highly engaged citizens in any smart city from my empirical sample. In statistics, a single success/failure experiment is drawn from a Bernoulli Distribution and forms the prior distribution for the sample of size n drawn with replacement from a population of size N. My sampling distribution helps to estimate the population statistic. The overall system of my interest, where a population of citizens can be divided into two classes (highly engaged and non-highly engaged citizens) and 366 independent data points, has a Probability Mass Function shown on the binomial distribution Fig. 71.

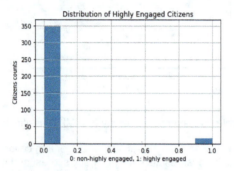

Fig. 71 - Probability Mass Function of my binomial distribution.

The *Central Limit Theorem* states that no matter the shape of the population distribution, the form of the sampling distribution will remain the same. This gives us a mathematical advantage to estimate the population statistic. The number of samples must be sufficient (generally more than 50) to satisfactorily achieve a normal curve distribution. Also, care has to be taken to keep the sample size fixed since any change in sample size will change the shape of the sampling distribution, and it will no longer be bell-shaped. As we increase the sample size, the sampling distribution squeezes from both sides, giving a better estimate of the population statistic since it lies somewhere in the middle of the sampling distribution (see Fig. 72). As for my study, the proportion of 4,4 % percent of highly engaged citizens over a random sample from a city population is already a mean generated from my 3 case studies. The Central Limit Theorem allows me to assume that if I were to investigate 100 Smart-Cities of the World with the same data collection protocol, the final mean of the proportions of Highly Engaged citizens would keep close to 4,4 %.

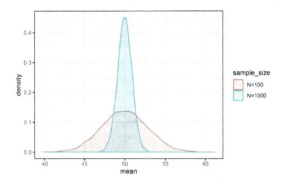

Fig. 72 - The central limit theorem states that the mean remains the same for x number of samples, and the standard deviation tends to reduce the bigger the number of samples are.

Inferential hypothesis testing

Hypothesis testing in inferential statistics consists of claiming the validity of a sample. With the advent of data-driven decision-making in business, science, technology, social, and political undertakings, the concept of hypothesis testing has become critically important to understand and apply. This method allows a sample statistic to be checked against a population statistic.

Inferential hypothesis testing is defined in two terms: a null hypothesis and an alternate hypothesis. The null hypothesis usually says that the inference is wrong, the alternate hypothesis says the contrary. In my case :

 - *Null Hypothesis*: My sample is not representative enough of the overall population, so I can't statistically validate my ranking model of citizen engagement so far.
 - *Alternate Hypothesis*: My sample is representative enough of the overall population, so I can't statistically validate my ranking model of citizen engagement so far.

The null hypothesis is assumed to be valid and statistical evidence is required to reject it in favor of the alternative hypothesis. What I am asking is how confident in the claim that my ranking model is correct am I? Or, what is the chance for any random sample of inhabitants in any Smart-City worldwide to reach 4,4% of highly engaged citizens?

This chance is represented by a *p-value* which I want to evaluate. Suppose this *p-value* is less than a predetermined critical value. Usually, a significance level α = 0.05. In that case, I gain evidence that the alternative hypothesis is accurate, and I can reject the null hypothesis.

The fact is that I don't know the real proportion of highly engaged citizens in the whole population of smart cities worldwide, so I can't compare my prediction with the reality. When the population parameters (mean and standard deviation) are not known, the best is to estimate it from samples by analyzing variances. Is there a significant difference in the proportion of highly engaged citizens between cities? (see Fig. 73 and 74). The overall proportion of highly engaged citizens is 4,37%. Taipei has 6,55% of them, Tallinn 4,92%, and Tel Aviv 1,64%.

```
highly_engaged  city_id
0                Taipei      114
                 Tallinn     116
                 Tel Aviv    120
1                Taipei        8
                 Tallinn       6
                 Tel Aviv      2
```

Fig. 73 - I have the distribution of highly engaged citizens of 3 samples.

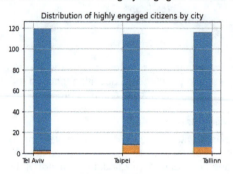

Distribution of highly engaged citizens by city

Fig. 74 - Distribution of Highly Engaged (orange) and not highly engaged citizens (blue).

Statistical Test :

The *analysis of variance (ANOVA)* tells whether two or more groups are similar enough to infer their results outside of the samples. It is based on their mean similarity and an f-score.

	Variable	N	Mean	SD	SE	95% Conf.	Interval
0	highly_engaged	366.0	0.0437	0.2047	0.0107	0.0227	0.0648

Fig. 75 - Overall mean and standard deviation.

	N	Mean	SD	SE	95% Conf.	Interval
city_id						
Taipei	122	0.0656	0.2486	0.0225	0.0210	0.1101
Tallinn	122	0.0492	0.2171	0.0197	0.0103	0.0881
Tel Aviv	122	0.0164	0.1275	0.0115	-0.0065	0.0392

Fig. 76 - Mean and standard deviation for each sample.

I am performing F-test to divide the variances together (see fig. 75 and 76) and compare the result with a critical value obtained from a table. Note that the matter should be more than one, and so we put the more significant weight on the top of the division (see Fig. 77).

```
stats.f_oneway(survey['highly_engaged'][survey['city_id'] == 'Taipei'],
               survey['highly_engaged'][survey['city_id'] == 'Tallinn'],
        |      survey['highly_engaged'][survey['city_id'] == 'Tel Aviv'])
```

F_onewayResult(statistic=1.8333333333333321, pvalue=0.16135700323789995)

Fig. 77 - One-Way ANOVA using SciPy.stats

The purpose of this statistic is to test the difference between highly engaged citizens from one city to another. Conducting a *One-Way ANOVA* using *the SciPy library*, I found *F-statistic* = 1.83 and a *p-value*=0.16. Considering the usual significance level at 0.05, I can't find enough evidence to reject the Null Hypothesis. So there is a statistically significant difference between my samples which does not allow me to attest that my predicting model will have the same satisfying accuracy score when used on other datasets. However, this result is not a point to the end of my study. The fact that my answers to the survey in Tel Aviv have been collected during the first Covid-19 pandemic could explain the drop of engagement feeling in the population. In a Mediterranean city in particular, where the way of life includes many word-to-mouth and outdoor meetings. Anyway, there are some more rooms to maneuver to validate this model. Reconsidering slightly the definition of a highly engaged citizen could have a significant impact. Collect more data points of the same cities, or other ones as well.

8. A predictive model of public opinion from Twitter mining

Natural language processing is a branch of artificial intelligence that deals with the interaction between humans and computers using natural language. I have been tempted to apply it to citizen engagement in smart-city. It results in a predictive model for public opinion in smart-city based on a lexical analysis of Twitter content.

To do so, I have collected 110,862 tweets (more than 19 Million words) over the 109 most advanced Smart-Cities worldwide, ranked by the_IMD Smart City Index 2020. My case studies are 3 of the 109 samples. I collected significantly more tweets than in other cities, riding up respectively to 2013 and 2012, representing almost all the tweets published in these cities on the platform. I am using this lexical content to extract numerical attributes on a text using Natural Language Processing (NLP) and Sentiment Analysis. Other calculations such as the weight of specific Bags-of-Words (BoWs) are tailored to urban topics. My model is built with Python's programming language, whose code and the initial raw data file are available on my_Github.

I am pursuing citizen engagement, and the spread of opinion started in the previous study by linking the ability to share its opinion in public with the sentiment expressed in tweets. Indeed, opinion mining algorithms are automating text analysis to extract and quantify the authors' affective states and degree of subjectivity. I will use the sentiment scores to create a new class of "highly engaged tweets," aggregated at a city level, and rank smart cities on their civic engagement. Machine learning algorithms will then predict highly engaged tweets.

Problematic :

Rather than asking people to engage through this or that app, or expecting them to use the official website of the local government to share their opinion, which often struggles to reach satisfying rates of citizen participation, another option is to catch the public opinion directly where it is: on social media. Suppose people don't have time to engage in in-person decision-making for their cities or trust their democratic representatives enough to join the usual political parties and meetings. In that case, they indeed use social platforms to express their opinion and communicate with peers. My research question would be: Can I use a Twitter mining model to detect citizen engagement in a smart city?

Hypothesis :

With this study, I would like to validate the following hypothesis:
 - Sentiment scores out of tweets are significant to classify cities on their civic engagement. The more citizens express their opinion online, the more cities collect a high engagement score.
 - Taking the weights of BoWs of urban topics is relevant to classify cities on their citizen engagement in a specific topic. The more the citizens use the words of a lexicon in their tweets, the more they are engaged, and so the more the city will collect a high engagement score.
 - The annual ranking of smart cities *Smart City Index* published by the_IMD Business School is significant to classify cities on their civic engagement. The more a city has a high position in the ranking, the more it collects high engagement from citizens on Twitter.
 - I can use some specific features extracted from tweets to build a predictive model for public opinion in smart cities.

Methodology :

First, I collected tweets mentioning in a hashtag my three case studies: #Taipei, #Telaviv, and #Tallinn. Then I have been concerned that I could use a similar technique to scrape the tweets from the whole population of 109 smart-cities classified by the IMD's Smart-City Index 2020. In the end, A has collected a dataset of 110,862 tweets from the four corners of the World, with a predominance of Europe, Asia, and the USA (see Fig. 78). As you can see on the following map, South America, Africa, Middle East, and Australia are also represented. Such a dataset will allow me to build solid statistical references to interpret my case study samples.

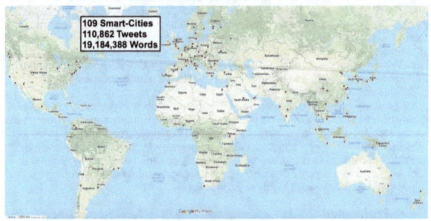

109 Smart-Cities
110,862 Tweets
19,184,388 Words

Fig. 78 - The map of 109 most advanced smart cities in the world.

The whole dataset represents 19,184,388 words, processed through natural language techniques and sentiment analysis to extract numeric features from tweets' content.

The tweet-level features will be aggregated at a city scale, dividing the total scores by the number of tweets for each city. This also avoids the unbalance between cities' samples and results in a series of average values expressed by float numbers on a standardized scale.

In the third step, I create a new variable, "engagement score," attributed to each city from the number of highly engaged tweets it has by the total number of tweets. This score allows me to determine the 20% of most dynamic cities from the engagement of the Twitter users acting on their behalf. Therefore, I have been able to use ranking algorithms of machine learning to predict the highly engaged tweets of a city based on other tweets' attributes.

Lastly, I will be using inferential statistics to test the probability of my model to predict public opinion on a global scale.

a. Feature Extraction—NLP, Sentiment Analysis

Natural Language Processing (NLP) is a subfield of linguistics, computer science, and artificial intelligence concerned with computers and human language interactions. It results in IT programs understanding the content of large amounts of textual documents expressed in a natural language. These programs can extract information out of texts and categorize and organize the documents themselves (see Fig. 79).

Fig. 79 - This NLP pipeline is indicative. I have proceeded more steps and in a different order.

Sentiment Analysis is one of the most popular insights extracted out of textual content, mainly used in the context of analyzing reviews from customers of a new product for a specific brand or company. Also called opinion mining, it uses NLP techniques to identify affective states and subjective information from texts of very different scales and various topics.

Fig. 80 - Three usual affective states detected by most Sentiment Analysis algorithms.

Tweet-level features

I extracted the following features for each 110,862 tweets:
- Tweet length
- Number of words
- Number of stop-words
- Number of sentences
- Average length of word
- Number of punctuation
- Number of hashtags
- Number of numerics
- Number of uppercase
- Percentage of Positivity, Neutrality and Negativity (0 to 1)
- Sentiment polarity (-1: very negative, 1: very positive)
- Sentiment subjectivity (0: very objective, 1: very subjective)

City-level features

Tweet-level features have been aggregated by city then divided by the number of tweets per city in order to create averages expressed as float numbers.
- Rank in Smart City Index 2020
- Number of tweets

- Average tweet length
- Average number of words
- Average number of stop-words
- Average number of sentences
- Average word length
- Average number of punctuation
- Average number of hashtags
- Average number of numerics
- Average number of Uppercase
- Average percentage of Positivity, Neutrality and Negativity
- Average sentiment polarity
- Average sentiment subjectivity

Lexical transformation

To extract more features at a city scale, I concatenated all the tweets of a city in a single text before processing it through a series of cleaning and transformation steps:
- Lower all characters
- Convert emojis to words (e.g. 😊 into smiling_face_with_smiling_eyes)
- Convert emoticons to words (e.g. :-) into happy_face_smiley)
- Remove punctuation
- Remove symbols
- Remove stop-words (common words which do not add any sense. E.g: a, the, or...)
- Remove urls
- Remove htmls
- Remove # (I do not remove the full hashtag which can contain interesting information)
- Remove @ mentions
- Remove digits
- Expand contractions (e.g. "aren't" into "are not")
- Number of clean words
- Average number of characters in clean words
- Average length of clean words
- Sentiment polarity of clean texts (to be compared with sentiment polarity on raw tweets)
- Sentiment subjectivity of clean texts (same)
- Tokenizing (converting strings to single words. E.g: The fox jumps => The, fox, jumps)
- Remove meaningless tokens. Non-words are "noise" which can be removed manually.
- Part of Speech tagging. Marking up a word as corresponding to nouns, verbs, adjectives...
- Most frequent 100 words. Counts and orders the most frequent words used in each city.
- Word embedding by enabling the preprocessing of text data into a matrix of numbers.
- TF-IDF vectoriser intend to reflect how important a word is to a document in a corpus.
- Weight of BoWs. A bag of words consists of a representative lexicon of a specific topic. I created lexicons of the 150 most frequent words for Smart-City, Civic-Tech, Infrastructure, Sustainability, Governance, and Entrepreneurship. So I have an overview of how much these topics are discussed in each city.

b. Descriptive Statistics

Once I extracted the above features from my dataset of tweets and created a new dataset of smart-cities with the corresponding numerical variables, I took an overall look at the data composition to identify some insights that could be visible with bare eyes.

Exploratory Data Analysis :

The average tweet length is about 180 characters, which is influenced by the social network standard format, of course. Still, we can see that the distribution is not normally distributed (Fig. 81), which shows testimonies of different behavior from the users in communicating on the platform. A subjective choice thus, which is also observed in the peaks over the distribution of the average number of words per tweet (see Fig. 82), meaning that this variable is not normally distributed either. The average number of sentences (see Fig. 83) and the average word length (see Fig. 84).

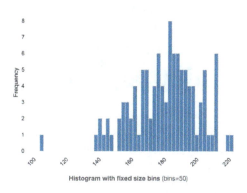

Fig. 81 - Average tweet length distribution (left)

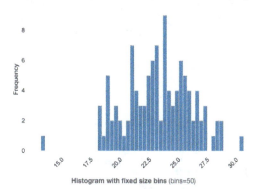

Fig. 82 - Average number of words per tweet (middle)

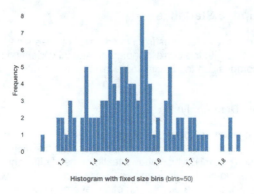

Fig. 83 - Average number of sentences per tweet

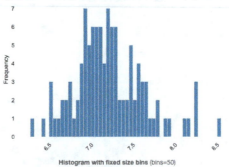

Fig. 84 - Average word length

The average number of stop-words (see Fig. 85), the average number of punctuation (see Fig. 86), and the average number of uppercase (see Fig. 87) distributions are also showing some peaks with insufficient regularity. The distribution of the average length of clean words (see Fig. 88) delivers a regular shape which probably depends on the nature of words rather than the users' behavior.

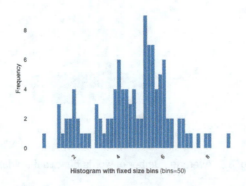

Fig. 85 - Average number of stop-words per tweet

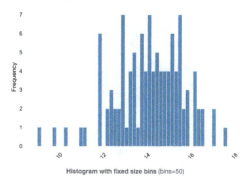

Fig. 86 - Average number of punctuation per tweet

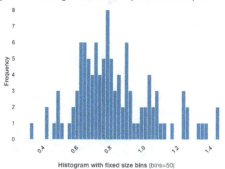

Fig. 87 - Average number of Uppercase per tweet

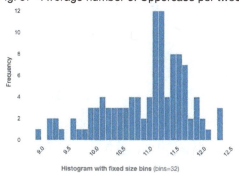

Fig. 88 - Average length of clean words

The average number of hashtags (see Fig. 89) and the average number of numerics (see Fig. 90) are subjective, such as the distribution of sentiment polarity scores (see Fig. 91) with a mean of 0.29, which says an overall moderation in expressing its opinion on Twitter, and this restraint seems to be very widespread with a standard deviation at 0.05.

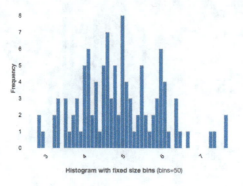

Fig. 89 - Average number of hashtags per tweet

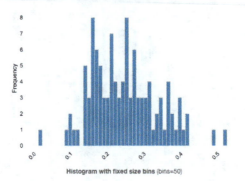

Fig. 90 - Average number of numerics per tweet

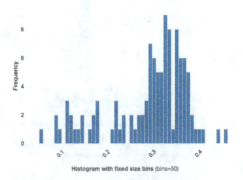

Fig. 91 - Distribution of sentiment subjectivity scores

The above assumptions can be tested by a simple look at scatter plots with the concerned variable and the average subjectivity score extracted with sentiment analysis. It appears that average tweet length, the average number of words, the average number of sentences, average punctuation, average hashtags, average numerics, and average uppercase are not depending on the average subjectivity (see Fig. 92).

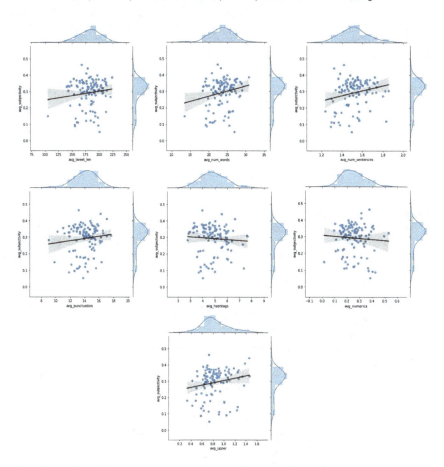

Fig. 92 - Subjectivity by average tweet length (upper left), average number of words (upper middle), average number of sentences (upper right), average punctuation(center left), average hashtags (center center), average numerics (center right), average uppercase (bottom).

Whereas stronger relationships are easily detected on scatter plots of pairs between the average number of stop-words, the average word length, and the average clean word length with average subjectivity (see Fig. 93). It is interesting to note that the average word length has a negative relationship with subjectivity. In contrast, the average word length has a positive one. Somewhat I can imagine that the 'noise' words, those being dropped while cleaning the text, such as stop words, are both the shorter ones (mean it goes from 7 to 11 before/after washing) and the ones expressing the less subjectivity.

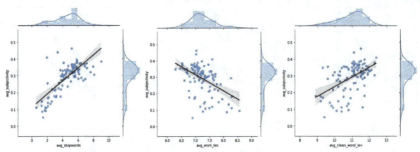

Fig. 93 - Subjectivity by average number of stop-words, average word length, average clean word length.

None of my hypotheses have been validated so far since I had no preconceived idea about the features and their distributions. Remember that I am primarily trying to prove that sentiment scores, the weight of BoWs, and smart-city index ranking will make sense at being used in a classification model for citizen engagement.

Correlation analysis

- The *Pearson's correlation coefficient (r)* is a measure of linear correlation between two variables. Its value lies between -1 and +1, -1 indicating total negative linear correlation, 0 indicating no linear correlation, and 1 indicating real positive linear correlation. Furthermore, *r* is invariant under different changes in the location and scale of the two variables, implying that for a linear function, the angle to the x-axis does not affect *r*. To calculate *r* for two variables *X* and *Y*, one divides the covariance of *X* and *Y* by the product of their standard deviations.

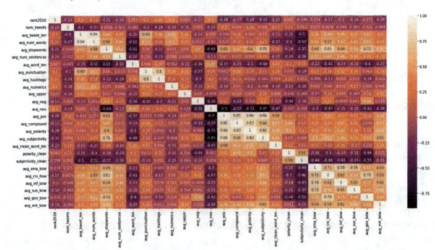

Fig. 94 - Pearson's R correlation matrix

I used three different correlation coefficients: Pearson's R (see Fig. 94), Spearman's ρ, and Phi K, to compare the matrixes' results. Overall correlation scores are similar, and I can already identify a few clusters of variables being correlated to each other:
- Average number of numerics, hashtags and punctuation are correlated with the average tweet length and the average number of words (raw).
- The number of punctuation, hashtags, numerics, and uppercase have no

correlation with sentiment scores and weight of BoWs.
- Average number of words, stop-words, sentences, and the average length of words are related to each other.
- Average number of stop-words is highly correlated with all sentiment scores and bags-of-words.
- Sentiment scores are all strongly correlated to each other, positivity globally more strongly than negativity.
- Weight of BoWs are all strongly correlated to each other.
- Sentiment scores and weight of BoWs are correlated to each other.
- The smart-city index ranking is not correlated with any variable.

So I can tell from this overall look at the correlation matrix that my features could somehow be remodeled in some combination of components to reduce the number of variables but without losing too much sense.
- The average number of stop-words could represent all the lexical attributes of the tweets (numerics, hashtags, punctuation, tweet length, length of words and number of sentences).
- The all sentiment scores could be reduced to the most representative of them, average polarity or positivity.
- The weight of Bags-of-Words could be reduced to one since they follow the same tendency, it should be the most representative which appears to be the entrepreneurship one, which is also the most correlated with sentiment scores.

It also looks like one of my hypotheses has already been invalidated: the rank of cities in the smart-city index 2020 can't be used to classify citizen engagement in smart cities since it is not correlated to any variables (see Fig. 95).

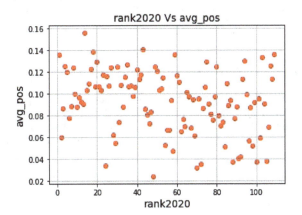

Fig. 95 - smart-cities index 2020 rank by level of positive sentiment expressed : no correlation

The correlation between the average weight of the CivicTech BoW and the moderate positivity expressed is much clearer (see Fig. 96).

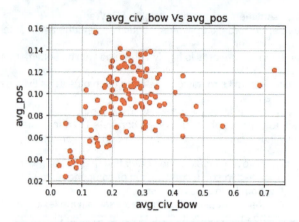

Fig. 96 - Average weight of CivicTech BoW by average positivity

Hypothesis 3 saying that the Smart-City index 2020 ranking is relevant to classify smart-cities on their citizen engagement is invalidated. How about my other two assumptions? Are sentiment scores and weight of BoWs significant to classify cities on their citizen engagement? So far, I can't answer with lots of certainties: on my correlation matrices, it appears that some sentiment scores are correlated to some weights of BoWs, but the correlation is not strong enough between all, and it also varies between coefficients. The average subjectivity is related to 3 on 6 BoWs: Smart-City, CivicTech, and Entrepreneurship. To validate my pending hypothesis deeper, I will perform linear regression analysis and reach more evidence of the relationship between variables.

Regression analysis

In this case, I will not use linear regression to predict values. The purpose of my regression analysis will be to infer causal relationships between a target variable and dependent ones. I will proceed with such multi-linear regression twice on my two pending hypotheses, meaning using average subjectivity and the average weight of BoW as y-axis.

The linear regression model performs the predictions of the target variable by using the other features of my dataset. It means that additional features easily predict the average subjectivity. So it proves that most components are depending on the average subjectivity.

The linear relationship between existing data of the average subjectivity and predicted ones by the regression model shows a good performance with an R2 of 0.94 (see Fig. 97 and 98).

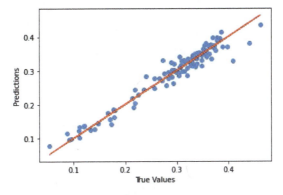

```
Intercept of model -349.95253906995276
The mean absolute error of the model in the test set is:   0.01
The mean squared error of the model in the test set is:    0.00
The root mean squared error of the model in the test set is:   0.02
The R2 of the model in the test set is: 0.94746
```

Fig. 97 - Linear relationship between average subjectivity values and the predicted ones

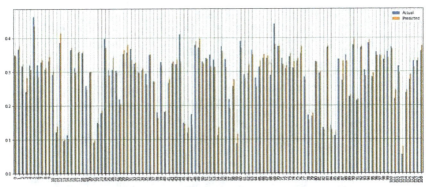

Fig. 98 - The histogram of both existing and predicted values shows the predictive performance.

Hypothesis 1 saying that subjective sentiment score is significant to rank cities on their civic engagement. Consequently, the more citizens express a personal opinion about their city on Twitter, the more the city can be considered highly engaged.

To test hypothesis 2 about the relevance of BoWs to predict such citizen engagement, I have had to choose one of the 6 BoWs created. I retained the one showing the best correlation with most variables, which is the entrepreneurship BoW. The linear relationship between existing data of the entrepreneurship BoW and predicted ones by the regression model shows a poor performance with an R2 far from 1 (see Fig. 99 and 100). It means that the average weight of BoW is not correlated to other features, so we can't use it as a basis to build a predictive model of citizen engagement in smart-city.

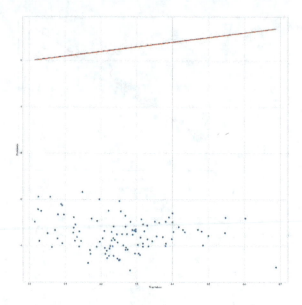

```
Intercept of model -796.9153788968592
The mean absolute error of the model in the test set is:    4.00
The mean squared error of the model in the test set is:  16.18
The root mean squared error of the model in the test set is:    0.02
The R2 of the model in the test set is: -960.34354
```

Fig. 99 - Linear regression between average entrepreneurship bow values and predicted ones

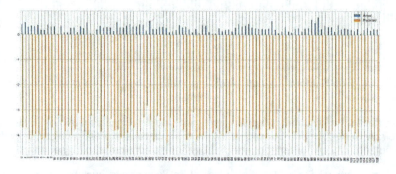

Fig. 100 - The histogram of existing and predicted values shows a poor predictive performance.

Consequently, hypothesis 2 is invalidated. The weights of BoWs are not significantly predicted from other features out of my Twitter datasets, so I can not say that weights of BoWs (which are highly correlated to each other) are relevant to rank cities on their civic engagement.

Suppose the weight of BoWs hasn't proven to be predictable from other Twitter attributes. In that case, they remain correlated to some variables, such as the average number of stop-words or different sentiment scores. Thus, I can think about some insightful ways to use these features for my predictive model, like using them to subsample datasets and look for sentiment scores in the specific topics they cover, rather than on the overall dataset. Indeed, a multiple regression line on my six weights of BoWs presents relationships with the average subjectivity score. It means that they all depend on the validated target variable sentiment scores with different intensities (see Fig. 101).

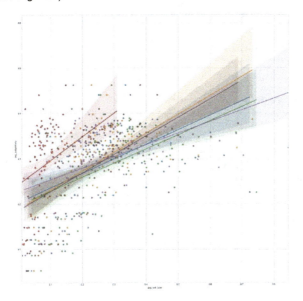

Fig. 101 - Weights of BoWs are (more or less) correlated to the average subjectivity score.

c. Machine Learning - Classification algorithms

To improve my ranking model of smart cities based on their civic engagement, I will create an engagement score for each city based on the number of highly engaged tweets. So far, I am defining a highly-engaged tweet as a tweet having:
- average sentiment polarity ≥ 0.5
- average sentiment subjectivity ≥ 0.75

Since the polarity is expressed from -1 to 1 and subjectivity from 0 to 1, I select the top 25% of potential sentiment expressions in a tweet. It appears that 7,574 tweets out of 110,850 are matching my definition. It represents 6,83% of my dataset. These highly engaged tweets are randomly distributed over my smart-cities dataset. As a precision on my case studies, Taipei has 1589 highly engaged tweets out of a total of 17,341 tweets, totaling 9.76%. Tel Aviv has 1485 out of 17,628, meaning 8.42 % of the total, and Tallinn has 705 out of 6,299 tweets, 11.19%. Therefore, I can attribute an engagement score to each city by dividing the number of engaged tweets by the total one. It gives a satisfying result that can be used to rank cities on their citizen engagement online. Then, I create a categorical variable called "highly engaged" to categorize the most dynamic cities of my dataset. This last variable will be used as the target of my machine learning algorithms. A statistical description of the "engagement score" variable is shown in Fig. 102.

```
count     109.000000
mean        0.054641
std         0.023315
min         0.004484
25%         0.038038
50%         0.058000
75%         0.068702
max         0.112311
Name: engagement_score, dtype: float64
```

Fig. 102 - Statistical description of the "engagement_score" variable

Fitting the data

Feature selection in machine learning and statistics is a process of selecting a subset of relevant features, variables or predictors, to build a performing machine learning model. The central premise is that the data contains some features that are either *redundant* or *irrelevant*
and can thus be removed without incurring much loss of information. The optimal number of components can be tested using Recursive Feature Elimination with Cross-Validation on a classifier algorithm. I did it on the random forest classifier and got four features (see Fig. 103).

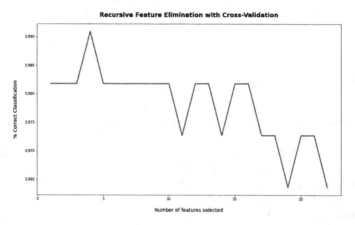

Fig. 103 - Using RFECV on a Random Forest Classifier, 4 is the optimal number of features.

The same Random Forest Classifier algorithm is used to rank the most important features of my dataset. The engagement score and the number of engaged tweets, as the average polarity and subjectivity, are the most important to predict the "highly engaged" cities (see Fig. 104).

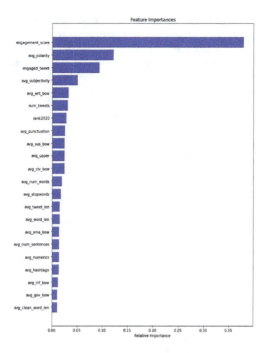

Fig. 104 - Feature importance ranking using Random Forest Classifier.

I will use Synthetic Minority Over-sampling Technique (SMOTE) to oversample the minority class in my target variable. As a result, I will have a new dataset of 174 data points, with the same proportion of highly engaged and non-highly dynamic cities (see Fig. 105).

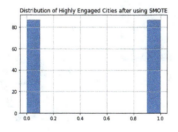

Fig. 105 - My dataset is now balanced with 87 data points for each highly-engaged city and not.

Predicting citizen engagement

To select the most performing model to answer my research question, I will run four algorithms and compare their accuracy scores. The four classifiers I will be using are:
- Logistic Regression
- K-Nearest Neighbours
- Multi-Layer Perceptron
- Support Vector Machines

The performance of each algorithm in predicting the highly engaged cities is evaluated through accuracy scores (see Fig. 106 and 107) and the confusion matrices (see Fig. 108). All in one, I can say that the K-Nearest Neighbours classifier is the model achieving the best performance in predicting the classification of highly engaged cities from my Twitter attributes. It has good accuracy scores and balanced proportions of errors. However, an accuracy score of 82% is not incredible, and I should try different combinations of features for the KNN classifier until I reach better scores.

	accuracy	f1	auc	recall	precision	mae	mse	rmse	r2	vif
Logistic Regression	0.706897	0.679245	0.723558	0.56250	0.857143	0.293103	0.293103	0.541390	-0.185096	0.843813
KNN Classifier	0.827586	0.843750	0.825721	0.84375	0.843750	0.172414	0.172414	0.415227	0.302885	1.434483
Multi-Layer Perceptron	0.706897	0.784810	0.676683	0.96875	0.659574	0.293103	0.293103	0.541390	-0.185096	0.843813
Support Vector Machines	0.689655	0.640000	0.711538	0.50000	0.888889	0.310345	0.310345	0.557086	-0.254808	0.796935

Fig. 106 - Accuracy scores of each of the four classifier models.

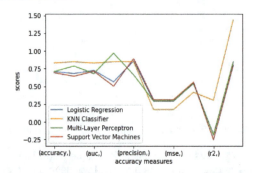

Fig. 107 - A line plot of difference of performance for my four models.

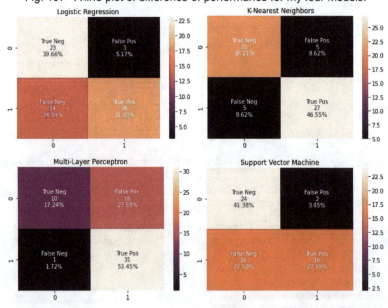

Fig. 108 - Confusion Matrices of my algorithms show the proportion of error.

Inferential statistics

With statistical inferences, it is possible to reach conclusions that extend beyond the actual dataset. Suppose the machine learning models are used to make predictions inside the dataset. In that case, probabilistic models are used to make predictions about extensive data, using the probability of an event to occur and statistical hypothesis testing. To proof-test my last hypothesis about my research question: I can use some specific features extracted from tweets to build a predictive model of public opinion in smart cities. I will formulate the following:

- Null hypothesis: I can't use specific features extracted from tweets to build a predictive model for public opinion in smart cities.

- Alternate hypothesis: I can use specific features extracted from tweets to build a predictive model for public opinion in smart cities.

Hypothesis testing techniques will be used to answer the research question.
- *F-test* (ANOVA): The t-test works well when dealing with two groups, but sometimes we want to compare more than two groups at the same time. For example, suppose we wanted to test whether voter age differs based on some categorical variable like race. In that case, we have to compare the means of each level or group the variable. We could carry out a separate t-test for each pair of groups, but you increase the chances of false positives when you conduct many tests. The analysis of variance is a statistical inference test that lets you compare multiple groups simultaneously.
The Anova is based on the mean similarities and variances (see Fig. 109).

```
# population
smartcities100['subjectivity_tweet'].describe()

count    110850.000000
mean          0.309158
std           0.320444
min           0.000000
25%           0.000000
50%           0.262963
75%           0.535714
max           1.000000
Name: subjectivity_tweet, dtype: float64
```

```
# sample 1
taipei = np.where((smartcities100['query']=='#Taipei'))

smartcities100.loc[taipei]['subjectivity_tweet'].describe()

count    17337.000000
mean         0.330454
std          0.330097
min          0.000000
25%          0.000000
50%          0.300000
75%          0.580952
max          1.000000
Name: subjectivity_tweet, dtype: float64
```

```
# sample 2
telaviv = np.where((smartcities100['query']=='#telaviv'))

smartcities100.loc[telaviv]['subjectivity_tweet'].describe()

count    17612.000000
mean         0.330184
std          0.330180
min          0.000000
25%          0.000000
50%          0.300000
75%          0.575000
max          1.000000
Name: subjectivity_tweet, dtype: float64
```

```
#sample 3
tallinn = np.where((smartcities100['query']=='#Tallinn'))

smartcities100.loc[tallinn]['subjectivity_tweet'].describe()

count    6295.000000
mean        0.360651
std         0.330555
min         0.000000
25%         0.000000
50%         0.350000
75%         0.600000
max         1.000000
Name: subjectivity_tweet, dtype: float64
```

```
from scipy import stats
stats.f_oneway(smartcities100['subjectivity_tweet'][smartcities100['query'] == '#Taipei'],
               smartcities100['subjectivity_tweet'][smartcities100['query'] == '#telaviv'],
               smartcities100['subjectivity_tweet'][smartcities100['query'] == '#Tallinn'])

F_onewayResult(statistic=22.51047492092302, pvalue=1.6949511362230516e-10)
```

Fig. 109 - Statistical description of my samples and the whole population. Resulting p-value.

Considering the usual significance level at 0.05, I can't find enough statistical evidence to reject the null hypothesis. The unbalance between my sample sizes can be a reason to weaken the performance of this ANOVA test. Anyway, suppose I have not proved it statistically using this hypothesis testing. In that case, I demonstrate clearly that the NLP and sentiment analysis techniques are adapted to rank cities based on the polarity and subjectivity detected on tweets.

9. Classifying citizen engagement in smart-city from social network analysis

The structure and the dynamics of individual social networks say a lot about individual behaviors, which can be taken widely and in the frame of citizen engagement. To conduct such social network analysis, I will merge all my Twitter datasets by cities: the ones from #Taipei, #Telaviv, and #Tallinn will be augmented with the ones from the respective representatives of each stakeholder category: public sector, corporate company, startup, academic sector, civil society, and media industry (see Fig.1). By doing that, I will collect more insights into the complex systems of digital interactions of citizens in smart cities. I will be able to sketch profiling attributes for my stakeholders' categories.

Each city has its networks of stakeholders, influencing the decision-making from a global to a local scale. The relationships between stakeholders are not dialogical but interconnected in a web of networks, where each user has a potential capacity to exercise a role of leadership on the whole. The moving interests of each stakeholder make them sometimes cooperating, sometimes challenging, or strongly opposing to influence the total in the direction to its closest interests.

Problematic :

The engagement on the platform and the popularity level are two indicators of social network activities I want to get insight from. Understanding better the complex dynamics of social network interactions will allow me to address the broader research question: Does the popularity on a social platform depend on the level of engagement? Can I predict the influence of a social media user from a topological analysis with graph-based machine learning?

Considering this problem, simple steps to answer would be:
- Determinate the influential nodes in a given network
- Determinate the impact of a message on the social network
- Determinate the influence of communities of nodes on the network

Hypothesis :

My primary hypothesis is that the number of tweets is a good indicator of the level of engagement on the platform. The number of followers is a good indicator of the popularity of a user. These two variables could be used as targets for a machine learning model willing to predict it from different topological network attributes. I will say that popularity and engagement are dependent on each other, even if I suspect the relationship is not regular.

My secondary hypothesis is that the different categories of stakeholders do not behave the same on the network. So it should be possible to predict the belonging type of a user or group of users based on different topological network attributes.

Methodology :

When a user follows, gives similar to, replies, or mentions someone in a publication, it creates a binary relationship from which I can build a graph representation. Different features will be extracted from the graphs to describe the social networks statistically. They will be processed through machine learning to predict communities of users and future links between them.

In the following infographic (see Fig. 110), I present the merging of my datasets into six stakeholder categories and three cities.

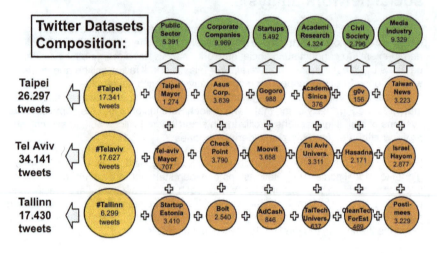

Fig. 110—Composition and aggregation of Twitter datasets

a. Feature extraction from network topology:

I will perform the network feature extraction in the programming language Python before using them as input in different machine learning algorithms to infer the evolution of the network topology. The Python libraries and steps are shown in Fig. 111.

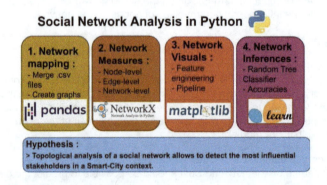

Fig. 111 - Python libraries used to conduct my social network analysis

Data Transformation

The first step of a social network analysis consists of transforming raw datasets of nodes into a file of edges with frequency, then turning the sheet into a 3D graph file (see Fig. 112).

tweetDate	twitterId	handle	text	profileUser	name	tweetLink
Mon Mar 30 17:	198436076	Ron_Huldai	שי הישטורי תקרים	https://twitter.cor	רון חולדאי	https://twitter.cor
Wed Mar 25 12:	198436076	Ron_Huldai	ארץ מוסהה בתום	https://twitter.cor	רון חולדאי	https://twitter.cor
Thu Mar 19 07:5	198436076	Ron_Huldai	T @Ron_Huldai	https://twitter.cor	רון חולדאי	https://twitter.cor
Thu Mar 19 07:4	198436076	Ron_Huldai	החולילאי המשט	https://twitter.cor	רון חולדאי	https://twitter.cor
Thu Mar 19 05:2	506585581	MiroHQ	Collaborate like	https://twitter.cor	Miro	https://twitter.cor
Wed Mar 18 17:5	198436076	Ron_Huldai	אותט מוסהס אותו	https://twitter.cor	רון חולדאי	https://twitter.cor
Tue Mar 17 12:1	198436076	Ron_Huldai	תושבים וחושבות	https://twitter.cor	רון חולדאי	https://twitter.cor
Sun Mar 15 12:1	198436076	Ron_Huldai	את כל התנועות ות	https://twitter.cor	רון חולדאי	https://twitter.cor
Thu Mar 12 17:0	198436076	Ron_Huldai	שי כמה עיוחומ יש	https://twitter.cor	רון חולדאי	https://twitter.cor
Wed Mar 11 11:4	198436076	Ron_Huldai	בימים האחרונים יע	https://twitter.cor -	רון חולדאי	https://twitter.cor
Wed Mar 04 17:5	198436076	Ron_Huldai	עיריית תל אביב-יפ	https://twitter.cor	רון חולדאי	https://twitter.cor
Wed Mar 04 16:5	198436076	Ron_Huldai	בכל מפגיה, רי בה	https://twitter.cor	רון חולדאי	https://twitter.cor
Mon Mar 02 18:x	198436076	Ron_Huldai	גאו להצביע!	https://twitter.cor	רון חולדאי	https://twitter.cor
Thu Feb 27 18:2	198436076	Ron_Huldai	נאשה גדולה! הבר ג	https://twitter.cor	רון חולדאי	https://twitter.cor
Wed Feb 26 21:x	198436076	Ron_Huldai	שפעם מה לעשות	https://twitter.cor	רון חולדאי	https://twitter.cor
Wed Feb 25 11::	198436076	Ron_Huldai	מברך על החדשות ג	https://twitter.cor	רון חולדאי	https://twitter.cor
Sun Feb 23 08:1	198436076	Ron_Huldai	אלי בסונם שות DoriaLampel@	https://twitter.cor	רון חולדאי	https://twitter.cor
Thu Feb 20 19:1	198436076	Ron_Huldai	שות DoriaLampel@	https://twitter.cor	רון חולדאי	https://twitter.cor
Thu Feb 20 18:2	3104837426	saradiv1	J @regev_min@	https://twitter.cor	פלתקה ▲	https://twitter.cor
Thu Feb 20 16:3	3245194376	zeev_elkin	אני מצינ, בהינט זו	https://twitter.cor	Zeev Elkin	https://twitter.cor

user	target	url	freq
Ron_Huldai	asaf_lib	https://twitter.com/asaf_lib	1
Ron_Huldai	GLZRadio	https://twitter.com/GLZRadio	12
Ron_Huldai	MoavVardi	https://twitter.com/MoavVardi	1
Ron_Huldai	NadavEyalDesk	https://twitter.com/NadavEyalDesk	1
Ron_Huldai	RavivDrucker	https://twitter.com/RavivDrucker	1
Ron_Huldai	amit_segal	https://twitter.com/amit_segal	1
Ron_Huldai	TelAviv	https://twitter.com/TelAviv	10
Ron_Huldai	talschneider	https://twitter.com/talschneider	1
Ron_Huldai	hootsuite	https://twitter.com/hootsuite	2
Ron_Huldai	iTelAvivYafo	https://twitter.com/iTelAvivYafo	23
Ron_Huldai	yaronsamid	https://twitter.com/yaronsamid	1
Ron_Huldai	ZSosenko	https://twitter.com/ZSosenko	1

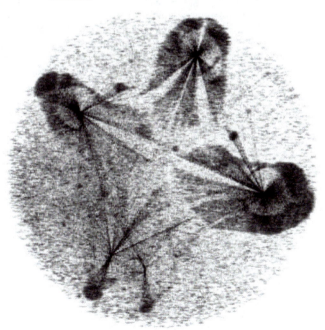

Fig. 112—Example on the city of Tel Aviv: raw dataset of tweets (upper left) into a list of edges with frequency (upper right) into a 3D graph representation (bottom)

Node-Level measures

The node is the first level of analysis of a network. It represents the entity whose you investigate the interaction with others. Different kinds of metrics can be taken on nodes. These will be the basis for the calculation of communities of nodes. In brief, degree centrality determines the most connected node(s), closeness centrality determines the fastest communicating node(s), and betweenness centrality determines the most influential node(s). Centrality measures have been taken for each node of each graph (see Fig. 11)

```
taipei_node_measures.head( )
```

	node	degree	deg_centrality	closeness	eigenvector	betweenness	load
0	Taiwan_Today	70	0.005220	0.220649	1.863455e-02	1.323426e-02	1.336112e-02
1	iingwen	24	0.001790	0.225682	2.129649e-02	4.798539e-03	4.670811e-03
2	KMCTaiwan	1	0.000075	0.000134	-2.833286e-18	0.000000e+00	0.000000e+00
3	Meetup	3	0.000224	0.000224	-2.171845e-18	3.337266e-08	3.337266e-08
4	diode_chain	13	0.000969	0.123291	1.707375e-06	1.286027e-03	1.286027e-03

Fig 113—Preview of node measures files. For each network, each node is evaluated.

Edge-Level measures

The second metric to take on a graph is at an edge level: each node is linked to at least one other, which means that some measures can be taken on this link. To prepare my data for machine learning algorithms to predict links in my networks, I will focus on adapted metrics. Taking these measures takes time and uses lots of computer resources since it has to calculate existing links and all the potential ones, which means the non-existing links between each node of the network. As a result, we get vast records of probabilities. For example, in Tel Aviv, my network contains 214.793.995 edges and non-edges (see Fig. 114).

```
telaviv_resource
```

	0	1	2
0	rothem	irmolicr7	0.000000
1	rothem	MarleeMatlin	0.000000
2	rothem	ChrisBarrett	0.000000
3	rothem	yoavshaham	0.000554
4	rothem	Fredoev	0.000000
...	...	...	...
23937	moovit	cluedont	0.000000
23938	moovit	transantiago	0.000000
23939	moovit	C_Fesen	0.000000
23940	moovit	SophieB_94	0.000000
23941	moovit	jadeepatersonn	0.000000

214793995 rows × 3 columns

Fig 114—Measure of probabilities of link between nodes of edges and non-edges in Tel Aviv.

Network-Level measures

Finally, the third level feature extraction from a network is the network itself. A series of metrics can be taken at the ensemble level, which helps detect similarities such as density and clustering. I will also aggregate the node-level and edge-level measures at the network level using mean, standard deviation, min, and max values for each network. Finally, I will add the number of tweets of followers and the maximum likes received on a tweet to evaluate the relationship between popularity and engagement taken as variables. All in one, I have collected 50 variables (see Fig. 115) on each graph and will look for relationships between them.

network_measures

etweenness_min	betweenness_max	load_mean	load_std	load_min	load_max	num_edges	num_nonedges	size	density	transitivity	edge_connectivity	b
0.0	0.210036	0.000106	0.002972	0.0	0.211673	12924	89894574	12924	0.000144	3.079020e-04	0	
0.0	0.349891	0.000085	0.003420	0.0	0.347741	26533	299718996	26533	0.000089	1.962362e-04	0	
0.0	0.351748	0.000176	0.005109	0.0	0.351872	9983	41027376	9983	0.000243	8.764435e-04	0	
0.0	0.760753	0.000532	0.016457	0.0	0.760753	2446	2951222	2446	0.000828	0.000000e+00	0	
0.0	0.712492	0.000285	0.010937	0.0	0.712153	7993	31406711	7993	0.000254	5.166839e-07	1	
0.0	0.897104	0.000236	0.011206	0.0	0.897022	8193	32687551	8193	0.000251	0.000000e+00	1	
0.0	0.977466	0.000357	0.015309	0.0	0.977174	4287	9016344	4287	0.000475	0.000000e+00	1	
0.0	0.924982	0.000737	0.020919	0.0	0.924876	2489	3071474	2489	0.000810	0.000000e+00	1	
0.0	0.889164	0.000703	0.020278	0.0	0.889164	2620	3386488	2620	0.000773	0.000000e+00	0	

Fig. 115—Network measures files contains 50 variables for each graph.

b. Statistical analysis of social networks:

First of all, I would like to see how the graphs look. To do so, I will use the drawing layout functionality of the network library to apply a node positioning algorithm. I chose the *spring layout*, which uses a *force-directed graph drawing* to position the nodes in a two-dimensional space where all edges are of equal length and have a few crossing edges as possible. It assigns forces among the edges and nodes based on their relative positions and uses them to simulate the motions. I will highlight the two nodes with the highest centrality in red and orange to ease the visual reading of the graph.

In the following figures (see Fig. 116, 117, 118, 119, 120, 121, 122, 123), I will position both the entire graph (left) and the largest subgraph (right) for each city and each stakeholder category. Visualizing the largest subgraphs aside from graphs makes it possible to get an idea of the size and the sparsity of the networks from a quick look. Suppose the full graph allows us to represent the nodes and the spread of the most influential ones. In that case, the largest subgraph deletes all poorly connected elements of the network. It makes the central relationships between nodes clearer. It is handy here about the categorical networks of the stakeholders since we can get a look at the connections between stakeholders between cities.

As we can see, the public sector and the media industry do not have a complete network of networks between cities. In contrast, the private sector (corporate and startups) has the strongest one. Academics and civil society have an existing but weak connection across cities.

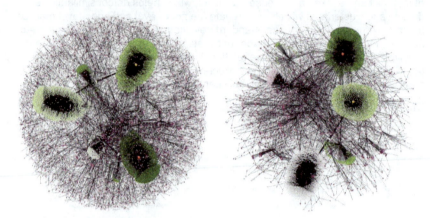

Fig 116—Taipei graph (left) and largest subgraph (right)

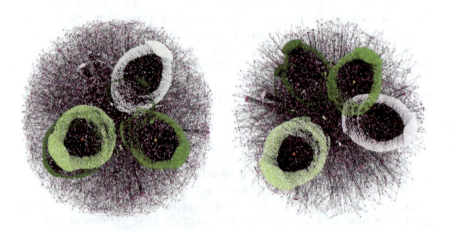

Fig 117—Tel Aviv graph (left) and largest subgraph (right)

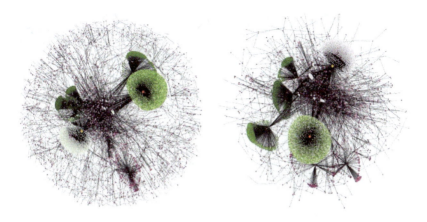

Fig 118—Tallinn graph (left) and largest subgraph (right)

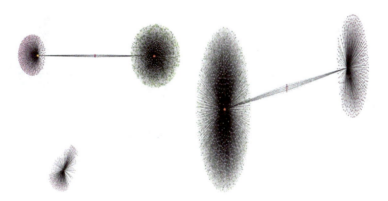

Fig 119—Public sector graph (left) and largest subgraph (right)

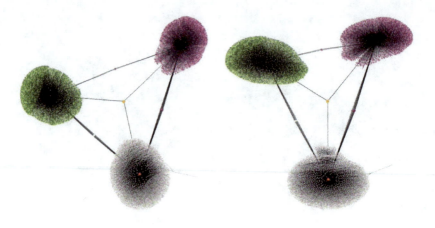

Fig 120—Corporate companies graph (left) and largest subgraph (right)

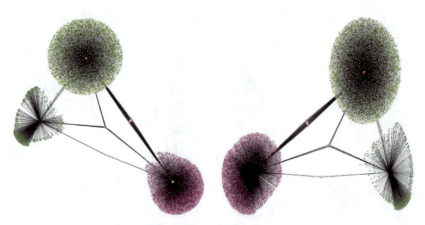

Fig. 121—Startups graph (left) and largest subgraph (right)

Fig 122—Academic sector graph (left) and largest subgraph (right)

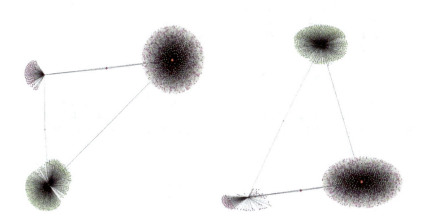

Fig 123—Civil society graph (left) and largest subgraph (right)

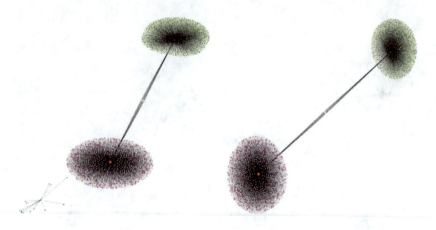

Fig 124—Media industry graph (left) and largest subgraph (right)

From this visualization technique, I can already tell that some networks resist subgraph filtering better: which means they spontaneously built more connections between influent nodes. It can come from a better animation of the sector as whole or similar strategies for digital engagement. As a result, these categories assure a better resilience to edge/node deletion and a better information flow between them. Surprisingly the public sector and the media, which are two professional communicators by definition, lack a connection to resist the largest subgraph filtering. We can argue that they focus instead on local engagement than an international one, while corporate companies and startups are thinking globally to grow their market shares.

Exploratory Data Analysis

From a first look, the number of tweets is correlated with the number of followers, and the maximum number of likes received (see Fig. 125). However, the quantity of data records is not enough (9 networks in total) to validate this assumption at a large scale.

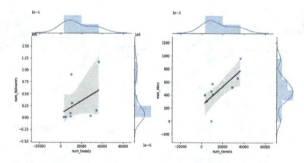

Fig. 125—Nbr. of followers by nbr. of tweets (left) and nbr. of followers by nbr. of likes (right).

Suppose the number of nodes and the number of edges is correlated to the number of tweets, which means that the size of an ego network is proportional to the user's activity (see Fig. 126). In that case, the number of followers is not correlated to the number of nodes, neither to the number of edges nor the size of the network (see Fig. 127). So the size of a network is not helping in terms of popularity. Since the number of connected components and the average shortest path length shows a clear correlation with the number of followers (see Fig. 128), I assume that the most popular users can also spread information more widely, thus being influential on the network whole.

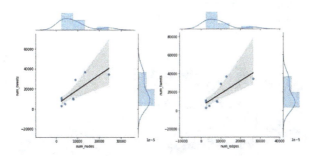

Fig. 126—The nbr. of tweets is correlated to nbr. of nodes (left) and number of edges (right)

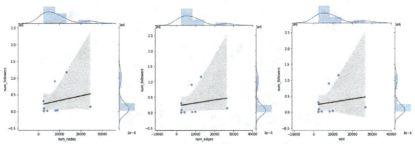

Fig. 127—The nbr. of followers is not correlated to the nbr. of nodes (left) nor to the number of edges (middle) nor to the size of the network (right).

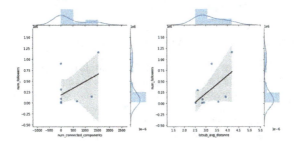

Fig. 128—The nbr. of followers is correlated to the nbr. of connected elements (left) and the average shortest path length (right).

In other words, the popularity on the social network measured with the number of followers or the maximum likes received does not react as expected: it is not systematically related to the engagement level in the network. Other factors may enter into a collision with the performance as an influencer on Twitter. This finding echoes previous assumptions from my research, saying that civil society, for example, is granted more trust than the media industry and corporate companies.

Correlation Analysis

A very polarised heat map (see fig. 129) indicates high positive and negative correlations between variables. From an overall look, I can say that the popularity metrics react together in a positive correlation. These popularity metrics are negatively correlated to all centrality measures (degree, closeness, eigenvector, betweenness, and load centrality) but highly related to the largest subgraph. It means that a well-connected network, rather than a dense one, will give better predictive results.

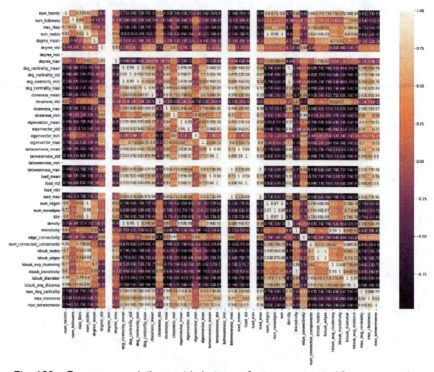

Fig. 129—Pearson correlation matrix between features extracted from my graphs.

Node-level and network-level measures are in a negative relationship. Still, I am not sure how to interpret these results. It might be a consequence of sampling: the more extensive the network of my representatives, the higher node-level scores, and so the lower network-level ones. This could theoretically be balanced by collecting all the relationships inside my cities, but this is practically impossible without an agreement from the social media platforms and a powerful computer.

On another note, the number of tweets (engagement metric) has a better multi-correlation with other variables than the number of followers or the maximum likes received (popularity metrics). This confirms my assumption that the popularity on the network is hardly predictable. The number of connected components and the total degree centrality are well correlated to the other variables, making them essential measures in a machine learning context, where multicollinearity tends to affect the model performance, so feature redundancy reduction is needed. This multicollinearity can be tested through multiple regression analysis.

Regression Analysis

I have run three multiple regression analysis on these three different independent variables:
- Number of tweets (engagement metric)
- Number of connected components (network connectivity metric)
- Maximal degree centrality (node influence metric)

All three achieve an awful performance taken as a unique independent target to predict other variables with a machine learning algorithm (see Fig. 130). It means that none of these variables can be directly expected from the other ones. I will need specific algorithms to make predictions on the network.

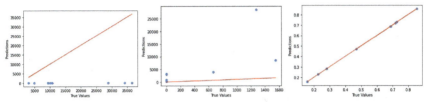

Fig. 130—Predictions of number of tweets (left), number of connected components (centre) and maximal degree centrality (right) from other variables. None achieves a satisfying predictive performance (the right one is too good to be true).

c. Probabilistic inference - Graph-based machine learning

Suppose we accept graphs as an essential means of structuring and analyzing network data about the world. In that case, we shouldn't be surprised to see them being widely used in Machine Learning as a powerful tool that can enable intuitive properties and power many valuable features. The main inferences to do with machine learning on graphs are of three kinds:
- node classification
- link prediction
- association between networks.

These predictive models can have direct applications in community detection, inferences on network evolution, and detection of similarities between networks. First of all, it is needed to prepare the data for it to reduce redundancy and multicollinearity.

Recursive Feature Elimination

As no variables seem to have the capacity to be predicted from the other ones, the recursive feature elimination can't find an optimal number of features other than 1 (the one we try to expect). Thus, there is no way to simplify my variables by combining them without losing the information it contains.

Feature importance

Anyway, a ranking of feature importance from a random forest regressor algorithm confirms that my independent variables have been appropriately chosen from the correlation matrix and the exploratory data analysis (see Fig. 131).

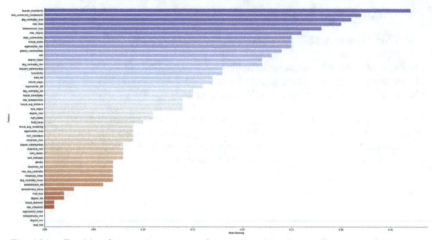

Fig. 131—Ranking feature importance from a Random Forest Regressor algorithm.

Community detection

To test the different methods for community detection on my graphs, I will cross the result of four different algorithms:
- Greedy Modularity algorithm
- Louvain Algorithm
- Maximal Cliques
- Label Propagation.

There are many ways of detecting communities in a network. Still, the most popular method is to use the modularity metric. Modularity measures relative density in a network: a community has a high density with other nodes within its hub but low density with those outsides. Modularity gives a score of how fractious a network is and can partition the web and return individual communities. Very dense networks are often more difficult to split, but most real-life networks are sparse and disconnected. Most community detection algorithms start with selecting the best partition of the web like the Louvain algorithm does in my case.

Greedy Modularity algorithm

This method determines the number of communities in a graph and groups all nodes into subsets based on these communities. There's one set for each group, and the sets contain the names of the people in each group.

I haven't represented the greedy communities visually but simply collected the number of communities detected by this algorithm in my graphs (see Fig. 132). We can see that many sub-groups exist among city networks. Still, the communities of the stakeholder categories are very isolated from one to another. Taipei got 1633 communities detected from the greedy modularity algorithm, Tel Aviv 1404 and Tallinn 726.

```
for l in greedy_communities:
    print(len(l))
```

1633
1404
726
3
3
3
3
3
3

Fig 132—Number of communities detected by the greedy algorithm in my 9 graphs.

Louvain Algorithm

The Louvain community detection algorithm was initially proposed in 2008 as a fast community unfolding method for large networks. This modularity approach tries to maximize the difference between the actual and expected edges in a community. It is working by iterations of the same two steps:
- Local moving of nodes
- Aggregation of the network.

In the first phase, the algorithm assigns a different community to each node of the network. Then for each node, it considers the neighbors and evaluates the gain of modularity by removing the particular node from the current community and placing it in the neighbor's community. The node will be placed in the neighbor's society if the gain is positive and maximized. The node will remain in the same neighborhood if there is no positive gain. The first phase of the Louvain algorithm stops when a local maximum of modularity is obtained. In the second phase, the algorithm builds a new network considering communities found in the first phase as nodes. I have plotted the resulting communities visually (See Fig. 133 and 134). All categorical networks have the exact shape of 3 communities, with different final modularities indicating the tightness of their networks: 0.44 for the public sector, 0.62 for corporate companies, 0.45 for startups, 0.26 for academics, 0.41 for civil society, and 0.43 for media.

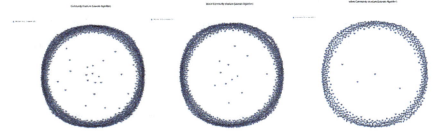

Fig. 133—Taipei has 1609 communities and a final modularity of 0.87 (left), Tel Aviv have 1331 communities and a final modularity of 0.81, Tallinn have 704 communities and a final modularity of 0.77.

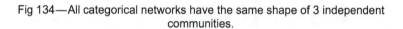

Fig 134—All categorical networks have the same shape of 3 independent communities.

Maximal Cliques

Cliques are one of the basic concepts of graph theory. They are used in many other mathematical problems and constructions on graphs. A clique is a subset of nodes in a graph so that every two distinct vertices in the clique are adjacent. That is, a clique of a graph is a complete subgraph of that graph. A maximal clique is a clique that cannot be extended by including one more adjacent vertex, a clique that does not exist exclusively within the vertex set of a larger clique. The maximal clique algorithm returns all maximal cliques in an undirected graph. For each node, the maximal clique is the largest complete subgraph that contains it. Maximal cliques for each network are visually represented below (see Fig. 135 and 136). Taipei has 12,227 for a total of 12280 communities, Tel Aviv 24,859 for 24,879, and Tallinn 8,857 for 8,868.

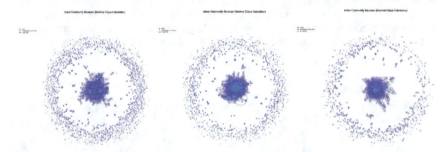

Fig. 135—Maximal cliques of Taipei (left), Tel Aviv (center), and Tallinn (right).

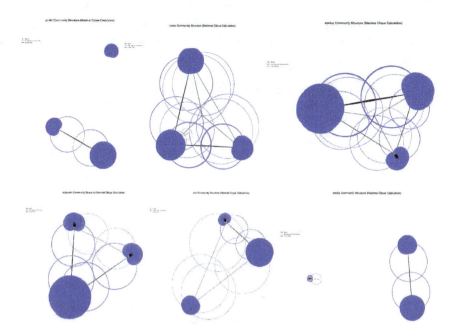

Fig. 136—Maximal cliques of public sector (upper left), corporate companies (upper middle), startups (upper right), academic sector (bottom left), civil society (bottom middle), and media industry (bottom right).

Asynchronous label propagation

A probabilistic semi-supervised machine learning algorithm assigns labels to previously un-labeled data points and then returns the communities detected. The algorithm stops when each node has the title which appears the most frequently in its neighbors. It is said to be asynchronous because each node is updated without updates on the remaining nodes. I haven't represented the results in a visual graph but collected the number of communities for each (see Fig. 137).

```
lpa_communities = [len(custom_asyn_lpa_communities(x)) for x in graphs]
lpa_communities
```

```
[2444, 2844, 1259, 3, 3, 3, 3, 3, 3]
```

Fig 137—Number of communities detected by label propagation on my 9 networks.

Link prediction

In terms of link prediction, I will use the four edge-level measures: familiar neighbors, Jaccard coefficient, resource allocation index, preferential attachment, to train a classifier algorithm of machine learning and compare the performances in predicting which non-edge is likely to be formed based on existing edges. This means determining which network topology allows the best link prediction task. Obviously, in a sparse network, there are much more non-edges than edges, so my dataset suffers imbalance. The first step will consist of balancing the datasets of edges and non-edges by using a downsampling technique. Indeed, considering the significant number of non-edges in a network (remember 214.793.995 edges and non-edges cumulated in Tel Aviv), oversampling the minority class would be impossible.

Downsampling:

Under-sampling, the majority class, can be helpful in big datasets or very imbalanced ones. It will randomly select data points from the majority class to have the same edges and non-edges (see Fig. 138).

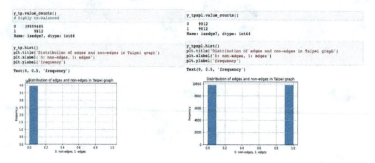

Fig. 138—Number of edges and non-edges before (left) and after (right) downsampling.

Accuracy scores

Accuracy scores are taken on the prediction of links in each network. They can be compared to evaluate which topology allows the best performance. It seems that Tel Aviv gets better performance in the link prediction task (see Fig. 139). It has a better accuracy score and more minor errors. However, the precision score in Tallinn is the best (where the network size is about half of Taipei and Tel Aviv).

	accuracy score	f1 score	roc aux score	recall score	precision score	mean absolute error	mean squarred error	root mean squarred error	r2 score	1/1-R2
Taipei	0.930876	0.930582	0.930909	0.922869	0.938424	0.069124	0.069124	0.262914	0.723501	3.616648
Tel Aviv	0.940136	0.939479	0.940174	0.942797	0.936185	0.059864	0.059864	0.244670	0.760496	4.175304
Tallinn	0.936178	0.935858	0.936221	0.926904	0.944986	0.063822	0.063822	0.252629	0.744708	3.917085
Public	1.000000	1.000000	1.000000	1.000000	1.000000	0.000000	0.000000	0.000000	1.000000	inf
Corpo	0.999791	0.999792	0.999791	1.000000	0.999584	0.000209	0.000209	0.014440	0.999166	1198.996664
Startup	0.999797	0.999798	0.999795	1.000000	0.999596	0.000203	0.000203	0.014262	0.999186	1228.941212
Academic	0.999223	0.999216	0.999230	1.000000	0.998434	0.000777	0.000777	0.027880	0.996891	321.599300
Civil	0.997323	0.997257	0.997321	0.997257	0.997257	0.002677	0.002677	0.051743	0.989284	93.320783
Media	0.998722	0.998723	0.998723	1.000000	0.997449	0.001278	0.001278	0.035749	0.994888	195.624920

Fig 139—Accuracy scores for link prediction algorithm on my graphs.

More insights will be extracted from this social network analysis by comparing the tendencies of each network in relationship with the local experiences recorded in the monographs and the one-to-one interviews of local experts. I will also use the network attributes to build agent-based models of citizen engagement in smart-city. My end goal is to simulate information flows in a web of networks representing my three cities of reference.

10. Computer simulation of citizen engagement and the formation of public opinion.

In my research on Citizen Engagement in Smart-City, I am experiencing how digital tools allow all kinds of inhabitants to participate in decision-making for the future of their city. When using computer simulations such as agent-based models, I intend to learn about the interaction of a crowd of citizens in a complex system of mutual influences like all cities are.

The previous data analysis led to some findings which will help writing the interaction rules among my citizens in the context of a simulation of engagement in their city. The ability to share one's opinion in public and change it in contact with others is correlated. The citizens feeling the most engaged tend to share their opinion in public more quickly. And the total sources of information to shape an opinion is an important variable to detect the highness of engagement in a population of citizens. Opinion mining algorithms combined with natural language processing on tweets allowed me to build a predictive model for public opinion. This makes it possible to rank cities on their citizen engagement dynamic using shared Twitter communication content.

In this study, I will be using NetLogo IDE to simulate the distribution of opinion in a population. Each voter will be influenced by others depending on various simulated behavior. Such social simulations will help us better understand the formation of public opinion.

Problematic:
Does citizen engagement influence the formation of public opinion at a city level?

Hypothesis:
Highly engaged citizens can increase influence over the whole population by gaining power from significant facilities.

Methodology:
An agent-based model (ABM) is a class of computational models for simulating the actions and interactions of autonomous agents (both individual or collective entities such as organizations or groups) to assess their effects on the system as a whole.

In the following study, we will use different models to simulate the formation of public opinion depending on various combinations of citizens' attributes and rules of interaction. Using ABM, we wish to answer these questions:
- What patterns do the models show ?
- How—through what mechanisms—do these patterns come about ?
- How do the patterns change depending on parameter settings ?

The following article has three parts: First, a presentation of the original Voting model from the NetLogo library and its extension. Second, a new model for citizen engagement was built from scratch. Third, data analysis to validate our model with empirical data.

a. The Voting model from NetLogo library

NetLogo is a programming language and Integrate Development Environment for Agent-Based Modelling (also called Multi-Agent Systems). ABM is a class of computational models for simulating the actions and interactions of autonomous agents (both individual or collective entities such as organizations) to assess their effects on the system as a whole. It can be used in a variety of scientific domains like biology, ecology, and social science. NetLogo allows scientists to program tailored models from scratch and proposes a library of validated models developed by its community of users. In this study, I will start using the voting model and then modify it by implementing some features to test specific hypotheses. I will finally develop my model from scratch using the NetLogo programming language.

The Voting model from the NetLogo library is a simple cellular automaton that simulates voting distribution by having each patch take a "vote" of its eight surrounding neighbors, then perhaps change its vote according to the surrounding majority. The simulation is composed of cells (agents) of either Blue or green color, which can represent a different kind of real-life situation where a population is divided in between two opinions:
- one can be FOR or AGAINST any proposition
- one can be a MAC or a WINDOWS user
- one can define its political position as left-wing or right-wing

An agent occupies each cell, and so each agent is surrounded by eight neighboring agents (this cell composition is called Moore Neighbourhood), and even if the software represents the model in a two-dimensional window for easiness, the actual space of our world is coded in a geometrical toroid shape, so there are no borders in our space. Each cell respects the assumption that it has eight neighbors (see Fig. 140). All the agents in the model update their opinion simultaneously, and an agent occupies each cell.

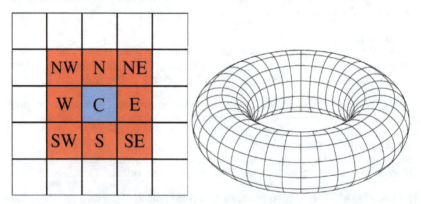

Fig. 140—Moore Neighbourhood cell composition and a Toroid geometrical shape.

The model starts with a random distribution of Green and Blue cells, representing any potential configuration of a population of citizens having one or the other opinion at an initial state. The underlying operation of the model is straightforward: each agent decides in consideration of its neighbors. Depending on the majority of Blue or Green in the surrounding eight cells, an agent will switch to Blue or Green. For example, suppose T=0, a green agent is surrounded by five blue and three green. In that case, such an agent will turn blue at time T=1, according to the surrounding majority. In case of equality in the neighbors: 4 blue and four green, the agent will stick to its previous state. This last parameter can be changed in the model. We will be able to simulate later what changes occur in the voting distribution when agents deliberately choose the opinion of the minority.

What do you think will happen ?
- Will all agents turn the same colour ?
- Will a stable distribution arise after a few or will it keep changing infinitely ?
- Will regular patterns emerge so we will be able to predict which cell will turn Green or Blue from the initial state ?

Running the original model in the look for patterns

When you run the model, you can see that clusters of opinion gradually and more and more arise. Blue cells and Green cells, which were perfectly mixed randomly from the initial state, tend to progressively aggregate by color until a stable distribution emerges where clear boundaries are visible between Blue and Green distribution. This is an elementary example of social self-organization. **A structure has formed from a random state, which is not random anymore** (See Fig. 141).

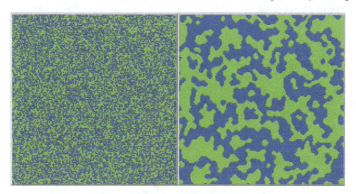

Fig. 141—Initial random distribution of votes (left) distinct structures of distribution (right).

Each time you repeat the process, you'll start with any random state and see that another distribution structure emerges. When we zoom in on a few cells to see what happens, we can observe that in some local places where there are many Green cells at the starting point, all cells will turn green. As a comparison, in some regional areas where there is a majority of Blue cells at the starting point, all cells will turn Blue. Somehow, the final voting distribution is predictable in some local places. Still, the final distribution of votes on the whole system is highly unpredictable. Indeed, the voting behaviors in many areas will depend on unknown intermediary states before the boundaries are set between groups of voters.

To understand what makes a group stable, we need to zoom in on a reducing cluster and observe the last stable configuration. The usual rule for stabilization is: when neighbors present an equal distribution of opinions (4 Blue and 4 Green) so the cells of the area do not change anymore. This is how stability arises in the system (See

Fig. 142). This resulting constant order does not allow us to predict easily from the initial state how the cells will merge and where the borders will be set.

Fig. 142—Stable cluster (left) and stable border configuration (right).

Two significant changes can be made in the parameters from the default version of the model. We will be able to change the switching rule in case of equality of opinions in neighborhoods and reverse the majority rule to ask agents to follow minority positions.

Change vote if tied

The default rule of the model is that when your neighbors show equality of Green and Blue opinions, you will stick to your last state and don't change your opinion anymore. The opposite rule can change this. If your neighbors show equality of Green and Blue opinions, you will systematically change your opinion. This change of parameter creates instability in the system, which results in a noisy equilibrium. Suppose the structures of clusters do not change anymore once they reach a stability point. In that case, the borders keep moving infinitely, giving the impression of vibration on the system. This excitement at the boundaries never stops, and the systems keep being noisy unlimitedly even if globally stable (See Fig. 143). Globally it does not change the scores of distributed opinions. Still, some agents are constantly changing their belief in this configuration.

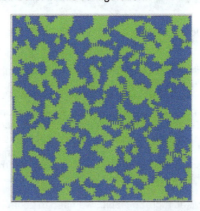

Fig. 143—Unstable borders keeps vibrating indefinitely.

Award close calls to loser

Another default rule of the model is that the agents will always follow the choice of the neighboring majority. This rule can be changed in the model, and we can ask the agents to choose the minority position systematically. With this kind of voting behavior, the results are pretty unexpected. We could imagine that a society of contradictory agents will necessarily result in a constantly changing, fractured world. The exact opposite happens: we first observe structures in the distribution of opinions, with a constant vibration at the borders. Soon, the forms start to aggregate themselves together in a few masses of similar views. But the system does not stop here since he can't reach a potential balance, and at the moment, one color takes a numeral advantage on the other. Once the unbalance becomes clear, the minority does not get back and reduces progressively in a few boiling blots. Suppose a few bubbles of minority opinions randomly split out of the reducing mass. In that case, the system constantly goes to a state where the whole population has turned to a single color, with a few tiny bubbles of minority opinions presenting high instability to their borders (See Fig. 144).

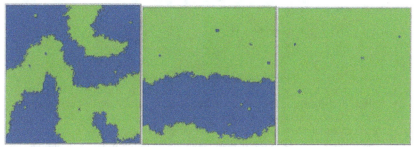

Fig. 144—When agents are asked to take the minority position, one opinion finally take the advantage on the other and embraces the whole population.

However, this constant output can take a very different time to advent since the two classes of voters sometimes cohabit for an extended period. Sometimes the loser class comes back to close equality with the winner. Sometimes it stabilizes between 8000 and 9000 votes against a majority of 13000 to 12000. We can understand from these variations of pictures in the public opinion of our population that from a constantly running democracy, the results of the votes at a particular moment are highly unpredictable and don't say about the poll products at another moment.

Extending the Voting model with more parameters change

I have tested the voting model deeper by varying different parameters settings:

- **Population size**: Are the patterns affected by the total number of voters ?
  In the settings button on the interface of the model (See Fig. 145), we can change the size of the world and the size of the patches. This results in variating the total number of patches (size of the population):
  - max-pxcor and max-pycor and the X and Y axes length
  - Patch size can be changed, it is measured in pixels.
  Original values were : X and Y = 75, Patch size = 3. For example we can try :
  X and Y = 25, patch size = 9. As a result we have the same size of window on the interface but the third of the size of the initial population. After a few tries, I can say that the size of the population does not affect the resulting patterns observed above.

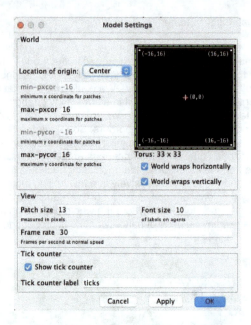

Fig. 145—Interface of model settings

- **Initial distribution**: The system reacts proportionally when it starts with a 50/50 distribution or an unbalanced one: it results in a stable distribution of opinions after a few turns, showing structures among the whole population. The main difference is the overwhelming level of the majority: If at an initial distribution of 60/40, the blue minority remains, it almost does not subsist to a 70/30 initial distribution and disappears from an 80/20 one (See Fig. 146).

Fig. 146—Results from a 60/40 initial distribution (left), 70/30 (centre) and 80/20 (right).

I have been curious to check if there is a combination of parameters to counter the initial imbalance? I tried to give more power of influence to the minorities with the *award-close-calls-to-loser* parameter. If this parameter makes it very unpredictable to guess from a 50/50 distribution which voting preference will take the advantage on the other, a small unbalance in the initial percentage of green make the issue very clear: even if the agents are asked to take the minority position systematically, the initial majority is taking the advantage on the whole population, which will turn uniformly to the majoritarian choice after some time (See Fig. 147). It seems that there is no way to counterbalance an initial skewed distribution of two opinions of a population.

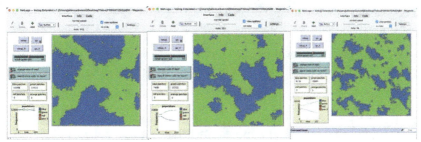

Fig. 147— With an initial balanced distribution (left) the result is not predictable. From 55/45 it is very clear already that the whole population will turn to the majority choice (centre). When increasing initial unbalance (60/40), the population will turn more quickly to the majority (right).

- **Four voting options**: how does the model react to a multi-class of voters ? This has been a trickier move since the model has been encoded on a numerical base: voters class from the original model was encoded as 0 = green and 1 = blue, and voters behaviors regarding its neighboring majority are built on sums of adjacent values:

  if total > 5, set vote 1 (means more 1 than 0 in 8 neighbours)
  - if total < 3, set vote 0 (means more 0 than 1 in 8 neighbours)
  - if total = 4, if change-vote-if-tied? set vote (1- vote)
  - if total = 5, ifelse award-close-calls-to-loser? set vote 1, set vote 0
  - if total = 3, ifelse award-close-calls-to-loser? set vote 0, set vote 1.

Creating a 4 class model on this numerical base asked me to make more calculations. I couldn't avoid all blind spots: some sums allow me to predict with certainty which value was majoritarian, some others could result from different combinations of values. I created 4 classes of voters like that: 0 = green, 1 = blue, 2 = red and 3 = orange (See Fig. 148).

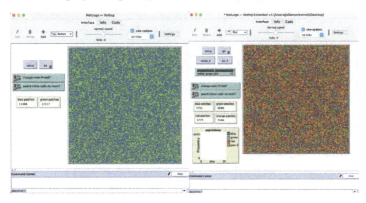

Fig. 148—Interfaces of the original Voting model (left) and my extension (right).

The result which comes out constantly is a majority of red. One acceptable explanation for this issue is the normal distribution of the probabilities: the sums of numbers of various sizes will always tend to their mean. Our system, full of random 0, 1, 2, and 3, necessarily tends to be close to value 2, attributed to the color red.

The two optional parameters of the system need to be adapted to the new opinion

configuration, for not resulting only in green and blue.
- **change-vote-if-tied** rule will ask the agents to take a new random colour in case of a blind spot in determining the neighbouring distribution.
- **award-close-calls-to-loser** rule will ask the loser to systematically take the second closest value to the mean.

The change-vote-if-tied rule is not changing anything to the issue: randomness in the change of colors results in the same advantage for the mean value. And the award-close-calls-to-loser does not unbalance the system but gives some more potential for the Blue (second mean value) to express itself. Both result in a stable opinion distribution after a few turns (See Fig. 149).

Fig. 149—The 4 class model constantly turns to the advantage of the colour which has its value the closest to the mean of all values (left). The change-vote-if-tied parameter does not change anything to this pattern (centre) but the award-close-calls-to-loser gives more room for expression of the second closest value to the mean (right).

I have concluded that this adaptation of an existing model can't produce more satisfying results and will not answer my research question with lots of certainties. To get some more insights, I will need to code the rules differently than on a numbers and sums basis by creating a categorical model, rather than a numerical, to observe the results of different categories of voters interacting. Coding a tailored model from scratch seems to be the best solution to test our hypothesis on contemporary democracy and citizenship.

b. Modelling Citizen Engagement from scratch

Building a model from scratch demands to think from its broader background theory to its most detailed parameters to find the best way to combine Theory, Data, and Experienced Reality. My model validity depends on its capacity to answer these questions: "Why do citizens engage? How do they interact with each other? What kind of benefit do they gain from engagement?" My previous research already gave some potential answers. The survey study on civic hackers presented in part 1 of this thesis can be re-interpreted through the Power and Status theory, which asserts that all human interaction can be reduced to those two fundamental dimensions.

The American sociologist Theodore D. Kemper gave this framework a new continuity: the "Power-Status theory of emotions" confirms the first and extends it to all human emotions. And this cross-cultural perspective looks pretty relevant in my case. In my survey study on the motivation of volunteer civic hackers, I found that *"Self-fulfillment: feeling good about what I do"* was the most common source of inspiration whether respondents were Americans, Taiwanese, or Russians. Combined with the idea of *"Contributing to the success of my organization,"* while *"Networking," "Up-skilling"* and *"Achieving a great work"* are three constant personal goals behind engagement, it says that the motivation of civic hackers finds a perfect echo in the Power and Status theory. Volunteer civic-hackers engaged to be part (networking, contributing to the success) of status-worthy groups (civic hackers communities) from which members receive a status-reward (self-fulfillment, performance), which can be augmented by a gain of power (upskilling, additional responsibilities) and the inspiration by a leader.

Thus my agents will gain some social reward and facilities which confers them some advantage compared to others. I also called my previous research on citizenship and democracy to describe the context of my model purpose best. Suppose an overall political apathy and a disinterest for political participation appear as a constant of contemporary democracies due to a growing feeling of inequality in the capacity to be heard by decision-makers and a resulting loss of trust the people grant to their electives and official media. In that case, some interesting concepts are introduced in the digital perspective for future democracies. The *post-democracy* conceptualized by Colin Crouch in 2000 designates the current state of the oldest democratic regimes where powerful minority interests have become far more active than the mass of ordinary people in making the political system work for them. The description of the *upcoming citizens* by Vincent Tiberj in 2017 depicts somewhat distant citizenship in contemporary democracies where a vast majority of well-understanding citizens keep far from traditional ways of political engagement but are very reactive to turn themselves in temporary powerful movements to engage spontaneously for issues that matter to them. My model will simulate these dynamics of the formation of public opinion, where a few highly engaged ones will influence a whole apathetic population with a neutral sentiment.

Composition of the Citizen Engagement model

The model composition is usually presented through an Environment-Rules-Agents (ERA) scheme (see Fig. 150).

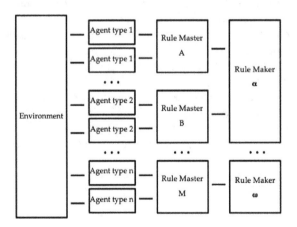

Fig.150—The Environment-Rules-Agents framework to present ABM.

- My environment is a geometrical toroid world with no borders, representing any artificial city hosting no spatial relationships but social ones.
- My agents are citizens of either positive/neutral/negative opinion about any kind of topic of public interest. An engagement-score and a social status are also attributed

to them.
- The rules of interactions are that citizens talk to each other in order to influence the opinion of peers, gain engagement points and social status, which both confer an increased influence over peers.

The citizen engagement model includes an input of empirical data to set up real-life combinations of citizen attributes collected from case studies in Taipei (Taiwan), Tel Aviv (Israel), and Tallinn (Estonia). The database can be extended in the future to simulate other smart-city contexts and compare the formation of public opinion between different existing cities. In the following study, I am using a manual setup to experiment with different plausible scenarios. Each agent has attributed some initial parameters:

- **opinion**: a random value between -1: very negative and 1: very positive, with a majority of neutral opinions (50%). This opinion represents any topic of public interest.

- **engagement score**: a variable inspired from the combination of variables of my previous studies pre-determine the social behavior of the agent. Each agent can be randomly more or less engaged from the setup. The manual version allows the user to choose the quantity of highly engaged citizens at the simulation start. The engagement level is represented by a value between 0: not engaged and 1: very engaged. Highly engaged citizens have a value > 0.75.

- **social-status**: equally starts at 1 for all agents. Then, each time an agent engages with another, the one with higher social status gains one point of social status. If both have the same social status, so both win one point.

Engagement score and social status are both rewards given to citizens for their engagement. They can confer them an advantage in the influence of others' opinion by two different facilities :

- **vision**: An engagement score above 75% results in a better engagement experience by the agent, which confers an extended vision. With this feature, the highly engaged citizen can contact another twice farther than the usual distance.

- **speed**: The increase of social status increases the speed of agent moves in the world. By moving faster in the model, he can get in touch with more peers than those with lower social status.

To be more realistic, each time an agent walks in to look for a peer to talk with, engagement scores and social status are decreasing. So the benefits are attached to them. To keep influential, an agent has to engage the most as possible! On the following flowchart (see Fig. 151), you can see a diagram representing the whole model process.

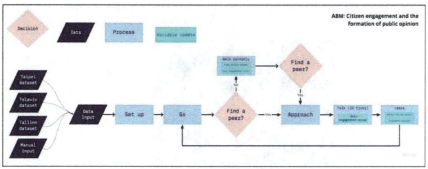

Fig. 151: Flowchart representation of the citizen engagement model.

Regular Patterns from different scenarios:

Experimenting with the Citizen Engagement model consisted in identifying the earliest insights which can be deducted from regular patterns. It needs to be taken carefully because each of these constants says at the same time a potential behavior of real-life societies and a technical result of the model parameter.

- After some time, a sentiment (positive or negative) takes advantage of the other. It ends up turning the whole population to its side.
- The final result is susceptible to slightly unbalanced opinion distribution at the setup.
- Engagement score and social status facilities have the potential to reverse an initial unbalance.
- Engagement score and social status took individually both increase the opinion formation. Still, they don't constantly get a better result when combined.
- The initial percentage of highly engaged citizens affects the formation of public opinion. It has the potential to reverse an initial unbalance. However, it is not regular: some values can reach an optimal speed in forming opinions while others get worse results.

As you can see from the following illustration (see Fig. 152), our model interface integrates different sliders and on-off buttons, allowing the user to simulate different combinations of features.

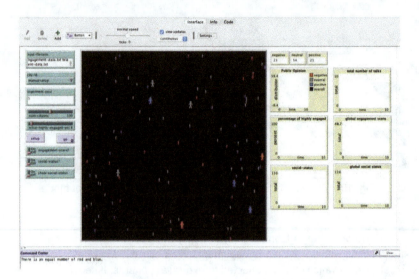

Fig. 152—Citizen Engagement model interface

In order to identify these patterns I have simulate different scenarios with manual settings :

1. **Opinion influence without facilities:** the result is pre-determined by the initial imbalance of red/blue. Even when we simulate a similar number of red and Blue at the beginning, but the neutral opinions are slightly skewed to positive or negative, the majority opinion will take advantage of the other, and the whole population will turn to a single opinion. In my model's parameters, it took 7965 ticks (unit of time) to form.

2. **Opinion influence with engagement score:** For some time, the result keeps unpredictable: with a gain of engagement score and the related extended vision facility, there is a possibility for a minority opinion to take the final position. Of course, and I should dig into it to identify the threshold values. From an initial equivalent number of red and blue, an opinion takes more easily the whole population when engagement score is enabled. It has been 6327 ticks for this time. However, the unpredictable minority/majority challenges at the beginning can lower or higher the result.

3. **Opinion influence with highly-engaged citizens at the setup:** As said above, different model combinations show no linear relationship between the level of highly engaged citizens at the setup and the efficiency of opinion formation. On the contrary, some initial percentages of highly engaged people can increase the model performance while others significantly decrease it. We will take a deeper look into it in the following data analysis.

4. **Opinion influence with social-status:** from initial equity in the distribution of social status, some agents will rapidly win a higher social status, and the related speed moves attached to it. This will significantly increase the formation of public opinion. In my model's parameters, it took 3897 ticks. Twice less than without any facility.

5. **Opinion influence with engagement score and social status :** When

combining both facilities, the formation of public opinion does not get better efficiency than in the social status only scenario. It took 3993 ticks with my models' parameters. There are two explanations for this: the facilities are not parameter correctly, and I should try different gain/lose values to normalize the effect of each facility on the society at scale. Or, this result of the combination of facilities is a natural reaction of the model, where engagement score and social status, which are not attributed to the same agents at the initial setup, tend to balance each other to produce a fairer society.

So far, the most influential variable on the formation of public opinion is the social status, which gives an increased speed to the agents when moving to a peer to talk with. The combination of engagement score and social status, which confers both an extended vision and increased speed, does not significantly improve the spread of majority opinion.

c. Statistical analysis

My first intention was to implement the NetLogo extension called PyNetLogo, which allows programmers to directly run their NetLogo model in a Python programming language, ideal for data analysis. Sadly the available PyNetLogo version was not yet compatible with my setup.

BehaviorSpace is an integrated software of the NetLogo programming environment. It allows users to run different experiments in a row, simulating some variable parameters in parallel, and collect data in a sheet format. This process of systematically varying the model's settings and recording the results of each model run is sometimes called "parameter sweeping." It lets you explore the model's "space" of possible behaviors and determine which combinations of settings cause the behaviors of interest.

Sensitivity Analysis—Causal relationships between input/output

Sensitivity analysis is the study of how the uncertainty in the output of a model can be divided and allocated to different sources of uncertainty in its inputs. The process of recalculating outcomes under alternative assumptions to determine the impact of a variable under sensitivity analysis can be helpful in a range of purposes such as testing the robustness of the results of a model, an increased understanding of the relationships between input and output variables, or simply calibrating complex models.

Model Validation—Closeness to reality

The model validation is the task of confirming that the outputs are acceptable concerning the empirical data. In other words, it consists of guaranteeing that the insights from the simulation have enough fidelity to the real-life phenomena we were investigating through the model.

The Citizen Engagement model already integrates different plots on its interface to visually follow different outputs. However, I have used my python environment and generated further correlation analysis and linear regression techniques to dig more in detail into the data. In short, it shows that the total engagement score of the population is correlated with the total number of talks between citizens, which attests somehow that the model behaves like it should: increasing individual engagement scores when two citizens talk to each other and lowering it when they walk without getting in touch with no one. Same for the total social status of the population.

As we've said about the regular patterns of different scenarios above, it is visually represented in the following illustration (see fig. 153). As you can see, the formation of public opinion without facilities (blue) takes twice more time than the best performance with social status and social status combined (green and red, respectively). The engagement score as the only facility still accelerates the model performance significantly. We can see the social status and social status combined with the engagement score because the first one takes a bit more time to accelerate. In contrast, the second one accelerates faster but slows at the end of the simulation and achieves a slightly longer performance.

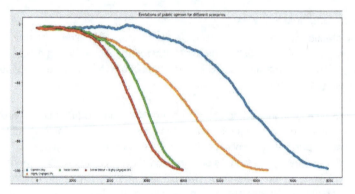

Fig. 153—speed of the formation of opinion in the different scenarios 1 (blue) 2 (orange) 4 (red) and 5 (green).

Otherwise, the linear regression accuracy calculated on a different series of simulations with an initial percentage of highly engaged citizens at 4%, 8%, 12%, and 50% reveals the relationship between this variable and the efficiency of the formation of public opinion is not linear. It is neither predictable (see Fig. 154).

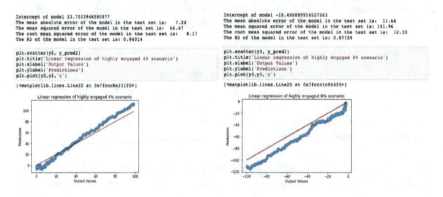

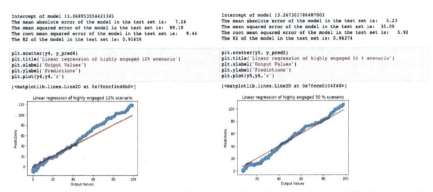

Fig. 154—Linear regression with 4%(upper left), 8% (upper right), 12% (bottom left) and 50% (bottom right) of initial highly engaged citizens.

Curious to better master this unpredictable result, I've been testing the performance of the model with all initial highly engaged percentages (5% scale) without the social status facility (see Fig.155) and with it (see Fig.156). It appears that some starting values like 25%, 35%, and 70% achieve a twice better performance than 30% and even more than the worst 65% without the social status facility. Another observation about comparing results between the opinion formation with and without social status is that this facility seems to normalize the model and make it more controlled and predictable. It decreases the differences of performance between populations with a different initial percentage of highly engaged.

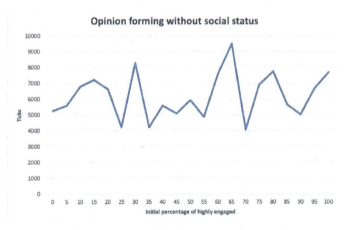

Fig.155 - Without social status facilities, 25, 35 and 70% of highly engaged increase significantly the speed of the formation of the public opinion.

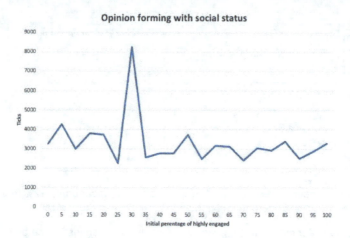

Fig.156 - With social status facilities, the speed of the formation of public opinion is globally better controlled, but there is a big gap of result at 30% of highly engaged citizens.

This last finding confirms our assumption that social status and engagement score tend to balance each other to create a fairer society. However, there are many rooms to maneuver to master the Citizen Engagement model at its full potential and lots of possibilities of features and political contexts to simulate from it.

It is a powerful tool for testing the probability of different hypotheses from samples more intuitively and interactively than most inferential statistics methods. This makes ABM a solid plan for prospective study, including a complex intertwined mix of dependent variables. At the same time, this method will help me fine-tune my definition of a highly engaged citizen developed in my previous machine learning models by testing the impact of different variable combinations on the formation of public opinion.

This model has been developed in two weeks in a 1-month program to learn ABM, and I'm already pretty satisfied with the early results. To make it better, I would suggest normalizing and re-parameter the facilities, master the experiment-seed feature to fix the "random" unbalanced distribution of opinions at the setup, and identify more threshold values in the model patterns. The fundamental research would also benefit from getting an answer to the question "Does engagement score and social status balance each other in the creation of a fairer society?" and to finalize the empirical data input to simulate different existing cities in the world.

11. Collective dynamics of decision-making in Smart-City with multi stakeholder engagement.

In the following Agent-Based Model, I integrate data from all previous studies of my research: survey, opinion mining, and social network analysis to represent six categories of stakeholders owning different levels of the same attributes in network behaviors. The six categories of stakeholders are the public sector, corporate companies, startups, academic research, civil society, and media. I already spotted that the popularity indicators are not directly correlated to the activity on the social networks. It suggests that the social reward from the other users does not follow a systematic rule, and some external factors might affect social popularity. In the following computer simulation, six representatives of these categories will try to influence the opinion of a population of undecided users.

The Stakeholder Engagement model observes how one can take advantage of others and how it potentially affects public opinion. It has been coded in Python. In my previous research, I found that civil society, for example, was granted more social reward proportionally than the professionals such as corporate companies or media. This made a perfect echo to the statement from former US senator Lloyd Bentsen when it used the name of the synthetic grass brand *Astroturfing* to qualify the fake grassroots initiatives orchestrated by professionals willing to benefit from the high credibility conferred to citizen movements in public opinion. However, all stakeholders are professional organizations that learn how to use social networks most beneficially and build strategies to adapt their communication behavior to their followers. To simulate the stakeholders' behaviors most accurately, I have integrated all the data collected for my previous studies to choose the best combination of them into profiling attributes of my different stakeholders. Five parameters have been built from nineteen variables out of three sources of data collection. Crossing the sources in a data collection process is a way to maximize the data quality and ensure the validity of a research model. These combined variables have been integrated as input parameters to my model, reflecting the capacity of each node to influence its neighbors in the formation of an opinion about any random idea. Agents receive an initial thought from the model interface. The ones presenting a view will try to influence the undecided ones.

Purpose of the model:

The stakeholder Engagement model experiments the power of influence of different stakeholder categories in forming public opinion on a social network.

Hypothesis:
- Network topology has an impact on public opinion formation.
- Some stakeholders have more power to influence the public opinion of a population in the direction of their interest is an assumption from my social network analysis that echoes the description of post-democracy.
- No single stakeholder can lead an urban project without the support of other categories of stakeholders, as pointed out in the survey study to the Civil engineer's Association of Finland.
- There are strategic positions in the network, which significantly increases the chances of one stakeholder to spread its opinion to the whole network.

- A conspiracy scenario saying that a coalition of professional stakeholders can reverse the opinion of a population must be wrong.

Methodology:

I already told a lot about agent-based models in the previous chapters. In short, ABM is computer simulations used for different research purposes to test inferences at a system scale, outside of the samples of empirical data. It consists of a distributed Artificial Intelligence among a set of interacting agents. Data can be exported and analyzed in variations of size, time, space, and other variables that can be set up manually.

a. Data Integration

Data integration involves combining data residing in different sources and providing users with a unified view of them. It becomes significant in various internet-based scientific research as much as the volume of the data becomes essential. The data being integrated must be received from heterogeneous databases and transformed into a single coherent data file that provides an overview of a transversal topic.

To simulate the ability of stakeholders to influence the decision-making at a society scale, I have been using three different data sources: survey, opinion mining, social network analysis, combined in four attributes:
- **engagement:** describes the networking activity
- **trustability:** represents the level of trust one is granted by the others
- **influenceability:** tells how much one is sensitive to others' opinion
- **recovery:** is the capacity of someone to recover their initial opinion
Influenceability is a constant value, while engagement and trustability vary along with the simulation, depending on the agent activity. Recovery is stable in itself but under the influence of the experience gained each time an agent recovers from an impact. The more an agent is experienced, the more easily it can recover its initial opinion.

Survey

I have been collecting 122 participants to a survey study on citizen engagement in my 3 case study cities. Each of these 366 participants said to feel part of one of my stakeholder categories, which allowed me to extract profiling attributes from survey variables.
- The engagement score from my ranking model for citizen engagement in smart-city is integrated into the engagement attribute.
- The quality of relationship others say to have with a category is integrated into the trustability parameter, together with the fact that others say to be influenced by it.
- Meeting citizens with other opinions online, the total number of meeting places, and the easiness to change its view, are integrated into the influenceability calculation.
- The total number of sources of information, the total social media used, the total influencers are used for combining a recovery capacity.

Opinion Mining

I have collected the tweets of 1 representative of each stakeholder category in my three cities.

- The number of tweets has been used as a metric of network engagement, the same as the average number of tokens in tweets and the subjectivity score.
- The number of followers and the maximum number of likes received has been integrated into the trustability calculation.
- The number of followings of each representative has been integrated into the influenceability score.

Social Network Analysis

The same representatives have been used for the social network analysis. I have been collecting their followings, the likes they gave, the profiles they have been replying to, and extracted the profiles they mention in their tweets. As a result, I get a network of their engagement over their city.

Different measures have been extracted from these networks:
- The number of nodes has been combined into the network engagement
- The closeness centrality means and the maximum closeness, which both translates the ability of a node to spread information in its network, has been used to complete the trustability score.
- The maximum node degree has been integrated into the recovery score.

I have been using means to calculate the stakeholder parameters from my three cities of reference. Combining variables from the three data sources from three different cities gives me a pretty representative overview of stakeholders' profiles. Since I want to observe the influence of professional stakeholders on a network of undetermined nodes, I have been creating a class called "undetermined," which is attributed to the average values of all participants taken on the source files. The results can already be appreciated with bare eyes (see Fig. 157). Corporate companies are the most engaged in networking. The startups get an impressive recovery capacity. The public sector has the highest trustability, while the academics have the lowest one with civil society and undetermined. Civil society has the highest influenceability score.

	category	engagement	trustability	influenceability	recovery
0	public	0.57	0.53	0.59	0.70
1	corpo	0.75	0.49	0.68	0.73
2	startup	0.69	0.29	0.68	0.97
3	academic	0.49	0.20	0.65	0.75
4	civil	0.43	0.21	0.69	0.72
5	media	0.50	0.23	0.65	0.71
6	undetermined	0.49	0.21	0.53	0.63

Fig. 157—Model parameters with stakeholder profiles from integrated data.

Giving the first look at these parameters, I can already invalidate the hypothesis that civil society has more power of influence since it is granted more trustability than professionals may be accurate but not validated at a network level: professional users globally have more opportunity to building an extensive and dense network, to adopt the best strategy of communication, which tends to balance their lack of trustability in the public opinion. This strategy must be good to ease the emergence of new influential nodes in an existing network. So even if hiding professional interests behind a civil movement or unaffiliated citizens, it might not have a long-term effect once the node network has emerged and stabilized to a professional scale.

b. Agent-Based Modelling in Python

I have chosen to code it into the Python programming language for this new Agent-Based Model at the difference from my last one. Suppose NetLogo is the most used programming language for Agent-Based Modelling. Suppose it is pretty easy to learn and has the most prominent model library. In that case, I feel that it is too much nested into its academic niche and that ABM would benefit from being more popular among the data scientist community.

It was challenging for me to choose Python rather than NetLogo for this last model because I knew I would face a crucial lack of resources. Python has a vast, growing, evolving community support worldwide, and AI gets much attention from mainstream audiences. Still, I also wanted to push my Python skills forward, and that was enough motivation.

Mesa framework

Mesa framework allows users to create agent-based models using build-in core components (such as spatial grids and agent schedulers) or customized implementations, visualize them using a browser-based interface, and analyze their results using Python's data analysis tools. We will go through a few steps for you to understand better how ABM in Python goes.

Setting up the model

To begin writing the model code, we start with two core classes:

- one for the overall model, which holds the model-level attributes, manages the agents and handles the global level of our model. Each model will contain multiple agents, all of which are instantiations of the agent class.

- one for the agents, which contains agents' attributes and rules of behaving at each unit of time.

Adding time scheduler

Time in most agent-based models moves in steps. At each step of the model, one or more of the agents — usually all of them — are activated and take their action, changing internally and interacting with one another or the environment. The scheduler is a particular model component that controls the order in which agents are activated. I use random activation in my model, which starts all the agents once per step, in random order.

Adding space

Most ABM has a spatial element: agents moving around and interacting with nearby neighbors. The space added to this model is one of a network of nodes. Each agent of my model will be added to a node of the network, hosting different interaction properties with neighboring nodes. Instead of interacting with random nodes of the graph, my agents will interact with agents they are connected with.

Setting up rules of behaving

In the Stakeholder Engagement model, an initial opinion will be attributed to each agent. We want the agents with a solid statement to influence the agents having a neutral sentiment. Thus at each step, agents are asked to:

- **Check Neighbours**: an agent as neighboring nodes linked to other nodes in a graph. This step creates lists of neighboring nodes for each agent and sub-sets them depending on the neighbors' opinion.

- **Try to influence**: The agents with a negative opinion (<-0.5) or a favorable opinion (> 0.5) will try to control their neighbors if the neighboring agent presents a neutral opinion (-0.5< x < 0.5) the agent influences it and gets some engagement points. If the neighboring agent shows the same view as trying to exploit it, he makes less effort, so it gets fewer engagement points. If the neighboring agent presents an opposite opinion, they battle in a debate. The one having the most decisive idea will win the argument and influence the other. It will collect the most engagement points, while the one who lost the debate will lose trustability. The engagement points won depending on the influenceability of the neighbor, so the more a neighbor is influenceable, the minor engagement point the influencer receives. The influence of the opinion of the other is depending on one's engagement and trustability.

- **Recover from influence**: when an agent's opinion is different from its initial opinion, it will try to recover its initial opinion depending on its experience and recovery capacity. Each time one manages to recover from an influence, one wins experience points depending on its influenceability.

- **Rescale values**: to avoid nonsense numbers, I set a limit to -1 and 1 in the opinion values. So agents are limited to a very negative (-1) or very positive (1) opinion. Same for experience and engagement, which can't overpass one, and trustability can't be decreased under 0.01.

Collecting data

Suppose we want to know the opinion of each agent at each step. In that case, we need to handle data collection and storage to make it available for further analysis.

The data collector stores three categories of data: model-level variables, agent-level variables, and tables (which are a catch-all for everything else). Model- and agent-level variables are added to the data collector along with a function for collecting them. Model-level collection functions take a model object as an input. In contrast, agent-level collection functions take an agent object as an input. Both then return a value computed from the model or each agent at their current state.

Setting up a batch run

To reach some hypothesis validation, you won't usually run the model once. Still, multiple times, with fixed parameters to find the overall distributions the model generates, and with varying parameters to analyze how they drive the model's outputs and behaviors. The BatchRunner also requires an additional variable running for the MoneyModel class. This variable enables conditional shut-off of the model once a condition is met. We instantiate a BatchRunner with a model class to run and two dictionaries: one of the fixed parameters (mapping model arguments to values) and one of the varying parameters (mapping each parameter name to a sequence of values for it to take). The BatchRunner also argues for how many model instantiations to create and run at each combination of parameter values and how many steps to run each instantiation. Unlike the DataCollector, it won't collect the data at every step of the model, but only at the end of each run.

Building a model interface

To watch the model run step after step, we will need to create an interactive interface. In Mesa, visualization is done in a browser window, using JavaScript to draw the different things visualized at each step of the model. To do this, Mesa launches a small web server, which runs the model, turns each step into a JSON object (essentially, structured plain text), and sends those steps to the browser. The visualization is the build-up of different modules :

- interactive model parameters: to play with variable input and simulate different scenarios
- visualization window of the model: to see the agents behaving in real-time.
- chart of variables: to follow the evolution of target variables step by step
- reset/start/stop buttons in the header: to control the model run.

Model Interface

Visualizing the agents asks to write the agents' portrayal, in which you define the shape, size, color of the agents. It also needs to instantiate a canvas network to host the agents and determine the width and color of the links between agents. Finally, this is how my model interface looks like (see Fig. 158).

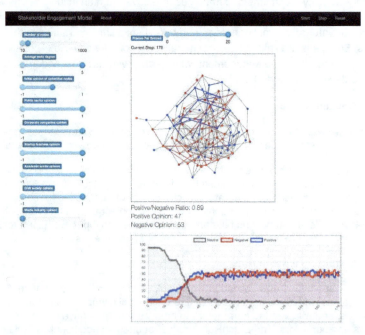

Fig. 158—The Stakeholder Engagement model interface has an interactive setup (left column), a real time visualisation of the network state (centre window) and real-time variable recording (bottom graph)

c. Model Validation

The average node degree directly influences the graph connectivity. With a moderate node degree of 1, the network is sparse and not mostly connected. At 3, it is denser with a few remaining unconnected nodes. At 5, it is much thicker and presents almost no chance for unconnected nodes (see Fig. 159).

Fig. 159—Average node degrees of 1 (left), 3 (centre) and 5 (right) impact network connectivity.

- In the formation of opinion, clusters appear, which stabilize sub-group opinion between nodes. The whole population never turns to a single opinion: a few neutral or opposite ideas always remain. Before a threshold value of average node degree between 3 and 4, no statement takes a dominant advantage over the other ones (see Fig. 160).
- With the average node degree at 2, it takes a long time and many tries for a stakeholder to fully convert a neutral user to a strong opinion. But an increase in average node degree will increase the speed of the formation of opinion to a stable state.
- The average node degree increases the speed of opinion formation. It decreases the proportion of neutral or opposite remaining and allows domination of one opinion on the others. Before a threshold value between 2 and 3 average node degrees, positive and negative tends to stabilize at an equivalent rate (see Fig. 160).

The hypothesis saying that network topology has an impact on opinion formation is validated!

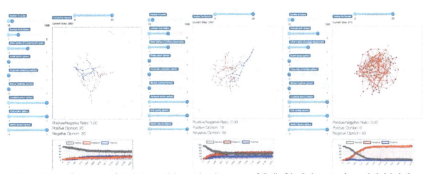

Fig. 160—Spread of opinion with node degree of 2 (left), 3 (centre) and 4 (right).

- Some stakeholders have more chances than others to turn the whole population into their opinion. So even if we start with three positive and three negative stakeholders, depending on who has what opinion, the entire population will not turn out the same (see Fig. 161).

The hypothesis saying that some stakeholders have more power of influence on public opinion is validated!

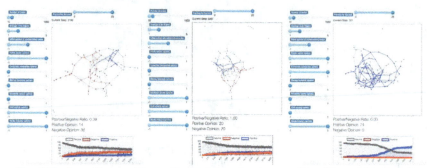

Fig. 161 - 3 positive and 3 negative opinion at setup result in different final result depending on the ones spreading it

- When a single stakeholder has a contrary opinion than the other ones, its chance to influence the whole network depends on its attributes, of course, giving him more or less power of influence on the others, but also its position in the network. Indeed, the more central it is, the more chances it has to take advantage of the network or to maintain a significant minority nested in the whole network (see Fig. 162).

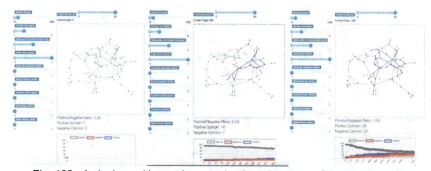

Fig. 162 - A single positive node can take the advantage of 5 negative ones depending on their position in the network.

The hypothesis saying that there are strategic positions in the network, which significantly increases the chances of one stakeholder to spread its opinion to the whole network, is validated!

- A regular conspiracy theory says that professional interests manipulate people. I have attributed an opinion to all population nodes and the contrary view to the six categories of stakeholders in my model. Despite their advantageous parameters, which give them an increased power of influence,

c. Model Validation

The average node degree directly influences the graph connectivity. With a moderate node degree of 1, the network is sparse and not mostly connected. At 3, it is denser with a few remaining unconnected nodes. At 5, it is much thicker and presents almost no chance for unconnected nodes (see Fig. 159).

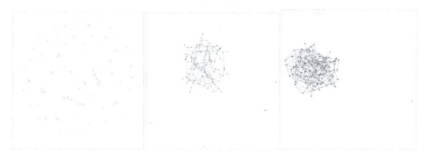

Fig. 159—Average node degrees of 1 (left), 3 (centre) and 5 (right) impact network connectivity.

- In the formation of opinion, clusters appear, which stabilize sub-group opinion between nodes. The whole population never turns to a single opinion: a few neutral or opposite ideas always remain. Before a threshold value of average node degree between 3 and 4, no statement takes a dominant advantage over the other ones (see Fig. 160).
- With the average node degree at 2, it takes a long time and many tries for a stakeholder to fully convert a neutral user to a strong opinion. But an increase in average node degree will increase the speed of the formation of opinion to a stable state.
- The average node degree increases the speed of opinion formation. It decreases the proportion of neutral or opposite remaining and allows domination of one opinion on the others. Before a threshold value between 2 and 3 average node degrees, positive and negative tends to stabilize at an equivalent rate (see Fig. 160).

The hypothesis saying that network topology has an impact on opinion formation is validated!

Fig. 160—Spread of opinion with node degree of 2 (left), 3 (centre) and 4 (right).

181

- Some stakeholders have more chances than others to turn the whole population into their opinion. So even if we start with three positive and three negative stakeholders, depending on who has what opinion, the entire population will not turn out the same (see Fig. 161).

The hypothesis saying that some stakeholders have more power of influence on public opinion is validated!

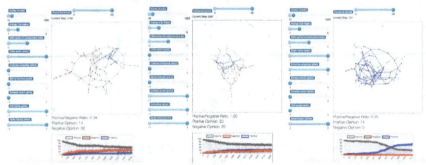

Fig. 161 - 3 positive and 3 negative opinion at setup result in different final result depending on the ones spreading it

- When a single stakeholder has a contrary opinion than the other ones, its chance to influence the whole network depends on its attributes, of course, giving him more or less power of influence on the others, but also its position in the network. Indeed, the more central it is, the more chances it has to take advantage of the network or to maintain a significant minority nested in the whole network (see Fig. 162).

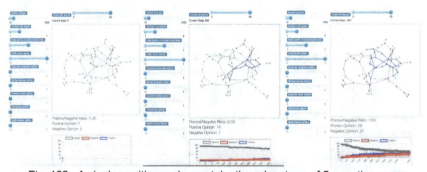

Fig. 162 - A single positive node can take the advantage of 5 negative ones depending on their position in the network.

The hypothesis saying that there are strategic positions in the network, which significantly increases the chances of one stakeholder to spread its opinion to the whole network, is validated!

- A regular conspiracy theory says that professional interests manipulate people. I have attributed an opinion to all population nodes and the contrary view to the six categories of stakeholders in my model. Despite their advantageous parameters, which give them an increased power of influence, the stakeholders haven't been able to reverse the opinion of the mass population and have rapidly aligned their opinion to the majority (see Fig. 163).

Fig. 163 - A coalition of stakeholders can't reverse the opinion of a population.

The hypothesis of the conspiracy scenario saying that a coalition of stakeholders can reverse the opinion of a population when it is formed wrong. Hypothesis validated!

FINAL DISCUSSION:

Comparing cultures is as much right as wrong as clichés are. I refuse relativism as much as I like to simplify complexity to find conceptual bridges to cross stereotypes. Studying the digital transformation of cities in far different cultures as the Asian, the Middle-Eastern, and the North-Eastern European, was a dream job. I am so grateful for all that I have learned on the way. All these meetings and experiences extended my sociability far beyond what it would have been if I did the same study settled in a research lab anywhere. In conclusion, I will speak broadly about each local society, sharing the richness and the beauty of each cultural uniqueness in the most accessible way to outsiders.

Suppose Tallinn is the city where most citizens say they do not feel engaged (more than ⅓ of respondents quoted the lowest score at the engagement feeling question) and Taipei is the city where they globally feel the most engaged. In that case, Tel Aviv is the city with the highest rate of using social media as a source of information to shape an opinion, and the only one ranking word-of-mouth as the second most important (70 of 122 in Taipei, 71 in Tallinn, 80 in Tel Aviv). However, in terms of the total number of influencers when deciding, most Tel Avivians say to be influenced by only one person (54%). In contrast, 25% of Taiwanese and 31% of Estonians say the same. This makes a real echo to my experience of Tel Aviv society and the functioning of their education. The "chutzpah" of the people, the outdoor living culture of the Mediterranean, combined with the necessity to include newcomers and to settle a territory, makes them direct, talkative, and bold. A city full of these like-minded people is both welcoming and chaotic, where social contact multiplies easily. Still, so you strengthen your personality and opinions individually. I have been seduced by this capacity of the Israeli to have at the same time a firm and personal opinion on everything and the sensitivity to coordinate as a whole people when necessary, without any top-down orders. I assume this results from the great inclusiveness culture at the core of the Zionist project, the mandatory non-hierarchical military service, the habits coming out of the first decades of Israeli people living in a kibbutz, and vital solidarity between Jewish, following an old. Still, demographically limited, worship, having been used as a scapegoat in recent history (XXth century). Suppose Tallinn is technically the most integrated state with all services available online for all citizens. In that case, the long and cold winter makes the social behavior very different. The people are way more introverted and have the highest proportion of respondents using the internet and emails as sources of information, making sense as they spend six months a year hiding away until spring. There is a need for coordinating these lonely people, but this is not a job attracting the most ambitious careerists. In a very successful liberal society, the low-hierarchy by design, since the Estonians are only 1.3 Million and 447,000 inhabitants in Tallinn, makes it easy to get in touch with your electives, even at a state level. So anyone can have a direct talk with the president or its ministers easily if they need to propose a project or suggest a reform. But this does not help them feel satisfied with being engaged in decision-making. I compare the Finnish, who are very close relatives, to Estonians, who joke about themselves being elected by the UN every year as the happiest people on earth. At the same time, locals can be very cynical towards their lives, struggling with the weather and the hardship of living in the middle of the snow. Somewhat Taipei presents the most balanced and satisfying results to my citizen engagement investigation. The availability of the technology, the attachment to its democracy, and the proudness of their independence from the Chinese government despite a lack of official recognition make them committed to their island. If they wish, they can engage in social movements or political parties and get support from the state to run a non-profit on any social cause. At the same time, the demographic size (22 million) offers enough possibilities to scale from the homeland. On another note, the Asian culture values wisdom and rational behavior, which is tangible in how Taiwanese envision citizen engagement in democracy. The people are not interested in how things are done but rather in the final result. They expect the governments to produce results. Some topics such as waste management and sustainability received great interest from the public, maybe because they live on an island that helps thinking autonomously. Taiwanese enjoy hiking in their semi-tropical forest, camping in the mountains or the sea on holidays and weekends. So the smart-city agenda took this turn to satisfy its people. In contrast, in Tel Aviv, where the people are looking for entertainment and fun, maybe to forget the wars, the smart-city model turned to prioritize leisure and cultural offers. But finally, the ease in sharing its opinion in public places is very closely the same for the three cities and the capacity to change its opinion in contact with others. Many citizens commonly say they would like to engage more in decision-making (85% in Taipei, 78% in Tel Aviv, and 72% in Estonia). Looking in detail, the inhabitants from Tallinn are the ones ready to spend the most time (between one hour a month to one hour a day) for civic engagement. In comparison, Taipei and Tel Aviv agree on less (between one hour a week to one hour a month). From the combined variable built for my machine learning model to rank cities on their citizen engagement, I found that Taipei has the most highly engaged citizens (8 out of 122), Tallinn is close (6). At the same time, Tel Aviv seems behind (only 2 out of 122). This could be a reaction to the first lockdown. Most people were worldwide feeling confused by their government decisions and being forced to stay at home. But another reason could be that even though being one of the most advanced startups and technological hubs of the world, the Tel Avivian lifestyle expresses it outdoors before everything. This gap of highly engaged citizens between my three samples led to a failure at the statistical test ANOVA which did not authorize me to certify that my predictive model is valid in all world cities without collecting more samples towards other cities to get better results. However, my classification model from the survey study achieves pretty satisfying machine learning results, as I get an accuracy score above 95% with a few percentages of false-positive predictions (4,76%).

While the Smart-City index 2020 from the IMD Business School considers my three cities of research, Taipei, Tel Aviv, and Tallinn, respectively 8th, 50th, and 59th in a ranking of the most advanced 109 smart-cities in the world, I found that this ranking does not take into account the informal citizen engagement on social networks. Yet my opinion mining research on Twitter revealed that Tallinn is the city with the most engaged tweets over all the smart-cities classified in this report (11.23% of active tweets). Taipei is 7th with 9.16%, and Tel Aviv 11th out of a total of 109 cities. As we said, Estonians living in the most advanced e-government of the world are experienced with digital communication. They know all the Estonian ecosystem takes care of its e-reputation. Communicating a cheering or blame online is, for them, a very efficient way to be heard publicly and receive a fast reaction to citizen engagement.

Also, Tallinn is one of my three case studies where topical lexicons are the most used in tweets. In terms of smart-city, civic-tech, and governance vocabularies, Tallinn is far more expressive (respectively 25th, 24th, and 28th) than Taipei (56th, 65th, and 61st). In terms of infrastructure vocabulary, Tel Aviv is the most discreet (80th) compared to Tallinn (44th), and this is probably due to the worst condition of the transportation system and public roads. Still, it is the most expressive in entrepreneurship vocabulary (61st) compared to Taipei (84th). Even if the use of specific lexicons evaluated by taking the weight of topical Bags-of-Words tailored to my urban studies has not proven to be representative enough to serve as an independent variable allowing to predict the sentiment scores in a linear regression analysis, this last finding pushes me to think that the lexicons used on a city tend to emphasize their best side rather than complain. With both the Vader Sentiment

Analysis algorithm and TextBlob Natural Language Processing package, Tallinn expresses more positive sentiment than Taipei and Tel Aviv (4th most positive ones with TextBlob and 7th with Vader, against 17th and 21st for Taipei, and 32nd and 68th for Tel Aviv). And again, the pervasiveness of the e-government in Tallinn seems to have increased the level of precision in which inhabitants communicate spontaneously online. We can identify what kind of sentiment they are having towards one or the other topic of a city. This tendency is confirmed by the average subjectivity taken out of tweets. Tallinn arrives 20th of the ranking on all smart cities. At the same time, Taipei and Tel Aviv are respectively at 43rd and 45th positions. Anyway, my three case studies end up filtering the 20% cities having the highest number of engaged tweets and so classified with the same value on the y-axis of my machine learning. After having tested four classifier algorithms, however, it appears that the Key Nearest Neighbors is the one reaching the best accuracy scores and the fewest errors in the task to predict which city is highly engaged from the lexical measures extracted from tweets. However, the performance of 83% is not astonishing, and I suggest that better predictions could be achieved by fine-tuning the feature selected as an input in the classifying algorithm. The gap of intensity in the correlations between clusters of values having a high redundancy of information, such as the different sentiment scores, and the other lexical attributes such as the number of numerical values or uppercase in a tweet, makes this predictive model very dependent on a few correlated variables. This is not the best way to achieve the most remarkable predictions. In this analysis, however, I have collected enough information to compare my sample values to the entire population of smart cities in the world. This allows me to say that Tallinn is more engaged in its tweets than the average cities in the world (mean value of 36% of subjectivity, against 31% worldwide).

In comparison, Taipei and Tel Aviv are also more expressive than the average (33% both) but less than the first. For your information, the standard deviation is the same for the three (0.33). This time, my three samples of tweets are close enough to each other in terms of variances for me to conclude on a functional inferential statistics test ANOVA. However, if the lowest p-value usually means that there is more substantial evidence in favor of the alternative hypothesis, in my case, meaning that "The sentiment scores extracted from tweets are good to automate the classification of cities based on their civic engagement," my p-value of 0.0 makes me suspicious. Therefore, I want to dig into more details to accept the validity of my inferences.

About the topology of the social networks across my case study cities, taken on the same Twitter datasets from the lexical analysis to which I added the records from representatives of each stakeholder category, I can say that Tel Aviv is by far the city with the biggest network. From some 34,217 tweets in Tel Aviv in total, averaging a total of 36,573 in Taipei and 28,862 in Tallinn, Tel Aviv reaches almost twice more nodes (24,485) than Taipei (13,410) and thrice more than Tallinn (9060). This is confirmed by the number of edges deployed, 26,533 in Tel Aviv, 12,924 in Taipei, and 9,983 in Tallinn. But this does not mean that Tel Avivian communications are mainly of one-shot since Tel Aviv is second in node degree mean (2.16) when Taipei has 1.92 and Tallinn 2.20. As I suspected in my hypothesis, the popularity of social networks is not systematically linked to the level of engagement. Indeed, considering the number of followers and the maximum number of likes reached as two main indicators of popularity on Twitter, it appears that Taipei is the city collecting the most support from its users, with a total of 1,162,578 followers and 957 likes reached on a tweet. Far behind, Tel Aviv collects 147,540 followers in its network and a maximum of likes at 658. In contrast, in Tallinn, the denser network collects 37,884 followers and 518 likes on a tweet at the maximum. Like a city, like a social network, Tel Aviv is vibrant, welcoming, and noisy. At the same time, Tallinn is dense and faithful to its users, while Taipei is the most balanced but shows the most effective results in the end. Speaking about density, Tallinn has one of 0.00024, so thrice more dense than Tel Aviv (0.000088), while Taipei is at 0.00014. A higher number of nodes comes with a higher number of potential edges, which led Tel Aviv to the highest number of non-edges: 299,718,996 and the resulting lowest transitivity score of 0.00019. Taipei has 89,894,574 non-edges and a transitivity at 0.0003, while Tallinn has 41,027,376 non-edges and a transitivity at 0.00087. For your recall, the transitivity of a network expresses the existence of tightly connected communities or clusters of nodes. By the way, sparsity has some advantages. Tel Aviv shows the lowest betweenness centrality mean (0.000085, against 0.00010 in Taipei, and 0.00017 in Tallinn), which means its network is the most resistant to node deletion and at least at risk of information flow compromission. Regarding the number of connected components, which is calculated by some nodes having more than two links, Taipei is again the city showing the best effectiveness: 1552, against 1275 in tel Aviv and 665 in Tallinn. Yet Tel Aviv shows great resistance to the node deletion on the largest subgraph filtering, and Tallinn shows the advantages of its nesting identity. In that task deleting all nodes in a dead-end or a single relationship with the network, Tel Aviv conserves 85% of its original network, Tallinn 79%, and Taipei 66%. Finally, Taipei has the largest network diameter (20), corresponding to the maximum distance between two nodes. In contrast, Tel Aviv has 17 and Tallinn 14. Proportionally to its size, Tel Aviv is the city with the shortest average path length, a measure used to evaluate the ease of spreading information in a network. Finally, is this helping a better prediction performance on the evolutions of respective networks by graph-based machine learning algorithms? At least on the link prediction task, yes. Tel Aviv gets better performance from a Random Forest Classifier algorithm having to predict which non-edge has the most probability of forming an edge with another node of the same network. Tel Aviv gets a better accuracy score (94%) and fewer errors (5%) than Taipei and Tel Aviv (93% and 93.6% respective accuracy scores, and 6.9% and 6.3% errors). In a community detection task, Taipei got 1,633 communities detected from the greedy modularity algorithm, Tel Aviv 1,404, and Tallinn 726. With the Louvain algorithm, Taipei has 1,609 communities and final modularity of 0.87. Tel Aviv has 1,331 communities and final modularity of 0.81, Tallinn has 704 communities and final modularity of 0.77. Taipei has 12,227 maximal number of cliques for a total of 12,280 communities, Tel Aviv 24,859 for 24,879, and Tallinn 8,857 for 8,868. All categorical networks have an equal number of communities and a maximal number of cliques, which means that no clusters have been detected in it from this technique. Using the asynchronous label propagation algorithm, Taipei has 2,444 communities, Tel Aviv 2,844, and Tallinn 1,259. All in one, this means that the clustering algorithms based on modularity scores achieve better performance in Tel Aviv, where communities include roughly 18 nodes. In contrast, it gathers 12 ones in Tallinn and 8 in Taipei. And the clustering algorithm labeling nodes on their neighbors' labels perform better in Tel Aviv, too, with 8.60 nodes by the community, against 7.19 in Tallinn and 5.48 in Taipei.

With the Citizen Engagement model, the first agent-based model built for this research, I am comparing the formation of the public opinion between cities by using the empirical data collected from the survey study. The distribution of engagement scores is not the same in Taipei, Tel Aviv, and Tallinn. So is the formation of public opinion. If Taipei has eight highly engaged citizens following my definition, Tallinn has 6 of them and Tel Aviv only 2. This tendency is observed in all the engagement scores and not only at the extreme top of it: Taipei is the city with the highest mean of engagement scores 0.69 (0 to 1 value), while Tallinn has a standard of 0.65 and

Tel Aviv 0.58. And the whole sample respects this tendency around the mean: the first quartile goes from 0.6 in Taipei to 0.52 in Tallinn, to 0.50 in Tel Aviv, the second quartile (the median value) goes from 0.7 in Taipei to 0.6 in Tallinn, to 0.6 in Tel Aviv, and the third quartile goes from 0.9 in Taipei to 0.8 in Tallinn to 0.7 in Tel Aviv. This tendency in the engagement scores of the samples' population has an impact on the simulation, such as the formation of the public opinion does not take the same time for each city. However, as we saw it when we were experimenting with the model from random values at the input, the formation of public opinion does not follow a linear relationship with the level of citizen engagement. This reaction from the model makes it hard to get any more insight from the simulation of populations having the empirical values or citizen engagement: indeed if the output depends on mastered data as engagement scores, it also depends on the random spread of opinions at the setup. By running different experiments, I found that it usually takes more time in Taipei than in Tallinn for a public opinion to form, but this is not always true, so if the Citizen Engagement model helped to understand the overall dynamics of the formation of public opinion influenced by citizen engagement, I wouldn't give much credit to the cross-city comparison through this computer simulation. The second agent-based model, called the Stakeholder Engagement model, coded in the Python programming language on the Mesa framework, is different. Indeed, it is clearly shown that the average node degree increases the speed of the formation of public opinion, and the nodes having the highest degree of centrality have an increased power of influence over their networks. With the Taipei network having an average node degree at 1.92, Telaviv one at 2.16, and Tallinn one at 2.20, it is clear that the last simulation ends up faster than the former ones.

The one-to-one interviews have been a great insight to balance my understanding of the local contexts. Like having small talks with locals, discussing with local experts in my field of research was a way to access an in-depth point of view directly. It helped me in catching the right picture of the local phenomena. In all cases, the provincial government supports startups and think tanks or private research to help them grow the innovation business ecosystem. Keeping the country's economic growth is a concern shared by Israeli and Estonians academics, which may be less valid for the Taiwanese scholars. They are more committed to the usual public education role. In Israel, all teachers have a double degree in their primary discipline (e.g., chemistry or engineering) and secondary graduation in business management. No teacher would lead its students in academic research that can't produce any business in the end. The professors have a practical background in the market. They are both mentors and academic professors. They do not practice research without looking for the best and shortest way to value it concretely. They are all in the best strategic position to know what happens in their industry. The whole scientific ecosystem is oriented to innovation production with great potential to create enterprises of fast scale-up. In Tallinn, the economic responsibilization of the academic ecosystem is a concern, as the teachers are asked to find support for their research alongside corporates and other enterprises.

However, Tallinn academics receive regular grants from the European Union at the difference with Israel since they are highly experienced in covering the demand in public administration innovation. In that vein, the three main think tanks in Taiwan are three branches of the same Institute for Innovation Industry, ensuring the private research to deliver reports and tailored research to public needs, under about 70/80% public grants completed by other personal missions the industry. The III is a platform that creates a transparent bridge of the collaborations between enterprises and the state. In practice, the average person has a good knowledge of what it needs in everyday life but does not think about how new technologies work and help them. But the government has to know how to improve its public services in the best way with minor investment and risks, so they delegate a consultancy mission to these private research think tanks in charge to ensure cross-fertilization between industrials, government and citizens transparently. Even if most citizens do not look for it, it is essential that the one who wants to understand the public choices on technology better can access all the information it needs.

In practice, much new technology fails. But when a government spends public money to invest in technology, it must work: the public can't tolerate uncertainty at the large scale of public services. So that's why the general ecosystems often prefer to choose older solutions, with more maturity and no risk of investment loss. When the public agrees on taking risks, the moment in history is when it has nothing else to lose, just like the Estonians at the fall of the Soviet Union. As the former prime minister of that time said in hindsight, the population was so desperate that they would agree on whatever plan to make them leave poverty. Since the government succeeded with its massive reforms, the civil society in Tallinn keeps quiet and comprehensive to its government nowadays. In Taipei, the government, such as in most Western democracies, has to face regular criticism. The decision-making in the innovation and the deployment of new technologies such as the 5G takes a much longer time in Taiwan than in the neighboring Mainland China because they have to deal with the social movements, ecologists, and completists. In Estonia, this kind of opposition people vs. government does not exist. Maybe because of the demographic size, or because of their history, but also the low-hierarchy by the design of their governments, the citizens trust that there is no one better placed than their government to defend their interests. However, we have seen in the survey studies that the people feel less engaged in decision-making. A positive side of mistrust existing in some democracies is that it encourages the government and think tanks to consult the entrepreneurs and the people directly by interviews and surveys to best answer their public mission. As a result, the population in Taiwan globally feels more engaged in decision-making than the Estonians do. In practice, much new technology fails. From our point of view, if the city government invests in technology, it MUST be successful. We can not tolerate the risk of uncertainty at the large scale of public services. Sometimes we prefer to choose the oldest solutions because they have more maturity and no investment loss. The mission of general advisors is to suggest to electives a technology vision that contains no risk of failure. The smart-city concept is blurry for everyone. It says many different things, and most people locally do not have an education or an experience to understand complex phenomena. The result is that globally the population and the public services do not have the exact definition or interests in smart-city devices, and this can create a sense of frustration, which can be increased by inadequate consultation with the citizens, where the citizens quickly think that the government will apply the ideas they have shared to their city in some open innovation event.
Estonia orients its communication in the direction of international recognition, as Israel does in another fashion. Taiwan branding is tricky because of its name after the "Republic of China" in post-WWII. It lacks support and understanding internationally when it thinks about replacing the name of its original institutions to include Taiwan identity, yet embedded in the population. As an answer, Taiwan tries to multiply its collaboration abroad to make itself more popular globally. From my experience, the Israeli companies rely more on themselves. Indeed, they reach impressive results in most domains like that. This is probably due to the history of the Jewish people, the Zionism at the core of their state, and the anti-zionism or anti-semitism which goes with it. Comparatively, Estonia's communication is clear and satisfying for all stakeholders since companies, startups, and academics gather

under the public sectors' communication agencies when they do not create the Estonian association of their field.

In Israel, the relationships between municipal government and the national one are not so good: Tel Aviv is often defying Jerusalem, and in a sense, do not respect the Zionist project at the core of the Israeli state: it is too much open to the world, too big and too liberal. But many decisions can't be taken by the municipality and depend on the national state. The buses and public transportation in Tel Aviv, for example, rely on the ministry of transport of Israel. So even if the city's growth needs to improve its public transportation system as soon as possible, the mayor can't move a bus station by himself. This decentralization of decision-making creates problems and delays in deploying effective solutions. As an answer, the municipality is hosting 50% of innovative transportation startups in its public incubators. They are investing massive resources in ways to solve their problem by avoiding the government. The IT department of Tel Aviv has 450 employees to develop more than 90% of the digital tools in-house. The municipality collects and owns all the data from citizens, private companies, and public services departments to make itself able to integrate all kinds of information on the city. Each public service department has its dashboard with access to geolocalized data helping in its shared mission. This attracts foreigners' companies willing to benefit from the local mindset in disruptive thinking and ease in deploying real-life experiments by the municipality. For example, a cluster of German car brands (Porsche, Audi, and Volkswagen) created an innovation hub in Tel Aviv, where the corporate intrapreneurs or most innovative executives can join for some months, the time to try and experiment with some innovation before bringing it back in the mother office in Germany or elsewhere. Like most big fish of their field, having a welcoming office in Tel Aviv is also a way to organize and attend events where the most promising startups are presented in their early stage to support their scaling up and collect part of the benefits. In Israel, there are about 300 innovation labs supported by foreign corporate companies like this one. If the American state and companies support each of these three democracies, I have been interested in meeting the French equivalent in my cities of investigation. The French Tech has an official hub in Taipei and Tel Aviv, not in Tallinn, where the French Institute in Estonia ensures the French presence. The two first have a mission from the French minister of the economy, to promote business exchanges between the two countries. In practice, it serves as a cultural window where local entrepreneurs can meet other expatriates and invite their local partners to the French folklore parties (Day of the new wine, Bastille Day). In Tallinn, the French Institute depends on the Education ministry. Instead, it proposes French lessons and partnerships in the academic field. None of them has extended possibilities of crossed-cultural projects since they depend on ministries based in France. So, the budgets allowed for this or that foreign policy. None of them has the mission to engage locally in decision-making, neither to filter the startups it hosts to orient its ecosystem toward this or that field of innovation such as the smart-city or transportation one. The social empowerment of citizens and youth, in particular, from the different internet movements, is priceless. All the skills they are learning from a startup experience, for example, are tremendous: storytelling, business development, self-fulfillment, global education, ambition, career-building. Entrepreneurship is a natural way of life achievement and empowerment for many people.

Some generations before had the music movements, like rock bands, to learn by experiment and build a living. Art and fashion were ways to do the same: they structured and empowered whole generations of youth. Nowadays, the startup movement and digital entrepreneurship is a worldwide movement to help the young people of our age who want to keep their heads above water, learn things and make a society. We can visit smart-city exhibition centers and startup hubs everywhere globally; nothing comes out of it because they do not have an old generation of doers to push the new generation forward. In Israel, the first generation of tech startups from the early 90s help the newbies: they give ideas, advice, and coaching. They know how to help because they have already processed the same way. And this double competence in scientific research and starting businesses is the typical mindset from the beginning of Israel: they had a country to build from scratch and defend from its neighborhood and world diplomacy. This is very specific in the world to have this passing of power between generations, except in silicon valley, where it is the same.

In Estonia, lots of support for public projects and academic research comes from the European Union. And the investment in startups is ensured by a tight community of successful entrepreneurs and founders who re-inject the benefit from their previous business into the new seeds. The cost of living in Tallinn is not high. The real estate market is growing carefully so that the value keeps stable. More and more inhabitants can buy their own comfortable houses or make investments in properties to rent. As a consequence, there is no insurmountable gap between the lowest and the highest prices. So the best house to buy in Estonia must be about 1.3 million euros. When you are very successful in your business and want to live in Estonia, you can afford the best of the country quite easily and spend the rest of your benefit in growing the ecosystem of innovative businesses. The attractiveness of Tallinn from an entrepreneur's point of view is also that compared to its neighboring capital cities, Helsinki in particular, Tallinn eases the deployment of innovation in real-life situations. If the South-European countries have a way more comfortable weather and lifestyle, such as Spain, Italy, and Portugal, the efficiency of its public administration is far beyond seducing. They are about ten years behind places like France, England, or the Netherlands and 20 years behind Spain and Italy. When you are a young Italian entrepreneur or aspiring to be, even if you love your country and wish to make a living in your hometown, you know that the ineffectiveness of public administration and banking services is a dead end to your ambitions. With the e-residency status, digital nomads and startups worldwide can enjoy the stability of the European currency and values in business. But Estonian ecosystem lacks inclusiveness, and the weather does not allow the outdoor culture of the Mediterranean. Consequently, some digital nomads report having made more friends in Portugal in two weeks than in Tallinn in two years. And the Estonian government knows they need to refurbish their offers regularly to attract students, entrepreneurs, and tourists worldwide. There is a community of 60.000 e-residents from the four corners of the world. Still, the program, even if technically unique in its effectiveness, lacks possibilities for cross-fertilization, joint projects to exploit the sleeping workforce better and take the best out of it. Furthermore, a recent reaction by the local population, not skilled enough to enjoy the startup ecosystem, has been revealed in votes. The presidential elections brought a conservative government in the replacement of the liberal one to answer the concern over the integration of Russian migrants from the east and the increase of local prices due to foreigners' migration with high income. So a part of the Estonian population is not that much open to Europe but rather focuses on national identity. The public administration and most officials often do not speak English, the same as the national newspapers. They will probably less tend to speak a foreign language in the coming years. The local youth are not much into mixing with foreigners. It creates three societies living in parallel: the Estonian Estonians, the Russian Estonians, and the expatriates. Their primary concern is to build their destiny, and independence is a critical issue to the population. This goal is very sensitive to the change of global geopolitics and national vision. A conservative government could lead to closeness in the global game. So the Estonian civil society, hosting the best experts of their fields, are very concerned in making the whole people and intern politics acknowledge these risks of not making the best decisions at the right time. This is also why the startups are so important to Estonia because they make them famous worldwide and ensure their liberty as an independent country. Of course, this does not affect the business hubs, which keeps evolving in parallel and is too important to the state to be left on the side of decision-making, but if the tendency to retreat in nationalism anchors permanently in the local countryside, both because the local Russian population is not comfortable with the western upstarts, and because the Liberal Estonians are not comfortable with having Russian tramps drunk to vodka besides their office, it might lock Estonian dynamic for disruptive innovation in public policy. Furthermore, a certain disillusion is coming from the EU. If Estonia is often designated as the gifted child of Europe in terms of digital state, their X-Road system has been built from their personal experience to cover their needs better. It is much advanced in data safety and privacy. Still, it does not match the European regulations of the GDPR imposed lately on all European states. Estonia does not want to step behind to align with a less advanced ecosystem. They want neither to limit themselves to the exploitation allowed by European commissions of electives with a poor technical background or understanding. By the way, the entrepreneurs' population of the '90s was ready to take lots of risks since they didn't have much to lose. Still, the gentrification of the middle-class makes them less adventurous and afraid of losing their top position. All in one, Estonia has become more conservative lately. It will have to confront its fear of being fully integrated into globalization despite its small demography and short independent history. The main issue for Estonia now will be to make itself important as a core player of the international game.

EPILOGUE:

As an epilogue, I distance my thesis built on developed countries since the advent of CIT in the '90s. I was questioning myself on the replicability of these models of economic development in less developed countries. I chose the African continent to take another perspective on civic technologies and smart cities. This study has been written to prepare a speech given to the Civic Tech Innovation Network based in Johannesburg, South Africa. The webinar is part of diverse events happening during the South African Urban Festival 2020 on "Empowering the Civic." It is supported by the South African Cities Network, WITS School of Governance, Konrad Adenauer-Stiftung (KAS) "Strong Cities 2030," and the African Center for Cities. It would not have been written the same if I hadn't reached local entrepreneurs who openly shared with me their experiences of the ongoing digital transformation in their respective countries and their opinions on African smart-city projects and policies. These talks helped me catch a grounded vision and strengthen my wish to visit the African continent soon.

The African continent will host one-third of the world population in the next generation. These last years went through social, economic, and environmental transformations at a spectacular size and speed. Trying to understand what makes contemporary Africa, identifying the most relevant African urban and digital developments are inspiring challenges to embrace. The African continent is plural, dynamic and undertakes its challenges, innovates, and inspires worldwide. However, Africa remains an unknown continent, often poorly understood. For a long time, Africa was presented as the continent of all difficulties: wars, famines, epidemics, desolation. However, it is nowadays living a profound transformation by its youngest peoples, which manage to present it as the continent of resilient creativity and a crossroad of possibilities.

With an annual urban population growth rate of almost 4%, Africa has the fastest urban growth worldwide. Cities such as Ouagadougou (Burkina Faso), Bamako (Mali), Addis Ababa (Ethiopia), and Nairobi (Kenya) are currently growing at an even faster rate. This process of urbanization brings both opportunities and challenges at an environmental, socio-economic, and political scale. In December 2019, the Ministry of Foreign Affairs of Finland published *Mega-trends In Africa*, a report providing an overall understanding of African challenges through 6 topics: Population Growth, Climate Change, Urbanisation, Migration, Technological Development, and Democracy. Regarding my research issue, I have been interested in reading more about urbanization, technological development, and democracy.
- **Urbanisation** process in Africa hasn't followed a straightforward path associated with structural transformation. The distinction between rural and urban areas is blurry, and cities tend to keep highly dependent on agricultural production. Many metropolitan areas have quickly developed a growing service sector which could be the foundation of an innovative economy. Still, it is not able to create enough formal employment alone. Consequently, many urban jobs keep informal, insecure, and poorly paid, resulting in less tax income and reduced potential for infrastructure investments. The rapid urbanization challenges, even more, the existing infrastructures and the public services are rarely able to follow the growth rate. As a result, the need for financial resources to invest in expanding cities is often lacking.
- **Technological development** has been exceptionally rapid in mobile banking since the unbanked African population has been able to use mobile money accounts with no intermediate. More widely, the spread of mobile phones has a transformative role on African societies by giving access to information, job creation, service delivery, and a more accessible business environment. However, regional variations are

significant. Moreover, the temptation of being provisioned by foreign technological solutions has attracted many African governments, accelerating the adoption of technologies and exacerbating existing inequalities. Furthermore, orienting Africa in a technology-driven continent while skipping the industrialization phase is not sure to produce the desired effects regarding African interests.

- **Democracy** did progress in several areas: political parties and elections, the increased role of women in politics, empowered civil society, but some political rights and civil liberties have also deteriorated over the past decade. Yet many problematic areas still exist, such as endemic corruption and the emergence of competitive authoritarian regimes. One of the central challenges lies in normalizing peaceful power-sharing and power alternation. Showing restraints towards political opponents and relinquishing power in due course is a political-cultural challenge for African democracies. Furthermore, a crucial battleground for governance ideas is the training of future African elites. At the same time, some foreign influences in the region may promote other models of governance than the democratic one.

This article aims to light on the Smart-City as a model for African urbanization and Civic Technology as tools that could strengthen democracies on the continent. I will first present the cultural context of innovation in Africa to set the basis of our reflection. Then I will propose a vernacular approach as an answer to the city and entrepreneurial development challenges. This will lead us to question the pertinence of deploying foreign innovation in the African context. Finally, we will look at the economic reality and compare the African sovereignty perspective with the foreign aid model.

a. What is contemporary Africa? Cultural Specificities of Innovation

The thesis saying that African culture has been a barrier to African development is nowadays widely denied. On the contrary, many humanists and African philosophers showcase arguments in favor of returning to the indigenous roots of African culture as the foundation of progress. In practice, the daily life of most African people is already a walk to innovation. Most African people are innovative since they develop their solutions by themselves, indirectly, without the aid of the state. And the African population is hyper resilient since they went through many difficulties.

Innovation, when it's not copy-pasted from somewhere else, can be defined as a cultural act. So Mario Lucio, former Cape-Verdean Minister of Culture, invites African decision-makers to impulse broad access to innovation on the continent to allow a better appropriation by the African peoples.

The best benefit to reach out of innovation is not the result at the end. It is the long-term process of collaboration between stakeholders, at different scales, the typical social and psychological changes nested in the acculturation, inspired by accessible leaders, supported by a community of daily makers, stimulating the virtuous dynamics of collective intelligence. This process necessarily needs a diversity of profiles and backgrounds to draw the strength and the inspiration at the source of its own culture. Indeed, innovation in Africa will not benefit from being embellished by all that technology can do. However, it has a lot to win by exploiting each opportunity nested in each problem, difficulty, and divergences. The young Africans who look for innovation and creativity have first to understand the African issues and culture. So they will be the best ambassadors for African values and a showcase of African talents.

Humanizing computation and solidarizing the peoples along the digital transformation process appears to be the best plan to tool up African people to answer the African problems with African skills and African-adapted supplies. Each difficulty faced by an African inhabitant has a corresponding solution to deliver by an African enterprise or other self-employment. By doing so, Africa will build its wealthiness from its realities. This is the pathway to development which is nested in the traditional communitarian contribution that we can find in the African culture. As Nelson Mandela said, "*Education is the most powerful weapon you can use to change the world.*" The best opportunity to tackle the global digital transformation challenges is to impulse a rise in the knowledge of technology within African youths.

To do so, some African innovators have built their own spaces for innovation, such as the WoeLab in Lomé, Togo, or Ouagalab in Ouagadougou, Burkina-Faso. These labs are educational spaces to learn new IT and Computation and startup incubators, where young entrepreneurs can host their businesses. Some Pan-African exchange networks also emerged, like Jokkolabs, to coordinate the innovation at the continent scale and support the ecosystem of African startups. African youths are the first doers of African development. They are the ones who combine a series of hacks to tackle everyday issues and shape the Africa of tomorrow. Some of them joined the Free Software Movement to redefine their computation in the shape of African realities. By doing so, they learn how the technology works and use it to solve specific African issues.

Open Data and Open-Source Movement

An Open Data infrastructure resulting from Open-Source Softwares with tools to navigate and manipulate the information would help the state and the people in the long term. Open Data repositories are many engagement mediums for all stakeholders: academics, civil society, non-profit volunteers, private businesses, and public servants. Behind the dynamic of data consulting, there is a dynamic of data sharing: the users of open data portals will progressively fill the datasets by sharing their own grounded experience, knowledge, and know-how. So the digital infrastructure will allow the transmission of values, living background, and cultural heritage.

Connecting the actors through new technologies and local memories of a place or a city strengthens the thought and social uses. In that sense, new communication technologies have the potential to record cultural ways of living. And then, networking will feed the cultural exchanges and spread the typical visions of the society and the city. The African culture is a lot about solidarity and physical contact between the people. To keep these social habits that make Africa, it is needed to re-create online this cooperative atmosphere that we can find offline in Africa. The actual embryonic level of development of the African digital experience will be financed by the indigenous populations in the form of contributions and will genuinely answer the needs of local people.

At the moment, there is no policy to regulate public access to information, even for experts and decision-makers. This means that there is no obligation or invitation to create open data repositories. The progress by the population exists, but it is still slowed by political and administrative reality. The digital transformation by the ground population is not strong enough for the moment to take the lead. In many places, the population is in advance of its administration. The citizens master the technology, but the state is not equipped for its use. In Guinea, for example, digital democratization made significant progress. However, the effects can't be seen since the population still needs to move in person to the administration office to fill paper forms. The link between the people and the state is not adequate. There are still many gaps to bridge between the infrastructure, the administration, and the people. But there are many chances that at one point, the brain drain may reverse to a movement of the comeback, and it will considerably enrich Africa. At that moment, the African states that have chosen to invest in human resources will benefit from having an educated and experienced workforce.

b. Urbanisation: A vernacular development for African cities

What is true for innovation is true for urbanization: the African Smart-City must be inspired from the African village, referring to collective construction in Africa. To do so, the African smart-city model needs to be developed in a vernacular fashion. This has been the spearhead of Sename Koffi Agbodjinou for the last ten years. Architect and anthropologist, founder of L'Africaine d'Architecture in Lomé, Togo, Sename insist: architecture and urban developments in Africa can't be blindly inspired by the Occidental vision. The African architects must develop their model of the city, leaning on the African culture of settlement and society. Most smart-city projects in Africa and elsewhere often promote a global vision of future housing with no connection with inhabitants' primary needs. To set a development strategy for African cities, it is needed to know its inhabitants better, identify their needs as clearly as possible, takes care of their deep aspiration, and deliver them the products and services that fit their daily reality. The core mission for urbanization in Africa is to ensure that the financial resources spent in the city infrastructures will positively improve the standard of life for the broader part of the African population. Thus, many initiatives on the African continent are labeled "Smart-City." Most capital cities have their own "Smart-City" projects ongoing. However, it appears to African watchers that the Smart-City promoters in Africa only think about physical infrastructure. It entirely skips the potential of digital platforms for social inclusion. At the same time, the latter could have much more impact on the people than the former.

Most urbanization projects become tools for strategic alliances between political powers that do not serve the people's interests first. Communicating on off-grounded projects can be part of a marketing strategy from governments to attract investors and foreigners' wealthiness. In developing countries such as in Africa, more than anywhere else, there are high risks to crash the yet fragile populations under debts and impoverish them a bit more than what they already are, to pay for projects that do not solve any of their needs and do not create any sustainable job market. This priority set on alliances between politics and business creates many other inconsistencies:
- Some projects are twice more prominent than the actual absorption capacity of the urban area, and most real estates can't be afforded with the actual buying power of the population.
- This will have the effect of increasing the wealthiness of a few officials, public servants, and some wealthy foreigners. The real estate value will inflate, and the indigenous population will be kept behind, even more impoverished.
- At a building phase, the game of political alliances between governments and private companies creates other inconsistencies: some urban infrastructure of second priority, like rainwater drainage, can be built before the wastewater treatment system, which is the priority.
- The construction sites are often offered to foreign companies, while these business opportunities must benefit African entrepreneurship.

- In the end, these urban developments risk impoverishing the African population a bit more than what they already are by contracting debts they can't payback.

The major challenge of African urbanization: the economic issue, is not considered in these Smart-City projects. They do not favor economic development. Even when incubators of enterprises are built, they have imposed constraints and do not answer the uses of the inhabitants. Indeed, the level of knowledge and intelligence of a city's population will never grow thanks to physical infrastructure. Unadapted on the form, huge smart-city developments are also often unadapted on the substance. No one knows if the model of Smart-City in Africa or elsewhere will bring the desired effects: there is not enough feedback. And these new city projects pushed by private-public deals, sprouting up like mushrooms in developing countries, pose a problem of governance. The most recent example is Akon City in Senegal: when a rich rapper, Akon, deals with the President of Senegal to build a private crypto-currency city, what will be the future government of that city? Does it have autonomous governance, or will it be included in the Dakar municipality?

In Angola, while most African projects lack investments, a new city has been financed by Chinese companies, allowing them to exploit local oil as a payment of the debts contracted by the Angola state for the building of a new port. The new city is empty since Angolan people can't afford the real estate price and Chinese people don't move to Angola. This shot-by-shot advancement does not consider the pan-African growing demography. On the contrary, it will accelerate the problem of municipalities overlapping in many African urban areas. There is no organization at the continent's scale, and cities are instead copying/pasted individually from global visions.

We already know that masterplans and huge models are not the way to drive urban growth anymore: technology is constantly evolving, and frozen building programs tend to impose too many constraints to evolve in the long term. They are not the right tools to follow the acceleration of technology and technology. In practice, there are a lot more opportunities to make smarter cities in Africa, no matter how smart the developed cities are. The unique pathway is to start creating a new initiative and showing the local inhabitants' potential. In some low-tech environments, the Smart-City is not a topic. There is no vital education on digital, houses are not connected to the internet. There are no offers such as in developed countries for monthly internet and mobile phone access. As an answer, some non-profit associations from civil society propose educational programs for the internet and support the digital transformation of local communities. Progress is being made in many different fields. They tend to create pilot projects to increase the digital penetration rate.

Like the Free Software Movement engages the technology users in a better acknowledgment of the logic behind computers, a citizen-focus city engages its inhabitants to become the first qualified workforce incapacity to make the most liveable cities. An increasing knowledge level of urban issues and how to fix them creates a network of enlightened citizens who participate in the maintenance of the town and support its municipal government. The combination of the open-source culture and the willingness of its youths will produce electives and academics "Made in Africa," highly specialized in addressing African challenges. This grounded experience will also lead the young Africans to achieve their professional integration by creating their jobs. Suppose the open-source software nowadays, and open innovation labs allow any young African to create a startup from scratch. In that case, they will all together progressively elaborate a digital economy based on their knowledge and skills.

Civic Technologies can help people to self-organize

The observation is more or less the same for CivicTech: it lacks digital platforms. The government will create a website for administrative requests (visas, passports). Still, it keeps top-down and does not take into consideration the emerging demands from the citizens. Some initiatives come from the private sector, but currently mainly from Arabian-speaking countries. There are not so many CivicTech developments in the French-speaking African countries. The OIF — Organisation Internationale de la Francophonie tried to do something internationally, but it didn't work concretely. However, there is a clear difference of advancement and success in the cities, countries, ecosystems where the public servants or government are aware of the talented people who deploy synergy and projects and get in direct touch with them to shape the better public policy with the best delay to follow fast innovation. In Africa, most public servants do not know anything about what people do on the ground.

In some countries, political stability is not always good. The advancement of many public interest projects depends highly on the political agenda and the elections. This is a constant that sometimes serves some bad political interests. When urbanization grows fast with no regulation, it becomes tough to find yourself in the city, even for locals. The names of the streets remain unclear, the number of houses and flats too, so it is hard somehow to identify the actual amount of population living in this or that area. The perimeter of the neighborhoods is not precisely defined. This stagnation has counterproductive effects at multi-levels :
- First, it is harder for the population to realize the delay they have in developing infrastructures and public services. The hospitals, the schools, the public buildings are not easy to find and identify. Thus it is not easy to report when it lacks equipment and contemporary technology or simply watch public budgets.

- Then, a clear identification of a territory helps for census and the fight against electoral fraud. Indeed, when the voters' demographic size and localization are not precisely known, it is much easier to fake the results.
- Small businesses also would benefit from a better identification on a map. Still, the authorities are not really in a hurry to do it. Many young people from civil society started to understand it. However, they are still not enough to claim the necessity and fix it. Even the low-tech countries such as Guinea host interesting Civic Technology initiatives: guineevote.org is an independent citizen initiative to watch and participate in elections. They can control and alert events in polling places. lahidi.org is another initiative to follow the acts behind the promises of the Guinean presidency. guineecheck.org is a fact-checking blogging website to counter public rumors and fake news.

c. African Economy: resourcefulness and dependencies

Most information on Africa is ignored, but we can see that the people manage to fend for themselves when we observe it from the ground. Yet, in many African countries, an extensive part of the population still lives informally regarding economics. In some places, the informal sector constitutes more than 80% of the activities. The inhabitants managed to build a house, pay the school, and create companies without any banking support. They can't access banking services because their production of values in the economy is not accounted for in the global financial system. They have no credit, no bank transfer, they pay everything in cash. Somehow, the failure of the institutions is opportunities for the private sector. There are many direct business opportunities to take. The revaluation of public spaces directly by the inhabitants allows the emergence of small underlying business models.

A city is made out of flows and exchanges between people, transportation, enterprises. All of them interact as in a market to trade goods and services. This micro-scale phenomenon is the daily reality on which macroeconomics is dependent. The new decentralization of powers which can be observed in many democracies is also palpable in Africa. Top-down governance tends not to be effective anymore in the digital transformation era. A new form of barter economy seduces many industrial nations. The population grows to bring more social equity and community building at the core of the consumer society. Locally initiated, the Local Exchange Trading Systems (LETS) now exist in many African countries. They allow people to negotiate the value of their goods or services and to keep wealth in the locality where it is created. Then the Community-based Exchange Systems (CES) provides the means for communities to trade across borders by allowing a currency exchange between countries. Founded in 2003 as an internet-based LETS in Cape Town, South Africa, the original CES had grown into a global network linking 82 active communities in 14 African countries. This system aims to foster the real wealth of communities and rebuild a sense of worth and self-esteem among their members. Sometimes described as a global complementary trading network that operates without money, this resettlement of the economy in the hands of those who make it daily will need to integrate itself with the official institutions to build a sustainable economy: when there is no business record, there are no taxes, and so the public infrastructures keep being financed by debts and the sell-off of state resources.

Infrastructure necessity and foreign aid

Only a performative infrastructure can sustain the long-term economic growth of developing countries. At the moment, it depends highly on foreign investments because it can be costly, especially in rural, sparsely populated Africa. If foreign aid has been an integral part of African economic development since the 1980s, the Aid Model has been criticized too, notably by the Zambian-American economist Dambisa Moyo, for supplanting trade initiatives. The even more radical Dependency Theory asserts that the wealth and prosperity of the superpowers are dependent upon the poverty of the rest of the world. The economists who subscribe to this theory believe that more impoverished regions must break their trading ties with the developed world to prosper. For example, in French-speaking Africa, the former governments bet on natural resource exploitation to play a global game. They didn't foresee that they were entering a top-down system where they depend on the buyers who can fix the prices of the deal and will be pressured by the financial partners. Regarding international responsibility, it is urgent to evaluate the ethics and sustainability of this development model.

To that point, 15 African countries still have their money owned by the French treasury, the CFA Franc. They can't become autonomous while they are bound hand and foot. By this dependency game, most African countries do not have control over their economic growth. This complex political situation locks the expression of opinions and inhibits growth by pure liberal entrepreneurship. The main issue is that most African states don't have a long-term vision, apart from a few of them who know where they want to go. All African politics is parasitic by financial bakers who don't look if their regulation fits the African reality. Some are sometimes asked to work with civil society actors. Still, they do not use the same organizational tools and are often seen as opponents. It is often problematic for locally launch initiatives to be understood and considered by development organizations coming from abroad. The locals usually host events to invite many people to learn new skills, while development organizations communicate by long reports. These are opposite methods that can hardly work together. Here again, the situation is nuanced since progress has been made these last years. The financial partners understand that a civil society supported by local youths can have a broader impact than the official structures. The local peoples slowly become unavoidable from the development process.

From another perspective, talking about African infrastructures, it will be necessary for African nations to break some frontiers and organize outside of former organizations. The highways, the 5G, will bring many opportunities to reconcile African countries. The question is, "Africa is it ready for this ?" It is essential to keep in mind that Africa has never been sovereign on its territory. They have no common money, regions, or armies; they don't even have clear borders between countries, which still creates many conflicts.

BIBLIOGRAPHICAL REFERENCES :

Introduction :

- *Analysis Matrix for Smart Cities*, Pablo Branchi, Ignacio R. Matias & Carlos Fernandez-Valdivielso (2014) Universidad Publica de Navarra.
- *Governing the smart city: a review of the literature on smart urban governance*, Albert Meijer (2016) International review of Administrative Sciences.
- *Social Smart City: Introducing digital and social strategies for participatory governance in smart cities*, Robin Effing & Bert P. Groot (2016), Saxion University of Applied Science.
- *A new collaborative model for a holistic and sustainable metropolitan planning,* Edi Valpreda, Lorenzo Moretti, Maria Anna Segreto, Francesca Cappellaro, William Brunelli (2018) *in* Techne Special Issue 01, European pathways for the Smart Cities to come.
- *D'une ville à l'autre, la comparaison internationale en sociologie urbaine*, Jean-Yves Authier, Vincent Baggioni, Bruno Cousin, Yankel Fijalkow and Lydie Launay (2019) Editions La Découverte.
- *Territoires intelligents: un modèle si smart ?* Didier Desponds and Ingrid Nappi-Choulet (2018) Editions de l'Aube.
- *Les concepts fondamentaux de la phénoménologie*, Claude Romano (2012), Revue de la philosophie française et de langue française, Vol XX, No 2 (2012) pp 173–202
- *Quelle phénoménologie pour quels phénomènes ?* Léo-Paul Bordeleau (2005), Recherches Qualitatives, Vol 25(1), 2005, pp 103–127.
- *La refondation de la phénoménologie transcendantale chez Marc Richir*, Alexander Schell (2010) Eikasia. Revista de Filosofia, año VI, 34 (septiembre 2010).
- *Un courant neurocognitiviste en phénoménologie ? L'acclimatation des neurosciences dans le paysage philosophique français*, Wolf Feuerhahn (2011) Revue d'Histoire des Sciences Humaines, Cairn.info
- *La quête du sens et du vécu: la phénoménologie en géographie*, Christian Morissonneau et Denis Sirois (1985), Département de géographie de l'Université Laval, *Cahiers de géographie du Québec*, 29 (77), 317–324.
- *Voir et percevoir à l'ère numérique: théorie de l'ontophanie*, Stéphanie Vial (2016), Université Paris Descartes (Paris 5)
- *Ontophanie et milieu perceptif*, Interview de Stéphane Vial (2017)
- *Naî(ê)tre au monde à l'ère numérique*, Conférence de Stéphane Vial (2015)
- *Herméneutique du digital: les limites de l'interprétation*, Alberto Romele (2015) Laboratoire Costech, Université de technologie de Compiègne
- *Le numérique comme milieu : enjeux épistémologiques et phénoménologiques. Principes pour une science des données.* Bruno Bachimont (2015)

Chapter 1

- *La citoyenneté*, Anicet le Pors (1999), Presses Universitaires de France
- *Démocratie antique et démocratie moderne*, Moses I. Finley (1976), Petite Bibliothèque Payot
- *Histoire des idées politiques*, Géraldine Muhlmann, Évelyne Pisier, François Châtelet, Olivier Duhamel (1982), Presses Universitaires de France
- *Les citoyens qui viennent. Comment le renouvellement générationnel transforme la politique en France,* Vincent Tiberj (2017), Presses Universitaires de France.
- *Usurpation de l'identité citoyenne dans l'espace public. Astroturfing, communication et démocratie*, Sophie Boulay (2015) Presses de l'Université du Québec.
- *Post-démocratie*, Colin Crouch (2004), Polity Press.
- *Democratie Electronique*, Stéphanie Wojcik (2013), in *Dictionnaire critique et interdisciplinaire de la participation*, GIS Démocratie et participation.
- *The Quickening of Social Evolution. Perspectives on Proprietary (Entrepreneurial) Communities*, Spencer H. MacCallum (1997), in *The Independent Review*, v.II, n.2, Fall 1997, pp. 287–302.
- *Smart Cities: Towards a New Citizenship Regime? A discourse Analysis of the British Smart City Standard*, Simon Joss, Matthew Cook and Youri Daot (2017) in *Journal of Urban Technology*, 24:4, 19-49.
- *Démocratie Liquide*, Arthur Renault (2013), in *Dictionnaire critique et interdisciplinaire*

de la participation, GIS Démocratie et participation.
- *Liberal Radicalism and Security Tokens: Quadratic Voting as a Governance Protocol,* Jesus Rodriguez (2018) hackernoon.com
- *Liberal Radicalism: Can Quadratic Voting be the Perfect Voting System?* nebulas.io (2018) medium.com
- *Liberation Through Radical Decentralization,* Vitalic Buterin (2018) medium.com
- *What makes Quadratic Voting an effective Democratic Voting Mechanism,* Eximchain (2018) medium.com
- *Radical Markets. Uprooting Capitalism and Democracy for a just society,* Eric A.Posner and E. Glen Weyl (2018) Princeton University Press.
- *Liberal Radicalism: Formal Rules for a Society Neutral among Communities,* Vitalik Buterin, Zoe Hitzig and E. Glen Weyl (2018)
- *Delegative Democracy Revisited,* Bryan Ford (2014)

Chapter 2 :

- *The next Era of Human progress. What lies behind the global new cities epidemic ?,* Cities (2019) *in* The Guardian 8 juil. 2019
- *Dynamiques publiques et privées autour des Smart-Cities en Inde,* Isabelle Milbert (2018) *in* Bulletin de l'association de géographes français, 94–1 / 2017, 5–22.
- *Smart Cities: Digital solutions for a more livable future,* McKinsey Global Institute (2018) McKinsey & Company
- *Smart-Cities: A conjuncture of four forces,* Margarita Angelidou (2015) *in* Cities 47 (2015) 95–106, Elsevier.
- *Dialogues: a virtual roundtable,* Paola Clerici Maestosi, Paolo Civiero (2018) *in* Techne "European Pathways for the Smart Cities to come" Special Series 01, 2018
- *A new collaborative model for a holistic and sustainable metropolitan planning,* Edi Valpreda, Lorenzo Moretti, Maria Anna Segreto, Francesca Cappellaro, William Brunelli (2018)
- *Smart-City: Quelles relations public-privé pour rendre la ville plus intelligente?,* Carine Staropoli and Benoit Thirion (2018) Terra Nova.
- Understanding of Public-Private Partnership Stakeholders as a condition of Sustainable development, Anna Wojewnik-Filipkowska and Joanna Wegrzyn (2019) in Sustainability 2019, 11, 1194
- *What is a Public Private Partnership?,* Raman Krishnan (2014) in Management Development Institute Gurgaon
- *The Concept of Key Success Factors: Theory and Method,* Klaus G. Grunert & Charlotte Ellegaard
- *Will the real Smart-City please stand up?,* Robert Hollands (2008)
- *Cook Book, recipes for agile piloting,* Veera Mustonen, Kaisa Spilling, Maija Bergström (2018) Forum Virium Helsinki.

Chapter 3 :

- *Stakeholder Engagement: Clinical Research Cases,* R.E. Freeman and al. (2017), Issues in Business Ethics 46, Springer International Publishing.
- *Théorie de l'acteur-réseau,* Aziza Mahil et Diane-Gabrielle Tremblay (2015) in *Sciences, technologies et sociétés de A à Z,* Presses Universitaires de Montréal
- *Decoding urban development dynamics through actor-network methodological approach,* Marija Cvetinovic, Zorica Nedovic-Budic, Jean-Claude Bolay (2017) Geoforum 82
- *On-Line Guide for Newcomers to Agent-Based Modeling in the Social Sciences,* Robert Axelrod and Leigh Tesfatsion (2019), Iowa State University
- *Agent-Based Modeling: a guide for social psychologists,* Joshua Conrad Jackson and Kurt Gray (2016) University of North Carolina at Chapel Hill
- *Agent-Based Modeling in Political Decision-Making,* Lin Qiu and Riyang Phang (2019), Oxford University Press
- *Data Action. Using data for public good,* Sarah Williams (2020), The MIT press

Chapter 4:

- *Internet Research Methods, a practical guide for the social and behavioral sciences,* Claire Hewson, Peter Yule, Dianna Laurent, Carl Vogel (2003), Sage Publications

- *Measuring Network Centrality*, Jesus Najera (2020) Medium.com
- *Generating a Twitter Ego-Network & Detecting Communities*, Shaham Farooq (2018) Medium.com
- *Determining the Happiest Cities using Twitter Sentiment Analysis with BERT*, Vladimir Dyagilev (2019) Medium.com
- *Deep Representation Learning for Clustering of Health Tweets*, Oguzhan Gencoglu (2018)

Chapter 5:

- *Russia's grassroots are more active than the West may think,* (2019) in New Eastern Europe, mars 2019.
- *Organizational behavior*, Stephen P. Robbins & Timothy A. Judge (2013) 15th ed. Pearson
- *The evolution of cooperation*, Robert Axelrod (2006)

Chapter 7:

- *Les approches du fait chinois par la géographie française*, Thierry Sanjuan (2008) in *Carnets de terrain. Pratique géographique et aires culturelles*, Paris, L'Harmattan, p.95–116.
- *A history of China*, Wolfram Eberhard (2004)
- *History of China*, wikipedia (2019)
- *Constructing Chinese National and Cultural Identities in the Age of Globalization*, Wang Ning (2007), Situations vol.1, Yonsei University
- *Harmony in contemporary New Confucianism and in Socialism with Chinese Characteristics*, Jesús Solé-Farràs (2008), China Media Research, Universitat Oberta de Catalunya
- *Taiwanese Indigenous Peoples*, Wikipedia (2019)
- *History of Taiwan*, Wikipedia (2019)
- *L'émancipation des aborigènes de Taiwan*, Olivier Lardinois (2012)
- *Les minorités ethniques en Chine, Entre inégalités sociales et croissance économique : quelles voies vers une société harmonieuse*, Xavier Qin (2011), China Institute.
- *Le paysage religieux de Taiwan et ses évolutions récentes*, Benoît Vermander (1995)
- *La Chine et ses frontières: Risk ou Monopoly ?* Michel Nazet (2015) diploweb.com
- *Bienvenue à Taiwan*, Documentation CCE (2013)
- *Disenchantment in Taiwan*, Mark Harrison (2019), ANU Press
- *Sharp power, youth power and the new politics in Taiwan*, Graeme Read (2019), ANU Press
- *Taiwan, au-delà des élections: identification plurielle mais citoyenneté Taiwanese*, Stephane Corcuff (2012)
- *Circulez, y a (pas d'Etat) à voir*, Françoise Mengin (2017), Sociétés politiques comparées, 2017, pp.1-29.
- *Sustainable economic development: The case of Taiwan*, Sorin-George Toma (2019), Annals of the Constantin Brâncusi University of Targu Jiu, Academia Brâncusi Publisher.
- *La situation économique de Taiwan en 2018 et ses perspectives pour 2019*, Bureau Français de Taïpei, Service Economique (2019).
- *Tout sur les affaires à Taiwan*, CCE (2014)
- *Une nouvelle génération de Taïwanais aux urnes*, Tanguy Le Pesant (2012), perspectives chinoises n° 2012/2
- *Hacker la démocratie Taïwanaise: Audrey Tang et la réinvention de la politique*, Emilie Frenkiel (2018), in Revue Participation , *Participer dans le monde chinois: une jeunesse connectée.*
- *Taipei Yearbook 2017*, Taipei City Government (2018), Taipei Yearbook Editorial Group

Chapter 8:

- Museum of Israel, Jerusalem
- Museum of David Tower, Jerusalem
- Museum of Jewish Diaspora, Tel Aviv

- *Histoire du Peuple Hébreu*, André Lemaire (1981), 10e édition 2019, PUF
- *Les manuscrits de la Mer Morte*, Ernest-Marie Laperrousaz (1961), 10e édition 2008, PUF
- *Zionism*, Wikipedia 2020
- *Regional Geopolitical Rivalries in the Middle East : implications for Europe*, Ellie Geranmayeh (2018), Foundation for European Progressive Studies
- *Le récit impossible. Le conflit israélo-palestinien et les médias*, Jerome Bourdon (2009), De Boeck / Institut national de l'audiovisuel.
- *Israel et la nouvelle donne géopolitique au Moyen-Orient, quelles menaces et quelles perspectives*, Roland Lombardi (2016), Etudes internationales 47.
- *The Geopolitics of Israel : Biblical and Modern*, Stratfor 2015
- *Kibbutz*, Wikipedia
- *Moshav*, Wikipedia
- *Rise and Fall of the Kibbutz*, Nir Tsuk (2000), The Hebrew University of Jerusalem
- *Israel, Startup Nation*, Dan Senor and Saul Singer (2009)
- *Digital Arab World : Understanding and embracing regional changes in the Fourth Industrial Revolution*, Whiite Paper (2018), World Economic Forum
- *The Middle-East in the Geopolitics of Digital*, Julien Nocetti (2019), IE MED, Mediterranean Yearbook 2019.
- *Tel-Aviv a cent ans ! 1909–2009 : un siècle de globalisation au Proche-Orient*, Caroline Rozenholc (2009), Hal archives-ouvertes.fr
- *Pour une lecture recontextualisée de Tel Aviv*, Caroline Rozenholc (2010), Hal archives-ouvertes.fr
- *Histoire de la ville blanche de Tel-Aviv : l'adaptation d'un site moderne et de son architecture*, Jeremie Hoffmann (2014), Hal archives-ouvertes.fr
- *The neighborhood of Florentin : a window to the Globalization of Tel Aviv*, Caroline Rozenholc (2010), Hal archives-ouvertes.fr
- *The emergence of a cosmopolitan Tel Aviv*, William Berthomiere (2005) Hal archives-ouvertes.fr
- *Tel Aviv Smart-City*, Tel Aviv Global, Tel Aviv Yaffo Municipality

Chapter 9:

- *Tallinn*, Wikipedia (2020)
- *Timeline of Tallinn*, Wikipedia (2020)
- *History of Estonia*, Wikipedia (2020)
- *New roman coin find in Estonia*, Mauri Kiudsoo (2012), Archaeological Fieldwork in Estonia 2012, 289–296
- *Migrants or Natives? The research History of Long Barrows in Russia and Estonia in the 5th—10th Centuries*, Andres Tvauri (2007)
- *Inhabitants of Saaremaa*, Wikipedia (2020)
- *The Estonian Economic Miracle,* Mart Laar (2007), Backgrounder, The Heritage Foundation
- *Demain, tous Estoniens ?*, Violaine Champetier de Ribes and Jean Spiri (2018), Cent Mille Milliards
- *Economic flows between Helsinki-Uusima and Tallinn-Harju regions*, H-TTransPlan (2013)
- *Lithuania, Latvia and Estonia : A Baltic Union ? About the cooperation between the Three Baltic States*, Julia Keil (2001)
- *Legacies, Coercion and Soft Power : Russian Influence in the Baltic States*, Agnia Grigas (2012)
- *The ethnic economy in CEE metropolises: A comparison of Budapest, Prague, Tallinn and Wroclaw*, Josef Kohlbacher and Patrycja Matusz Protasiewicz (2012)
- *Relationships between organizational culture and individual values of the Russian-speaking members of organizations in Estonia, Latvia and Lithuania*, Elina Tolmats (2004)
- *Digitalized and smart city—Tallinn*, Toomas Sepp, Head of City Office, Workshop 2017
- *OpenCity*, Krista Kampus (2019) Head of Smart-City Projects Competence Center
- *Smart Twin Cities via Urban Operating System*, Ralf-Martin Soe (2015)
- *e-Residency as a Nation branding case*, Margarita Kimmo (2017), Tallinn University of Technology
- *Estonian state's approach to cryptocurrency : The Case Study of EstCoin Project*,

Yuliya Polyakova (2018), Tallinn University of Technology
- *Blockchain from Public Administration Perspective : case of Estonia,* Parol Jalakas (2018), Tallinn University of Technology

Chapter 11:

- *Estimating Probabilities with Bayesian Modeling in Python*, Will Koehrsen(2018), medium.com
- How to use statistics, Steve Lakin(2011) Pearson

Chapter 13:

- Scott Allen Mongeau: *What information is gained from social network analysis? in* "Adopting Analytics Culture 6/7" (2013), sctr7.com
- John R. Ladd, Jessica Otis, Christopher N. Warren, and Scott Weingart: *Exploring and Analyzing Network Data with Python,* (2017, 2020), programminghistorian.org
- Euge Inzaugarat: *Visualizing Twitter interactions with NetworkX*, (2019), medium.com
- Valentina Alto: *Introduction to Network science with NetworkX*, (2020 a, b, c), medium.com
- Stephano Mariani: *A gentle introduction to NetworkX with Python*, (2020), medium.com
- Will and Al.: *Combining social network analysis and agent-based modelling to explore dynamics of human interaction: A review*, (2020), in Socio-Environmental Systems Modelling, vol. 2, 16325

Chapter 14:

- Wilensky, U. (1998): NetLogo Voting model. Center for Connected Learning and Computer-Based Modeling, Northwestern University, Evanston, IL.
- Colin Crouch: "Post Democracy", 2004, ISBN 0–7456–3315–3
- Theodore D. Kemper: "Power and Status and the Power-Status Theory of Emotions". In: Stets J.E., Turner J.H. (eds) "Handbook of the Sociology of Emotions." 2006, Springer.
- Vincent Tiberj: "Les citoyens qui viennent. Comment le renouvellement générationnel transforme la politique en France?", 2017, PUF
- R. Lau et al: "Measuring voter decision strategies in political behaviour and public opinion research", 2018
- Julien Carbonnell: "GRASSROOTS MOVEMENTS: The motivation of American, Taiwanese and Russian civic-hackers compared", 2019, medium.com
- Julien Carbonnell: "CIVIL SOCIETY: Evolutions of Citizenship and Democracy along history", 2019, medium.com
- Julien Carbonnell: "CIVIL SOCIETY: The futures of Citizenship and Democracy through Digital Perspective", 2019, medium.com
- Gert Jan Hofstede: "A relational view on culture and transculturality". In Wieland, Baumann, Montecinos (eds) "Relational economics and organisational governance" 2021, Springer.

Chapter 15:

- Mesa: Agent-based modelling in Python 3+ https://mesa.readthedocs.io/

www.ingramcontent.com/pod-product-compliance
Lightning Source LLC
LaVergne TN
LVHW051733050326
832903LV00023B/906